The Bradford Commission Report

The Report of an inquiry into
the wider implications of
public disorders in Bradford
which occurred on
9, 10 and 11 June 1995

November 1996

Applications for reproduction should be made in writing
to The Stationery Office Limited, St Crispins, Duke Street,
Norwich NR3 1PD

ISBN 011 702077 X

Contents

Section 3 Bradford's population as it now is and as it will be

Section 4 The Disorders of 9-11 June 1995

Part 1 Introduction

Part 2 Friday 9 June 1995

Section 5   Shared Problems; Perceived Divisions

Section 6 The Public Services

Section 7 Local Politics and Self-Government

Section 8 What Next?

Appendices

Section 1

Introduction

1.1 Our Terms of Reference

1.1.1. Over the weekend of Friday 9 June to Sunday 11 June 1995, disorders occurred in Manningham and spread to the city centre. Although the scale of these disorders was limited, the fear that they caused to local people, and the damage that was actually done to local properties and to the local economy, shocked many in the city. Underlying this response was a concern that those involved in the violence appeared to have been of one ethnic group and that the victims had been from other ethnic groups.

1.1.2. Many Bradfordians were proud of Bradford's reputation as a multi-ethnic city in which tensions were managed successfully, and, in these circumstances, the Bradford Congress, a voluntary association of representative Bradford institutions which includes the city council, decided to appoint a Commission of Inquiry, given the refusal of the central government to do so.

1.1.3. The Terms of Reference of our Inquiry were:

"to conduct hearings to consider the wider implications for Bradford of recent events in a part of the inner city of Bradford, in order to help to create a better future for all the people of the district and to promote peace, harmony and understanding between the communities of Bradford."

We have therefore been concerned to establish what happened, and what valuable lessons can be learnt.

1.1.4. The Congress, in a press release, gave the following reasons for establishing the Commission:

"The disorders of June were shocking to all Bradford's people. They were immediately destructive. They were potentially intensely damaging to the local economy and to our city's reputation. They might rupture the human values and relationships upon which we all depended.

As a community we might have ignored what had happened and hoped it would all blow over. The alternative was to hold some form of inquiry in which all should have an opportunity to participate. New courses of action might emerge.

When it fell to the Bradford Congress to recommend, after taking such soundings as were possible in the circumstances, the alternative was chosen – a 'Commission to hold hearings'."

1.2 A Bradford Commission

1.2.1. The Commission is a **Bradford** Commission. Its work has been generously supported by Bradford institutions in providing the Commission's accommodation and personnel. The consequence is that the actual cost to the bodies constituting the Congress, excluding printing costs, has been minimal, and we note this generosity as an important indication of the loyalty to the city which so many people have. The Commission has confined its attentions to within Bradford, and this Report is made formally to the Bradford Congress.

1.2.2.   The Commission is grateful to the *Bradford Telegraph and Argus,* and to other media, for helping to publicise our wish to hear from local people. On the assumption that the Congress will publish the Report, it is also to the individual citizens of Bradford as well as to the Congress. Many of them have supported the work of the Commission by taking the trouble to make their views known to us in a constructive and careful manner.

1.2.3.   We also acknowledge the assistance given to us by Mr Allen Sykes our Secretary, by Mrs Elaine Appelbee who opened many doors for us, by Mr Yusuf Karolia who provided administrative support during the latter stages of our inquiry, and by Ms Julie Williamson who arranged our complex programme of hearings.

1.3   The Manningham Focus

1.3.1.   Because of the origins and nature of the disorders our work has concentrated significantly, but by no means exclusively, on what is usually referred to as the Pakistani community in Manningham. Although our initial focus was Manningham, itself a variously defined area without official boundaries, the materials we gathered eventually related to many parts of Bradford, and this Report is therefore not just about Manningham. So much of the Manningham background, including the ethnic characteristics, is replicated throughout the inner city, and indeed beyond.

1.3.2.   For practical reasons our work has been confined to within the city of Bradford as it was defined before 1974, and we show these boundaries in Map A (Appendix 2). Unless, therefore, the context requires otherwise, the reader should assume that this restricted definition is applicable in any reference to Bradford in our Report, though the interdependence of all the communities which constitute the Metropolitan District cannot ever be sensibly ignored.

1.4   Our Proceedings

1.4.1.   The appointment of the Commission was announced on 7 September, and we began to hold hearings in October 1995. In relation to the disorders of 9–11 June 1995 our analytical objective was to understand why a minor policing incident, on an apparently normal Friday evening in Manningham, was followed by two nights of public disorder. But disorders of the kind which took place are not a rational, nor, in Bradford, a common activity, and the Manningham disorders cannot be understood merely by describing the time sequences of immediate causation on that weekend.

1.4.2.   Our overall objective, therefore, was to understand and to present the continuing tensions which existed both within Manningham and more generally within Bradford society. These tensions existed as background to the disorder, and as likely causes of the frustrations and anger which fuelled the violence, and there is an urgent need to develop more appropriate responses to these tensions. Even if all the tensions on which we report were not the basis of the disorders, they undoubtedly do exist, and *"a better future"* depends on their resolution.

1.5   Our Sources of Information

1.5.1.   Our Report is of a situation as it existed in 1995 and early 1996. This situation is constantly developing, and in the year that has elapsed since we began our work much of relevance has continued to change. Our Report may already have been overtaken in some details; it can be neither a start, nor a finish.

1.5.2.   As is to be expected, we have read a mountain of books, research papers, and official reports. So many of the situations which we have examined have also been the subject of previous investigation in Bradford and elsewhere. We have rarely set out the relevant parts of our background reading, but we were struck by similarities of the situation in Bradford in 1995 to that described in other Inquiry Reports into Public Disorders, notably Brixton 1981 and Darnall, Sheffield 1994. It is 15 years since Lord Scarman's *Report on the Brixton Riots (Cmd 8427)*, was published, yet so much of that Report has still to be digested and acted upon adequately by the authorities. We have, therefore, drawn attention to some of the parallels with the Scarman Report.

1.5.3.   We were given, and at times have felt submerged under, a wealth of written information relating to contemporary life in Bradford. There is a superabundance of statistics, analyses, articles, and books, about life in Bradford, but their very number, and the lack of consistent focus on key concerns, makes their content inaccessible in practice to the general public, and to busy public policy makers. We have not attempted to reproduce all this information in this Report.

1.5.4.   As a broad strategy we decided to invite members of the Bradford public to tell us of their experiences and views, before we heard from officials or the representatives of relevant organisations. An example of one of our leaflets is shown at Appendix 1. This sequence enabled the agenda to be determined by the public, rather than by officials and representatives. We should stress that, apart from a standard general introduction as to our purpose and status, we left these members of the public largely to an agenda of their own choosing. We merely asked questions to clarify any ambiguities.

1.5.5.   Our profound gratitude is owed to each of the 76 members of the public who were prepared to devote between one and two hours for their individual interviews, and to the 189 members of the public who attended lengthy small group meetings to put forward their individual views. In addition, there were larger semi-public or public meetings, and several very helpful written submissions. To the 119 officials and public representatives who generously gave time and effort to assist us we also express our thanks. They were asked to present their views and to respond to the agenda set by the members of the public.

1.5.6.   All these interviews and meetings, which took place between October 1995 and April 1996 inclusive, gave us a clear insight into the concerns of the people who spoke to us, and the many more whom they represented. Since the end of April we have been writing this Report, and have held further interviews to clarify some of the details.

1.5.7.   This method, though very time consuming, has also been very worthwhile. In terms of the scale on which it has been carried out it is, so far as we know, unique. The Commission's decision to listen primarily to the voices of Bradford's citizens, from any part of the District and from any walk of life, was taken in the firm belief that all of them had an equal right to be heard, in terms of their experiences, concerns and perceptions of the present, and ideas or visions of the future. Their contribution was considered to be vital to Bradford's social, economic, political and cultural way forward. This way of proceeding gave rise, predictably, to a variety of views, a range of perceptions and discrepant experiences, and positive as well as negative visions of future possibilities, but also to some clear priorities of concern.

1.5.8   Wherever appropriate we have quoted, without attribution, from the written materials supplied, or from our notes of the information we were given orally. Even where we do not quote directly, the text has been heavily influenced by what we heard. In this way we hope to emphasise that this Report is based almost entirely on contributions from Bradfordians. This also reinforces our indebtedness to the many people – citizens, public officials, police officers, informal representatives, councillors, Members of Parliament – who assisted us, and indicates that our Report should provide some realistic starting points for open public discussion.

1.5.9.   We have tried to make our Report self-contained for the general reader, rather than to give the impression that it is a research paper. We have avoided the use of footnotes. Specialists will be aware of the research literature in their own fields on many of the subjects covered in this Report. Any worthwhile debate will require some consideration of these sources which we are not able to provide in this Report.

1.6   The 'Evidence'

1.6.1.   This Report is about the city, not about individuals. It is mainly about collective forces and processes, which we have identified by listening to the experiences of individuals. Holders of public office, such as The Chief Constable, the Leader of the Council, or the MP for Bradford West, are readily identifiable as individuals, but we have preferred to use only their official titles. We guaranteed to all those who spoke to us that we would not identify them in our Report, nor openly attribute to them what they said to us, unless we first obtained their agreement. Our guarantee of confidentiality was intended to protect individuals whose vulnerability was such that, without such a guarantee, they would have been deterred from talking to us. This was in contrast to the procedure available to Lord Scarman, but in line with that of the Kerner investigation *(The National Advisory Commission on Civil Disorders Report, Washington D.C., 1968)*. We have followed this guarantee meticulously. We have tried to anonymise all individuals who are referred to in our Report unless it was already public knowledge, as in, for example 'the Honeyford affair'.

1.6.2.   We should explain the limits of our information insofar as we attempt a factual reconstruction of the disorders themselves. When we heard from people who witnessed these events we were not a Court of Law. This means that we had no power to compel people to tell us what they knew, and so we are very conscious of loose ends which we would have liked to pursue further. Nor did we follow a normal forensic process, whereby witnesses were openly subjected to cross-examination on behalf of those with an opposing view. We are not an 'official' inquiry. This means that we have no authority to determine formally where the truth might lie in matters of dispute, in the way that the formal verdict of a jury, or the formal judgement of a court, has to be accepted for all official purposes.

1.6.3.   In trying to understand both the events and the circumstances surrounding them we have been concerned about perceptions as well as facts. Perceptions influence people, even if they are wrong.

1.7   Terminology

1.7.1.   One of the obstacles to discussion about, and between, people of different ethnicities is the inadequacy of the descriptive language available. It is one of the signs of Bradford's failure over the past 30 years to accept on equal terms the settlement in the city of groups of immigrants and their British born descendants, that descriptions of the different groups involved are, in common speech, so vague, and so often inaccurate. Nor can the categories used for national ethnic monitoring do justice to Bradford's needs.

1.7.2.   One issue which therefore confronted us during our investigations, and in the writing of this Report, was what terminology to use for the different groups who necessarily figured in our work. It is a complex issue, with no simple or universally acceptable answers. Indeed, what is acceptable changes with circumstances, and depends on who is using a particular term, and the way it is being used. This is well illustrated by the robust attitude of one group of older women whom we met who were studying English. So much depends, they said, on the spirit in which a term is used. A wrong term may reveal ignorance, but it will not be taken as insulting or abusive if goodwill is obviously present.

1.7.3.   We at first tried to avoid using the word 'Asian' as being of little meaning in most cases. The term Asian is so often used to cover the user's ignorance of the specific background of anyone who vaguely appears to have roots in the Indian sub-continent, itself only a small part of Asia. 'White' readers might like to reflect on the consequences if all variations of Europeans were to be lumped together for all serious purposes of description.

1.7.4.   The shortcut term, 'Asian', is nowhere more misleading than when it is used in conjunction with the equally short cut term 'culture'. There are many cultures from the Indian sub-continent substantially present in Bradford and many other cultures, too. None is fixed and static, and none is homogeneous.

1.7.5.   Differences within cultures are important, and are most marked along class lines and by gender divisions. For example, the children of the successful and prosperous, both boys and girls, as with the White population, are more likely to be educated at private schools, along with their Western peers, than at inner city comprehensives.

1.7.6.   The term 'ethnic minorities' is, in Bradford, used almost always to mean people whose roots are in the Indian sub-continent, or occasionally in the Caribbean, although the city's population includes many citizens whose ethnic origin is from Polish, Ukrainian, or other Eastern European societies. Should these, or those of nineteenth-century Irish descent, still have an 'ethnic minority' status in Bradfordian conversation?

1.7.7.   The terms 'Asian', 'White', and 'ethnic' minorities are in daily use both in official circles and in popular speech. These are crude labels which will rarely be descriptively adequate. They can mislead, ignoring more powerful social factors, causing misdiagnoses of practical situations and social problems, and the development of negative stereotypes.

1.7.8. Unfortunately the use of these terms is too widespread for us to avoid them when reporting on past events. We have had to retain them in quotations from others, or where our sources were not more specific, or where such vagueness seemed unavoidable.

1.7.9. We have attempted to use more appropriate and accurate terms wherever possible. For instance, rather than 'Asian' we have referred to the region of origin of those who migrated from the Indian sub-continent. Sometimes an even more local description was appropriate. Many of those correctly referred to as Pakistanis are from Kashmir; many of them came from the very rural area surrounding the old city of Mirpur, when the building of the Mangla Dam flooded their villages in the 1950s. To describe someone's family background as Kashmiri, or Mirpuri, may sometimes be much more appropriate than 'Pakistani', and almost always more appropriate than 'Asian'.

1.7.10. For the children and grandchildren, born and educated in Britain, there are, as yet, no terms readily available which meet the criteria of acceptability and accuracy. We have, therefore, albeit reluctantly, adopted the same terms as those we use for their parents. We note here that this convention is rarely, if ever, used in official or popular language for those of Bradford's White population whose parental origins were in other parts of Europe.

1.7.11. Changes have taken place in recent years, such that some of the population are designated by, and describe themselves in terms of, religion. This is at present notably the case for some followers of Islam. We have tried to use such terms only when relevant to the matter under discussion, for example in the case of Hindus and Sikhs. Very little of our subject matter is best described by using descriptions of people's religious loyalties.

1.7.12. Even using as accurate a description as we can has often proved inadequate when applied to an individual person. The range of normal cultural diversity within any generally defined group is very great, and Bradford's historical reputation for individual non-conformity appears to be widely upheld by its present population, whatever their ethnic background! The **range** of attitudes in each of the different ethnic groupings in Bradford is remarkably similar, and they all have their unrepresentative individuals who appeal to the media. The widespread failure to know each other as individuals is both a cause and a symptom of the widespread ignorance which hinders our capacity to acknowledge our fellow citizens appropriately.

1.8. Nothing New

1.8.1. Although we have ordered our material in this Report under different headings the main themes often overlap, for better or for worse feeding off each other. Our artificial division of the material is almost entirely dictated by the perceptions and frameworks of those who spoke to us.

1.8.2. None of this material is new; indeed, our disappointment is that it is of long standing. Each theme is already the subject of much concern and effort, but we have to say that not enough is being done to understand the problems, to explain the choices, and to focus relevant skills.

1.8.3.   These themes flow inevitably from the two major changes which have affected Bradford over the last 30 years: the unprecedented decline in its staple industry, and the settlement of groups of citizens from the Indian sub-continent whose children and grandchildren have been born here. Only if there is a widespread willingness to accommodate these changes will there be the possibility of a satisfactory future for those who live in Bradford. Despite the many instances of public and private initiative of which we are aware we are critical of the slowness of many citizens, of all backgrounds, to adapt constructively to the present situation. An inevitable consequence is a lack of clarity in the city's self-governing policies and priorities.

1.9   Other Reports

1.9.1.   Several reports appeared in the wake of the disorders. Two by voluntary groups, *The Voices Must Be Heard (Foundation 2000)*, and *Powerful Whispers (Bradford Metropolitan Faith in the City Forum)*, made very telling points based on listening to people.

1.9.2.   The former report, published as we began our investigation, emphasised *"loss of confidence in the police"* as the immediate cause of the disorders, but spoke of a deeper anger at the injustices which members of the local communities in Manningham face every day. Other findings in that report are of hardships suffered by many people, with poor accessibility to services and political representation; of the cultural struggle which young Asian people have in *"being born into eastern tradition and living in western society"*; and of lack of trust by the local community in local politicians.

1.9.3.   The latter report was published shortly after we began our inquiry. We adopt the message of that report which encourages the people of Bradford to take the initiative, rather than wait for solutions to appear.

1.9.4.   A report requested by the Leader of the Council from officers in June 1995 and dated 5 September 1995, *The Riot Area Reviewed*, is referred to on several occasions subsequently in this Report.

1.9.5.   *'Race' and Housing in Bradford*, which was published by the council just as we were finalising this Report, also raises issues of relevance to some of the material in our Report.

1.10   Criticism

1.10.1.   It is inevitable that a report of this kind should express or imply present deficiencies, and therefore criticisms of those struggling with the problems, particularly those in public positions. Indeed, the institutions represented in the Bradford Congress are the most likely to be the subjects of any such criticism, and we welcome their openness to our Report as part of their disciplined response to the challenges which the Manningham disorders undoubtedly presented. The criticisms which we make, however, are not just of public institutions; they frequently relate to life in Bradford in general – to its commerce, industry and people.

1.10.2.   Nor should any criticism be allowed to diminish the excellent work and brave initiatives which have been, and are being, undertaken in Bradford by concerned citizens and organisations. There is so much good being achieved within the city by many agencies, and we have only been able to draw attention to a few examples. The very considerable challenges presented in this Report are not as daunting as at first sight may appear, so long as the constructive determination of sufficient people is mobilised.

1.11   The Main Concerns

1.11.1.   We have not concerned ourselves with firefighting – the important and necessary work of coping with the day to day problems which are a feature of life in any city. We have seen our task as one of surveying the local scene with the help of those who volunteered their assistance; then reporting publicly on what are often suppressed concerns, articulating the themes which need to be addressed as an important part of the processes of local self-government.

1.11.2.   We were surprised at the near unanimity of our witnesses in identifying their main concerns. It became very clear at quite an early stage in the hearings that there was a small list of themes which was, at least in part, likely to be raised by each witness. We do not pretend that those who spoke to us were necessarily representative of all Bradford people, but they certainly came from almost all typical localities and from almost all the major social and ethnic groupings in the city.

1.11.3.   There are, of course, many important facets of the life of the city which are not clearly within our remit, for example the National Health Service, or transport, and which we have not considered in any depth. The recently published study *'Race' and Housing in Bradford*, which has quite separately paralleled much of the general information in this Report, alone raises many serious problems which will have to be faced. The themes on which we report are not to be seen as excluding others.

1.11.4.   It is inevitable that the underlying nature of our remit – the disorders – exercised a limiting discipline on the topics raised by those who came to speak to us, so that they may have considered other important topics to be irrelevant to our purposes. We are, however, satisfied that the themes to which we draw attention cannot sensibly be ignored. The cost of not clearly selecting and pursuing priorities will, if the present trends which we identify are left to gather momentum, be very high.

1.11.5.   Establishing priorities means that some projects will receive attention and investment. But others will not, and there is an inevitable price to be paid, including that of political unpopularity. That is why we advocate a more conscious public participation in the local processes of self-government.

1.12   A Bradford Strategy

1.12.1.   Bradford's population mix in present economic circumstances is creating distinctive pressures which need a Bradfordian long term strategy to deal with them. We are confident, from our experience of the people we have met, that Bradford people can create and implement an appropriate strategy, building on the many separate initiatives which people are already taking to deal with the problems. Bradford's commerce, industries, and people have the capacity to tackle many of the problems, and where there is the dominance of a remote central government over many of Bradford's public policies there is also required, in response, a clearer local expression of public concerns and priorities.

1.12.2.   The problems involved are complex, and need opening up to awkward questions and informed discussion. The authority for the judgements we have made is, we believe, well established in the information which we have received and summarised in this Report, but we recognise that there will properly be discussion and differences of opinion about some of the things we say. Indeed, we hope that this will be the case. We are seeking to stimulate public interest in important matters of public concern, not to provide a political equivalent of painting by numbers.

1.12.3.   The critical political deficiency we have found is that there is no adequate process to link the concerns of responsible members of the public, or those working at the problems 'on the ground', with the means of participating effectively in developing the local solutions. We challenge the city to produce, **at many levels**, the leadership and the co-ordination which can channel the undoubted strengths of Bradford to deal with the problems we identify in this Report. There is a very serious situation, which Bradford must confront. It has faced similar situations in its not very long history, and pioneered solutions which have been widely adopted by others.

1.12.4.   We want to see more constructive and focussed processes replace a general public ignorance, and a presently diffused expertise. We are asking Bradford people to understand their circumstances more clearly, and then to think, to choose, and to monitor the achievement of their choices by themselves and by their public representatives. We have no quick-fix solutions.

1.13   An Outline Summary

1.13.1.   The main themes identified by those who spoke to us as being of major concern to them in relation to the disorders were:

(i)   ethnic conflicts and misunderstandings in Bradford

(ii) the lack of employment opportunities, and most particularly the extent and unfairness of racial discrimination in the labour market

(iii) street culture and criminal behaviour by boys and young men

(iv) the problems of appropriate policing

(v) the poor educational level of some schools, and the consequences for the educational attainment of many young people

(vi) the ineffectiveness of local political processes.

1.13.2.   We summarise our conclusion about these themes: Bradford's social divisions are inadequately perceived, and inadequately bridged, and Bradford's problems are actually shared across wrongly perceived divides, with the result that Bradford's economy, public services, and local politics have not come to terms with the nature, the circumstances, or the potential of Bradford's present and future population.

1.13.3.   This Report is organised in Sections. Section 2 amplifies the outline summary just given, but no summary can be a satisfactory substitute for the content of the Sections in which we report at greater length. Sections 1 and 2 are intended as no more than a convenience for those who will bother to grapple with the whole Report.

1.13.4.   Section 3 presents a brief historical and statistical description of Bradford, developing in particular the situation of youth unemployment. Section 4 gives our account of the disorders. In Section 5 we deal principally with the first and third of the themes just set out in para. 1.13.1. Section 6 deals principally with the fourth and the fifth themes, and Section 7 with the sixth theme. In Section 8 we consider how the Report may be disseminated and acted upon.

Section 2

An Amplified Summary of the Main Conclusions

2.1 Unrest

2.1.1. The disturbances to public order which occurred in Bradford on 9–11 June 1995 were a particularly disconcerting consequence of tensions and disorder which are present in many parts of Bradford, but the extent of the disorders has been exaggerated. If not dealt with, many of the present predispositions to such tensions and disorder will increase in the coming years. The disorders have been almost universally condemned throughout the city as morally wrong and practically self-defeating, but how can future eruptions be prevented if the same predispositions continue, or worsen?

2.2 The 'Causes'

2.2.1. The direct cause of the disorders, obviously, was the unacceptable behaviour of those relatively few people who behaved so antisocially. The particular occasion for this misbehaviour arose from a failure to police by consent, and a widespread local misunderstanding of the accepted protocol for protest. The police showed their ignorance of the local population, and of its concerns; the protesters showed their ignorance of the means of acceptable protest; some representatives of the local population showed their ignorance of necessary and proper police procedures.

2.2.2. We reject as superficial, and diversionary from the real problem, the suggestion that has been made that the disorders occurred because the police are racist, though we accept that in too many individual cases too many people experience such racism. Such a generalisation ignores the positive steps taken by the police both on the specific occasion, and generally. Ignorance about Bradford's population is not confined to the police, nor is the ignorance within the local population and its representatives confined to Manningham, nor to the subject of how to protest. This widespread ignorance can be understood as an unfortunate stage in a difficult transitional process of groups from different traditions learning to live together. It has lasted for too long, and it must now be rapidly supplanted by knowledge.

2.2.3. We also reject as superficial the suggestion that the disorders occurred because Asian parents had lost control of a generation. This generalisation ignores the small number of people involved in the violence of the disorders compared with the total Asian population such a generalisation necessarily and indiscriminately includes. The same reasoning must also apply to the very widespread social pressures of poor education, overcrowded homes, poverty, and unemployment, all of which relate to young men with particular emphasis. We classify these pressures rather as predispositions to tension and violence which have an unfairly heavy impact on a substantial number of young people from the ethnic minorities.

2.3   Ethnic Diversity

2.3.1.   The ethnic diversity of Bradford is both a potential strength and a problem; it is at all times capable of being used by all citizens and groups positively or negatively. Tensions are likely; apart from a degree of ignorance there is also uncertainty and hostility to recognising legitimate but different ways of life and different identities as equally valid. Fear and alienation exist, and both must be tackled.

2.3.2.   At a personal level, widespread mutual ignorance of the changing nature of Bradford's population needs to be met by an understanding of its reality, based on greater experience of the varied individuals presently identified in stereotypical blocs, to deal with exaggerated negative attitudes, and to assert and increase the many positive potential advantages. This needs a conscious effort at all levels of Bradford's life as a city.

2.3.3.   Statistically, Bradford needs to build up a most rigorous and openly constructed system to monitor, analyse, forecast, and implement policies appropriate to its changing profile. In developing the basis of such a system, and in the presentation of its findings, expert advice is openly required.

2.4   Constructive Response

2.4.1.   The disorders shocked many people into realising the inadequacy of the arrangements and initiatives which have hitherto prevented or minimised eruptions of disorder flowing from public frustrations. The city must use this response to identify and build on the many separate initiatives of good practice already established, so that the good practice becomes standard. The wide, and deep-seated, nature of the challenge means that there is no quick-fix solution. Identifying good practice, and establishing it, will require dynamic leadership.

2.5   The Basis for Progress

2.5.1.   We note the slowness of many citizens, of different backgrounds, to come to terms with the city as it now is. Increasingly, the members of the ethnic minority communities are citizens who were born and raised in Bradford, for whom it is their permanent home. The main obstacle to their commitment to the city is the lack of acknowledgement they receive from the majority of the population, leading to an unfair and unequal citizenship. The result on all sides is, with important exceptions, at best a polite but ineffective superficiality in relationships. At worst it is antisocial behaviour, promoted by a depressed economy and insufficiently responsive public services.

2.5.2.   It is necessary to understand the issues which the existence of an ethnically diverse city creates, on grounds of elementary courtesy, and of effective commercial dealing, and of effective public service delivery. The differences between cultural groupings should not be allowed to obscure the much weightier similarities which occur in the burdens borne within every ethnic group. Similarly, the range of opinions, of attitudes, of abilities, and of a desire for peace and harmony which exist in each group should be seen as a basis for political concern and mobilisation, rather than the incorrectly assumed homogeneity of ethnic groups. Only then can there be clarity in the city's self-governing priorities and policies. In particular, we assert that there is little enthusiasm for extremist politics, from pseudo-religious or nationalistic motives, amongst Bradford's people.

2.5.3.   Many citizens wish to overcome the apparent barriers, but do not know how to begin. The various shared and separate histories, and the present day artistic and intellectual insights of different backgrounds, offer stimulating shared opportunities to create a positive and vibrant multi-ethnic city.

2.6   The Role of Voluntary Groups

2.6.1.   Voluntary groups, in the wide sense of all voluntary associations of citizens – charitable, cultural, political, religious, social, and sporting – have a major role to play in setting an appropriate atmosphere in which mutual understanding and individual identities can develop constructively. Present performance is patchy. In some such associations it is excellent; in many it is non-existent. All organisations should have openly on their agenda the building of bridges amongst a divided populace.

2.6.2.   We recognise the importance of a more vigorous exercise of responsible citizenship to meet communal needs which cannot be met by expensive public services at a time of restraint on public expenditure. In particular, we look to adults to volunteer a greater interest in the education and development of the younger generation, in partnership with the public services.

2.7   The Role of the Local Public Services

2.7.1.   The conceptual basis for public service provision should be an equal emphasis, by an ethnically and religiously neutral state, on matching appropriately the agreed general standard of service to each recipient's needs in each case. At the present time, with some exceptions, the consequences of having to recognise the consequences of ethnic diversity are regarded as exceptional public service provision, rather than made an integral part of proper and normal service organisation, planning and delivery.

2.7.2.   The domination of service provision by Whites has led to adaptations negotiated with unofficial representative figures on behalf of previously inarticulate sections of the public. This short cut in communication is rapidly losing credibility, as new generations grow up who rightly expect to be consulted directly, and to be recognised individually, on equal terms with other citizens. In the absence of clear leadership, established ways exert too strong a drag. It is time for another stock-take in preparation for politically determined progress.

2.8   The Local Economy

2.8.1.   Any recovery of Bradford's struggling local economy will be inextricably linked to a proper appreciation of all of the city's present and future population. The two major changes of the last 30 years have been the decline in Bradford's staple industry, and the settlement of groups of citizens from the Indian sub-continent whose children and grandchildren have been born here.

2.8.2. This Report is not directly concerned with the difficulties of economic regeneration. We note, however, the significance of such regeneration to building improved relations across the city. The task of economic regeneration remains, in our view, one of the most crucial for the Congress and its partners. A city divided into a traditional White economy and a separate Asian economy, with African Caribbeans struggling to find a place, is not capable of realising its potential. The city centre, in particular, reflects this lack of synergy. Progress will necessarily include having a realistic regard for fairness in creating and giving appropriate opportunities for education, training, and employment across all groups who live in the city, and an end to racial discrimination.

2.9   Young Bradfordians

2.9.1. Friendships across ethnic boundaries are not uncommon in Bradford, and they appear to be growing amongst young people. However, strong pressures remain which prevent young people of different backgrounds from exploring life in Bradford together. The effectiveness of investment in them, particularly in their education and appropriate training, and their involvement in the political processes of the city, will largely determine Bradford's future.

2.9.2. In particular, the changing attitudes, needs, and circumstances of many young Asian women require attention in relation both to domestic and work patterns.

2.9.3. Some young men from most ethnic backgrounds engage in unsocial, ill-disciplined and, at times, unlawful behaviour, and this is widely experienced to the detriment of normal life, particularly in public places. It is a cause of considerable concern. Serious crime is the work of a very small minority, and increasingly results from the use of, and dealing in, drugs.

2.9.4. The growing number of young Asian Bradfordians deserves special mention, since the views of many of them are more strongly asserted, and more attuned to present circumstances, than those of their parents. Those young men who took part in the disorders of June 1995 were only a small proportion, both of those protesting and of their total group. They were quite unrepresentative of the constructive hopefulness of young people, though probably motivated by the anger felt by many at their unfairly blighted futures.

2.9.5. Of immediate concern is the problem of the lack of work for many people, which leads to a large number of unemployed young men spending their time mainly on the streets. Encouraging this available energy and time to be used constructively is a major challenge insofar as jobs are unavailable and cannot be created. We have been impressed by the positive influences brought to bear by youth and liaison officers, though they are few in number and limited in the scope of their activities. The contradiction of so many unmet needs in disadvantaged areas and the inability of current processes to provide jobs is all too glaring.

2.9.6. More generally, the movement of ethnic minorities appears to be following the same slow pattern as was followed by workers who came to Bradford in the last century. Long-term thinking is needed to prepare for a future which is at least partly foreseeable.

2.10   Local Politics

2.10.1. Local politics and self-government have wider implications than the activities of the city council, but the council is the formal expression of local democracy, and so we have tended to concentrate our attention upon its activities. In terms of local politics, we are critical of the failure to open up to constructive discussion issues which are thought to be controversial, of the failure to prioritise existing expenditures, of the failure to process public concerns, and of the failure to drive public services to be responsive to the needs they are supposed to meet. The ethnic tensions, and the means of dealing with them, raise difficult local political issues, yet there is no clear, accountable, prioritised, co-ordinated public strategy to cope with the causes or the strains of the tensions, or to build on the city's ethnic diversity.

2.10.2. We look for the creation of a realistic long-term strategy for Bradford as the culmination of a process which is only partly achieved. Given the civic financial dependency increasingly promoted by central government, such a strategy is vital for attracting the external funding which is so obviously needed, as well as for making local decisions clearly, consistently and accountably. Although the city council is now only a minor partner with central government in the local governance of Bradford, it is constitutionally designed to sort out local priorities. It should concentrate on being a central counterweight to the confusions created by separate pressure groups and initiatives, instead of encouraging such confusion by its processes.

2.10.3. These criticisms are made as pointers to what needs to be done. They are not necessarily criticisms of individuals whose involvement in exposed positions is often very demanding. The widespread lack of public knowledge about the limited choices which are available makes the local politicians' tasks even more difficult. The development of very local democracy which extends the understanding of the options available to public agencies is needed.

Section 3

Bradford's population as it now is and as it will be

3.1 Bradford

3.1.1. Bradford in the 1990s is much like many other British cities and metropolitan districts, but it has its own distinct features stemming from its history and geography. Geographically and socially it is very varied, ranging over villages and towns, moors and dales, redundant industrial buildings, crowded inner city streets, and housing estates both public and private. The Bradford Metropolitan District lies north of the trans-Pennine motorway, and west of Leeds. East and north of Bradford is North Yorkshire, with its landed estates, farmlands, spa towns and ancient cathedral cities, and to the west and northwards is Lancashire, and the Lake District.

3.1.2. Bradford's economy was for many decades dominated by the woollen textile industry, with some engineering and chemical plants, many of which supplied the needs of textile production. It was, by and large, a low wage economy and from the last quarter of the nineteenth century mainly a working-class city.

3.1.3. As an independent municipality, Bradford, in the field of public health, in housing, and in town planning, had at some periods a notable record of achievement, and in education Bradford is rightly recognised to have led the way in many respects. It is noted for its early provision of nursery education, was the first to develop a school meals service, and provided the first school swimming pool. Alongside this, art and design played a central part, and music and the theatre flourished.

3.1.4. The Bradford Mechanics Institute, later the Technical College, grew up in close association with the textile industry, becoming a centre of discovery, invention, and innovation. When the College of Advanced Technology gained university status in 1966, a dream of the city fathers for many decades, it continued the tradition of educational innovation, and encouraged staff to use their knowledge and skills for the benefit of the locality.

3.2 Its People

3.2.1. The centre of the woollen textile industry from the late eighteenth century, Bradford developed global links with the colonies and elsewhere, importing wool for processing and re-export, and these links were maintained well into the mid-twentieth century. Bradford, as part of this process, imported not only wool, but people. Its mix of faiths and ethnicities owes a great deal to this industrial base on which its wealth was founded.

3.2.2. The textile mill owners and the non-manual employees moved from the city into surrounding towns and into fast-growing suburbs. After World War II extensive schemes of slum clearance were undertaken by the council, and several large housing estates were built on the outskirts. During the 1960s and 1970s parts of the city centre were redeveloped with an emphasis on office blocks and motor traffic.

3.2.3.   The fine houses of the wealthy became multi-occupied dwellings, or were used for commercial or public sector offices, and the terraced and back to back houses, formerly homes of artisans and operatives, provided accommodation for migrants from Eastern Europe, Ireland, and parts of the Commonwealth, as well as students. Manningham was one such area, but retained on its borders a more prosperous sector of detached houses with large gardens, housing middle class professional families.

3.2.4.   The movement often referred to as 'White flight' is, in fact, a movement of Whites, Pakistanis, Indians and others who are upwardly mobile or middle class, and continues a movement out of the inner city which has been a constant feature of Bradford. Crucial factors in such movement today are concerns with educational provision, and with the poor image of the area and its effect on chances for employment. Such movement is not available to the unemployed or to those on low wages, nor is it desired by those who wish to remain, for whatever reason, where they were born and grew up, nor to those whose accommodation and other needs are not met by the housing or amenities available on suburban estates.

3.3   The Data; Demographic and Socio-economic Indices: 1991 and beyond

Existing Surveys

3.3.1.   The Commission did not carry out its own surveys on the social and economic conditions to which this section refers, nor was it able to make its own systematic analyses of the statistical data produced by others in Bradford, or nationally. We consulted as many of the publicly available reports and projects as possible, giving particular attention to those which contained policy advice or where, because of the source or the comment, they were likely to influence policies. The publications were frequently not commensurate with each other for several reasons, including the geographical area and/or the time period covered, or the definitions of the population adopted.

3.3.2.   We understand that some revisions to official forecasts are being discussed even as we finalise our Report. The indices which we have used are those which were available to us during our investigation, and we discuss them at three levels: the Bradford Metropolitan District; the inner city; and in particular the Manningham area.

Presenting Statistics

3.3.3.   Why, we asked, was forecast demographic change in Bradford so frequently seen as a problem? One paper presented to us contained the following observations:

"The best estimates are that the ethnic minority population will begin to level out by 2030 at a figure of 150,000, or 25–30% of the district's population.

By the year 2000 the population will be 96,000, or a growth of 25,000 on 1989 figures. Meanwhile, the white population will fall by 15,000...

*The problem is that this growth will not be evenly distributed. The growth in the inner areas will be tremendous while in the outer areas the population will be falling. Also the **distorted** [our* emphasis] *age structures will be continued. The white population will be ageing but the black population will be predominantly young."*

3.3.4.   Major consequences for housing and educational provision were predicted which, it was argued, might provoke racist jealousies unless carefully explained and understood.

3.3.5.   Other papers or oral evidence point to such instances as:

- *by the year 2000, 50% of school leavers would be Asian;*

- *that the Black and Asian population is predicted to grow from the current 89,000 to 138,000 by 2011;*

- *that growth of this magnitude is unique to Bradford;*

- *that with depressing economic statistics, but a dramatically growing population, the emphasis must be on these young people, on education and vocational training;*

- *that 700 or 1,000 new jobs per year were needed to maintain current levels of employment, and many more if unemployment was to disappear altogether;*

- *that increasingly those in work are projected to be females rather than males, and more from minorities than from the White population.*

3.3.6.   The population increases most frequently referred to relate clearly to changes in the ethnic composition (as recorded in the 1991 Census), not to overall increases.

The Need for an Open, Understood, System

3.3.7.   We are acutely aware that careful judgement is always required in preparing, analysing, and drawing conclusions from statistical material and projections. It is not unknown for specific sectional interests, whether good or bad, to lead to selecting, overstating or understating the figures to strengthen their case.

3.3.8.   We understand from one paper we have read that these dangers are known to the council's demographic researchers, but that fears of racist reactions, in particular, leads to caution in discussing and publicising data. We have concerns about the development, publication, and use of statistical information to, e.g. strengthen Bradford's case for more financial support, and which lead to false linkages between ethnicity and problems. Furthermore, whilst statistics are necessary and useful for policy making the official use of statistics constructed on different bases leads easily to confusion and suspicion.

3.3.9.   Where strong arguments can be made to pursue a particular policy as part of an overall strategy, it is our firm belief that the statistics used should be rigorously and openly constructed, and their limitations fully explained. Statistics on ethnic differences are some of the most complex to collect, analyse and interpret. In many cases, in a city like Bradford, their construction and interpretation is no easy task, as will be evident from this Report. The first step to improving this is to recognise the difficulties, and then for politicians and officials to follow expert advice on how to proceed, how to use, and how to present such material, especially where it is open to distortion. This is not simply a matter of statistical technicalities, but of enabling policy making on the best available data.

3.4   The Metropolitan District

Population Growth

3.4.1.   In 1991 the metropolitan district was the fifth largest of the 36 in England, with a population officially calculated at 475,500. By mid-1993 it had overtaken Liverpool to become the fourth largest metropolitan district after Birmingham, Leeds, and Sheffield. The Metropolitan District population forecast for 2001 is 498,600, and for 2011 is 523,850.

Population Changes – Similar to the National Trend

3.4.2.   Forecasts of population changes between 1991 and 2011 given in one official report indicate similarities with national trends; a 4% increase in the numbers of children under 16 by 2001, and slow growth in the population of working age, but a change in the composition of those of pensionable age, so that by 2011 there will be a 12% increase in those over 75.

Overall Age Distribution – Negligible Change

3.4.3.   If we look at the age distribution in Bradford Metropolitan District, using statistics prepared by the Chief Executive's Research Section in 1994, they show that in 1991 some 80,150 (17% of the total population) were above retirement age, and the estimates for this group are 79,700 (16%) in 2001, and 81,950 (16%) in 2011. For the same years, those aged 15 and under are given as 111,200 (23%), 118,200 (24%) and 123,450 (24%). Those of working age, 16 years to retirement (60 years for women and 65 years for men), numbered some 284,100 (59.7%) in 1991, and forecasts indicate an increase to 300,750 (60.3%) by 2001 and to 318,400 (60.8%) by 2011. These statistics show negligible change in the overall age structure.

Ethnic Composition

3.4.4.   The 1991 Census provided six categories of ethnicity for respondents to choose how to define themselves. These were White, Black African/Caribbean, Indian, Pakistani, Bangladeshi and Other. Such categories are inadequate in many respects, both for our purposes and for the decision-makers of Bradford. In some cases they can lead to serious distortions of the actual causes of social and economic problems and have deleterious consequences for relations between people. Nevertheless their use is widespread and often they are the only source of statistical data available on ethnic differentiation. We therefore use them, albeit reluctantly.

3.4.5.   In 1991, 84% of the population of the district were defined as White, and the 1994 forecasts estimated that this proportion would decrease to 79% by the year 2001, and to 73% by 2011. The proportions for the other categories for which estimates are given for the same three years are as follows:

	1991	2001	2011
African Caribbean	1.2%,	1.3%,	1.3%;
Bangladeshi	0.8%,	1.2%,	1.5%;
Indian	2.7%,	2.8%,	2.9%;
Pakistani	10.3%,	14.4%,	20.0%;
Other	1.1%,	1.3%,	1.6%.

3.4.6.   If these estimates prove to be roughly correct then, in 15 years time, just less than three-quarters of the population will be White, with the only sizeable minority Pakistani

Negative Net Migration

3.4.7.   A point that is stressed in some publications about Bradford is the in-migration from overseas, particularly from Pakistan, but overall net migration is negative. The concern appears to be about young men and women coming as spouses from the Indian sub-continent. For example, the Bradford Education Policy and Information Unit put this concern in 1996 as follows:

> "What has happened is that young Asian men and (since the 1985 European Court of Human Rights 'equal treatment' decision) Asian women have been taking marriage partners from South Asia. The great majority of immigrants in the last few years has been young men and women aged between 17 and 25. Between 500 and 600 marriages a year are 'international', between an Asian born here and a spouse from the sub-continent... There are two predictable consequences. One is that the proportion of Asian children in the local population will increase because a high proportion of married women of childbearing age are either Pakistani or Bangladeshi. The second is that, since the home language in the 'international marriage' is most likely to be an Asian language, there will be a continued demand for language support for pupils entering school."

3.4.8.   The educational consequences predicted are dealt with in Section 6, Part 1. Here we are concerned only with the implicit assumptions in this passage underlying the demographic predictions. These appear to us to be overstated. They ignore any changes in attitudes to family size by the Bradford-born spouse, and the changes taking place in this regard on the sub-continent.

3.4.9.   The forecasts of population change made by the Chief Executive's Research Section assume a slow reduction in Asian fertility rates, and caution that figures for future births are the *"least reliable of their estimates"*. We share this reservation about birth rate forecasts, which are based necessarily on averages of past behaviour. Migration from rural to urban settings brings many changes, one of the most likely being a falling birth rate. This has already been evidenced during the past three decades across all population groups. None of this is simply a technicality – birth rate predictions are used as one basis for political arguments. It is therefore imperative that Bradford does not allow alarmist presentations of such figures, or their misuse in political debate.

Unemployment and other Measures of Stress in the Metropolitan District

3.4.10. In October 1993 a report entitled *Areas of Stress within Bradford District* was published by the city council. On the measures of deprivation/stress used, Bradford District was below the average for the metropolitan districts, but had a higher average than England as a whole. For instance, its unemployment rate was 12.7% compared to 14.1% for the other metropolitan districts and 10.6% for England. The comparative youth unemployment rates (16–24 years) were 21.6%, 24.8% and 19.1%. Within the district some 20% of the population lived in areas of stress and the inequalities between different areas remained much the same in 1991 as they were in 1981. Changes in unemployment rates, and in the percentage of lone parents and of overcrowding, had increased, however, between electoral wards.

Areas of Stress

3.4.11.   The City of Bradford, as we have defined it for the purposes of this Report, has three parliamentary constituencies, and statistical analyses are often related to constituencies and to electoral wards, based on Census Enumeration Districts. None of these precisely defined areas necessarily forms a meaningful social unit, such as a community or a neighbourhood, nor do they indicate discrete labour markets. The constituencies and wards are units of political organisation and the locations in which citizens exercise the right to vote, so in these respects they are relevant to decision-making within the city.

3.4.12.   The report just referred to, *Areas of Stress*, found 202, out of a total of 927 Census Enumeration Districts, to be areas of multiple deprivation, measured by 10 poverty indicators. Indicators of four aspects of poverty (income, economic, social and housing) were used, and where an Enumeration District had very high levels on two or more of these it was deemed to be affected by multiple stress. Not surprisingly, the 20% of the population so affected were not equally distributed, geographically or socially. 94% (i.e. 189 out of the 202 multiply deprived areas of stress) were highly concentrated in ten areas of Bradford and Keighley, with the inner city and (former) council estates on the outer fringes figuring prominently in both.

3.4.13.   Using the ethnic categories the distribution showed 43% of African-Caribbeans, 81% of Bangladeshis, 25% of Indians, 53% of Pakistanis, and 14% of Whites, living in areas of stress. The percentage for those born in Ireland was given as 24.6%, but it is not clear if this was included in the 14% of Whites or in addition to it. No figure was given for the Census category Other. The overall figure for non-Whites was 48%.

3.4.14.   47% of council tenants and 32% of other tenants, but only 9% of owner occupiers, and just over 9% of those buying their homes, were resident in these areas.

3.4.15.   The unemployment rates in areas of multiple stress averaged 32%, compared to the 12.7% average for the District as a whole. In some of the electoral wards in the city, including those covering Manningham, the rates were considerably higher, both for total unemployment and for youth unemployment. A quarter of those under pensionable age with a long-term illness, health problem, or handicap, were resident in the areas of multiple stress.

3.5   Inner City Bradford

Definition

3.5.1.   The boundaries of the 'inner city' are drawn in a number of different ways by different bodies, according to those matters for which they have responsibilities, the institutional arrangements by which they carry them out, and the ways in which they prioritise problems and interests. The police, Education, Health, Social Services, and voluntary bodies, work with diverse boundaries. The boundaries are also influenced by different methods of funding. Moreover what is seen as the inner city changes with time, and reflects economic and social changes external to it, as well as political decisions taken by local and central government with reference to it.

3.5.2.   Some official publications classify the inner city in Bradford as composed of five electoral wards and the outer city as composed of some 15 wards, on the basis of demographic trends (Research Section, 1996). Although inner city Bradford, defined in this way, is often portrayed as an area inhabited predominantly by Pakistanis, the majority of residents are White.

3.5.3.   It is worth noting that one of the wards included in the inner city by some official publications, Bowling, appears to have a lower natural increase in population which is much closer to four outer wards (Eccleshill, Gt. Horton, Tong, and Undercliffe) than to the others in the inner city, and it has more land available for housing than have six of the outer wards (Bolton, Eccleshill, Heaton, Odsal, Shipley E., and Thornton). Therefore if demographic trends and land available for housing are the criteria, as appears to be the case in some official publications, this ward does not fit the inner city profile. Is it that the ethnic composition of the population determines Bowling's place in the inner city?

Population Changes

3.5.4.   The changes in the 1981–91 decade show an overall decline in the inner city population and in the district as a whole, of the Whites, Blacks and Indians, and an increase among Pakistanis, Bangladeshis and Others. A point which is often stressed is that the inner city has a high natural growth rate, amounting overall to 12 per 1,000 during the 1980s compared to 3 per 1,000 in outer Bradford. Standardisation, taking account of the difference in age structures, would provide a more useful comparison of differential birth rates in these areas, and be relevant to the conclusions to be drawn, just as age at marriage, birth of first child, and completed family size, are relevant to the projections made.

3.5.5.   There was a net loss through migration from both inner and outer Bradford. For the inner city the natural increase amounted to 10,896, and the net loss through migration was 5,519, leaving an overall population increase of 5,377, just less than 6%. We have not obtained figures on outward migration by race, age and gender.

3.6   The Manningham Area

"Amongst the Most Disadvantaged"

3.6.1.   The area where the June 1995 disorders began, Manningham, has no precise authoritative definition, though local people have their own individual views of their local community's boundaries, as do some reports produced by professionals working there. We have had to take references to Manningham as they defined it. However variously defined, its profile reflects, in many respects, that of other areas of the inner city of Bradford and of Keighley, and of some outer city wards. The question was often asked, by those we saw, whether Manningham was the most deprived area in the inner city. Others told us firmly that it was. A report produced, at the request of the Leader of the Council, by an Officers' Co-ordination Group some three months after the disorders, described the area as *"amongst the most disadvantaged in the city"*, a view we certainly share.

3.6.2.   The indicators used in the *Areas of Stress* report show this to be the case for the relevant electoral wards and Enumeration Districts in the Bradford West Parliamentary constituency in which most of Manningham lies. Manningham contains all or part of each of three electoral wards: Heaton, Toller and University (see Map B Appendix 3). Bradford West constituency has a total population of 96,646.

3.6.3.   In the Manningham/Toller area, as the officers' report notes, the majority of residents were from ethnic minorities, of which by far the largest number – 12,894 (55%) – are of Pakistani origin. Though described as 'Pakistani', the majority of the young people were, of course, born in Britain, and for the most part are the children and grandchildren of those who migrated to Britain in the late 1950s and early 1960s from Kashmir, though some also have forebears whose arrival was more recent. Other residents are White 7,013 (30%), Bangladeshi 1,163 (5%), Indian 1,064 (4.5%), African-Caribbean 725 (3%), and Other 705 (3%).

3.6.4.   Out of 5,720 young people between the ages of 9 and 19 in 1995, some 4,178 were Pakistani and, of those under 30 years of age, 70% were of Pakistani/Kashmiri/Bangladeshi origin. Conversely, three-quarters of the elderly were White.

3.7   The Challenge to Bradford

3.7.1.   The most important inference we draw from the data we have reviewed in our Inquiry is the extent to which the indicators of deprivation are focussed on particular locations and on particular ethnic groups. Those involved in the disorders which began in Manningham on 9 June 1995 were from such locations.

3.8   Youth Unemployment

Its Significance

3.8.1.   We dealt with the statistics relating to unemployment in Bradford generally in paras 3.4.10 and 3.4.15. Not only does Bradford fare badly in comparison with many other parts of the UK, but the position of young people in the inner city is much worse than those in the rest of Bradford. In Manningham, 45% of the young men in the local Asian communities are recorded as unemployed. Those from the most disadvantaged circumstances are the most likely to be without jobs, and to feature among the long term unemployed and the never employed. An address in Manningham, or an address in council estates, is known to deter many employers from even offering an interview.

3.8.2.   Because of our focus on the disorders we discuss Youth Unemployment with particular reference to the young men of Pakistani and Bangladeshi background. Whilst they are particularly affected, because of a general background of poverty and educational disadvantage, the impact of youth unemployment is, of course, on young women as well as men, and it will increasingly affect young women from these particular groups as time goes by. Our particular focus means that our informants, and therefore we also, have perforce tended to concentrate on the position of the young men.

3.8.3.   The background of Asian young men inevitably affects every part of their lives, and we have found a high value placed by representatives of different Asian backgrounds on what are traditionally seen as the masculine virtues of self-reliance, assertiveness and the ability to provide for one's family. A man's position is to a large extent defined by this ability.

3.8.4. This creates a situation where any employment is seen as better than none. It should not therefore come as a surprise that a hidden economy exists, including both lawful and criminal activities. It explains why unemployment is resented so profoundly, because it is not seen just as an economic misfortune; it strikes at the root of a man's perceived masculinity. It destroys his claim to be considered a meaningful part of his community.

3.8.5. We do not support the view (does anyone?) that unemployment should cause violent behaviour. Later in this Report, using a phrase from Lord Scarman's Brixton Report, we describe it as a social condition which creates a predisposition to violent protest. As one of the smaller Asian Associations put it:

"The Manningham area is one of the deprived regions of Bradford. There are many other inner city areas which have experienced similar problems. High unemployment breeds resentment, particularly amongst the youths. This is, however, not an excuse for this type of behaviour. We understand that children as young as 10 to 12 years of age and people from outside of Bradford were also involved. The latter obviously had little or nothing to do with the local community and involvement of these groups can't be justified on grounds of deprivation and unemployment alone."

3.8.6. Of all of the 'predispositions to violence' mentioned to us there is no doubt that the overwhelming majority of our informants from outside Manningham singled out unemployment, and the boredom, aimlessness, hopelessness, frustration and anger that it breeds, as the most significant factor. Those from Manningham most frequently put resentment at the behaviour of the police in first place, closely followed by youth unemployment. Furthermore, from the little that we do know about those involved in the violent protests in June 1995 who came from areas other than Manningham, we suspect that most of them also came from a similar economic background as the locals. They too would therefore be subject to similar frustrations as the unemployed youth in the area where the disorders began.

3.8.7. We have noticed relatively little anger at the mere existence of widespread unemployment in the interviews we held, though it was obviously strongly regretted. Some of the young people who spoke to us had a general and sophisticated understanding that international economic forces were at work which could not readily be countered. But unemployment is a key issue for us because its inevitable consequences are poverty and an untypical dependency on state benefits, and there was widespread justifiable anger at the common discriminatory practices and poor educational achievements which add so heavily to the general level of unemployment for many in the Asian communities.

The Future

3.8.8. One of the consequences of lack of employment prospects, whether from the sluggish local economy, poor education, or unlawful discrimination, is the large number of Asians who are self-employed, in shops, taxis etc. But these jobs cannot be multiplied indefinitely, and there is a limit to which each of the small family businesses set up by older people can continue to provide profitable employment to younger family members. To the present level of unemployment has to be added for the future the increasing number of Asian young men there will be in Bradford entering the job market. Similarly, there will be an increasing **number** of young Asian women, of whom it is most probable that an increasing **proportion** will enter the job market. To make the challenge even greater, the shift from manufacturing to service industries requires a well-trained and educated workforce, which Bradford is not sufficiently providing, as the concerns about Education show (see Section 6, Part 1).

A Sense of Rejection

3.8.9.   Some youths will not even bother to apply for jobs that might be available, because they see selection procedures as being 'rigged' against them and apprehend hostility within the workplace. One very experienced Headteacher of a largely Pakistani/Bangladeshi Upper school put it to us in these terms:

> *"There is a feeling of optimism amongst upper school pupils, despite all the problems. But some are worried that if they engage with British society and its opportunities they will be rejected. They won't face rejection, and so they go to work for uncle."*

3.8.10.   Several young Asian men who were employed told us that their next battle was to be taken seriously for promotion by employers who had recruited them merely *"to make the numbers look alright"*. We are looking for more far-sighted employers than that in Bradford's response to this critical situation.

Narrow Career Horizons and Poor Career Advice

3.8.11.   The Head teacher of another almost entirely Pakistani/Bangladeshi Upper school told us that the jobs, and job aspirations, of male school leavers were almost entirely restricted to Asian service industries. The school was trying to widen the horizons of its students, but wondered how far it was succeeding. Outside these existing narrow horizons were mainly dreams about becoming a professional footballer or snooker player. On one recent occasion only one parent had turned up at the school for a special meeting about careers, although the school admitted that it might have chosen an inconvenient time for parents.

3.8.12.   We met a centrally located employer who had offered to stage mock job interviews for the benefit of local school students, but the offer had not been taken up. Is this evidence of the perceived pointlessness of such an exercise, given the expected attitudes of the students, or of lack of concern, by the schools concerned? Either way, we are disappointed.

3.8.13.   Many schools find work placements to widen career horizons, although some also reported meeting with racial discrimination when trying to place pupils from some ethnic minorities. Some police initiatives gave pupils opportunities to shadow police officers, but at the time we enquired we were told that a particularly well regarded scheme no longer operated. There is obviously a great deal of scope for new ideas and initiatives for schools, colleges, the university, and employers generally to develop actively.

3.8.14.   Many parents, particularly Asians who are themselves unfamiliar with British education and careers, can offer no practical guidance to their children, and have no ready means of knowing how their children are progressing, nor what opportunities are potentially realistic. We were told, by teachers and others, that some young people continue in formal education beyond the age of 16, often in a very nominal way, rather than be seen as unemployed. We cannot estimate the size of such hidden unemployment, which is thought to exist in all ethnic and class groups. The lack of employment opportunities is, however, real, and continuing in education to gain relevant qualifications is seen by many, including politicians and parents, as the only possibility of competing in the current labour market.

3.8.15.   Parents in minority groups share this view, but may have to contend additionally with the view among teachers and others that they are being unrealistic in their career aspirations for their children and so the problems they face are compounded. This interpretation shifts the problems arising from the labour market onto the shoulders of the most disadvantaged, and fails to focus on the deficiencies of the educational system, the lack of employment opportunities and the existence of racial discrimination.

3.8.16.   Too many young people are not getting wise career guidance. This professional failure, despite many exceptions, is a problem for Bradford which is a major challenge to the integrity of the Education and Training sectors, given their dependency on 'bums on seats' dominated income. The nonsense is widely understood by the people professionally involved, and we have seen some evidence that the failure is being taken seriously within upper schools, and by some firms and trainers. We underline this distortion as an important matter, to be pursued with greater vigour than at present. Both the Careers Service and teachers have commented to us on the lack of knowledge of both parents and children about the range of possible careers for pupils, apart from certain professions, such as medicine and the law.

3.8.17.   A relevant example of good practice in relation to the vocational ambitions of schoolchildren is that provided by Quest for Education and Development (QED). We were particularly impressed with its ethos, methods, and achievements generally. It was founded in 1991, primarily as a training organisation, is financially supported by the Bradford and District Training and Enterprise Council (TEC), the Home Office, and other public and private bodies, and is technically and professionally supported by people from many sections of Bradford's working population. It is developing new ways of enabling Bradfordians, mainly from the Asian communities, to gain access to mainstream economic activity. In 1994/95 QED devised a 10-part mini-television series, in partnership with Yorkshire Tyne Tees Television, to increase information, particularly for parents, about the **range** of jobs potentially available for their children.

Lack of Commercial Synergy

3.8.18.   One factor which was quoted to us as causing 'non-Muslim' owned businesses to be attacked in the disorders of June 1995, and not 'Muslim' businesses, was that there were many of them in the area which were perceived never to employ local Muslim people. This perception may be only partly true; we were told that some of the businesses attacked did employ local Asian people, but it is sufficiently true that it may have had an influence. We have quoted, in para 4.27.3, from a letter to us from a local White woman, her surprise that no Asian people were employed in many White businesses with Asian customers.

3.8.19.   It has been suggested to us that Asian businesses are just as likely to be discriminatory in their employment practices as those run by Whites, but that would not be an answer to the folly of the present situation, merely a mirror image. In any event, most Asian businesses have been built up by individuals to provide employment almost exclusively for themselves and their immediate families, with unattractively meagre rewards. Many still provide sole employment. Most, in number, deal with local people of the same background culture. One large, successful, Asian business which deals commercially across the ethnic groups, did, we found, employ a multi-ethnic workforce.

3.8.20.   It is surprising to us that many businesses fail to see the advantages of employing a workforce which reflects an increasing proportion of the local populace, not only to improve custom, but also to improve security, and inter-business links. The danger is that Bradford is developing at least two separate formal economies, one based on the traditional, but numerically contracting, White society's needs and contacts, and another based on the presently more limited needs and contacts of the growing Asian groups.

3.8.21.   Surely local Asian businesses need White customers if they are to expand, just as local White businesses need Asian customers if they are to cope with the changes in the make up of the local population? The economic future of the whole of Bradford, and of present investment in it, is bound up with the proper acceptance on equal terms of the growing, and permanent, ethnic minority communities. Unless the inevitable nature of Bradford's unique population mix is purposefully turned to advantage then hope for the future health of the local economy must be diminished.

3.8.22.   But local employers who do recognise the need to reflect more realistically the Bradford population in their workforce do face difficulties. They may be under-resourced to cope with tackling the proper implementation of equal opportunities on their own. Turnover of jobs is often small, natural wastage being the most acceptable way of downsizing. The existing workforce may be prejudiced. Potentially qualified people may need encouragement to apply. Religious and other practices may be unknown, and therefore may need clarification to avoid misunderstanding.

3.8.23.   We understand that the need for help to prospective employers is being met by bodies such as the TEC, through its support of 'Bradford's Untapped Riches Partnership' – a group of private and public sector organisations committed to promoting the training and employment of job seekers from the inner city, and by QED; we commend urgent pursuit of this support.

3.8.24.   Our remit confines us to comment on the skewed accessibility of the jobs that are available, and we can only note in passing the acute need for more jobs. The large and growing number of locally based young people ought, if those people were suitably educated, to be an important attraction to investment.

Section 4

The Disorders of 9–11 June 1995

Part 1 Introduction

4.1 Our Account

4.1.1.   In this Section we give an account of what happened in the disorders of the weekend of 9–11 June 1995. Map C (Appendix 4) may prove helpful in following our description.

4.1.2.   We have listened to many firsthand, voluntary, accounts of what took place, from people who were present at different stages of the events, and it is upon these that we have based our account. In doing so we have been conscious of some self-interested editing in the accounts given to us, and a shortage of firsthand evidence from those who were convicted of criminal behaviour. What follows is, we believe, reliable for the general purposes of our Report, but we certainly do not claim precise accuracy for all the illustrative details, and in particular for some of the timings. Our purpose is to explain to the reader the general flow of events.

4.1.3.   To help us explain the events which led from a minor policing incident to major disorders we have divided the sequence into separate stages. It is important to remember that there were, in practice, both continuous and overlapping sequences of events, and that the time involved in each described individual event may bear little or no relationship to the length of our description. The people involved may have had to make decisions very quickly, and on the basis of inadequate information and understanding, whether as members of the public or as police officers. A trap we have tried to avoid is that of criticism based on hindsight. We have had the advantage of many months of reflection, the recollection of many points of view, and knowledge of how choices worked out, on which to base our Report. Those involved at the time did not.

4.2 'The Manningham Riots'

4.2.1.   During the nights of 9–10 and 10–11 June 1995 considerable public disorder occurred in Bradford. Although no one has been prosecuted for the criminal offence of rioting, some of these events were later classified by the Chief Constable as a riot for the purposes of dealing with claims under the Riot Damages Act 1886, and it is also clear to us that some rioting technically did take place on both nights. The popular phrase 'the Manningham Riots' is sometimes used as a general description of the disorders, even though many of the disorders which took place may not have been a riot, and even though not all of the events took place within Manningham.

4.2.2.   The definition of a riot, for the purposes of the criminal law, is contained in Section 1 of the Public Order Act, 1986, based on the old Common Law definition as amended in 1714:

"1. (1) Where 12 or more persons who are present together use or threaten unlawful violence for a common purpose and the conduct of them (taken together) is such as would cause a person of reasonable firmness present at the scene to fear for his personal safety, each of the persons using unlawful violence for the common purpose is guilty of riot.

(2)   It is immaterial whether or not the 12 or more use or threaten unlawful violence simultaneously.

(3)   The common purpose may be inferred from conduct.

(4)   No person of reasonable firmness need actually be, or be likely to be, present at the scene.

(5)   Riot may be committed in private as well as in public places.

(6)   A person guilty of riot is liable on conviction on indictment to imprisonment for a term not exceeding ten years or a fine or both."

4.3   Other Inquiries

4.3.1.   Certain parts of these events have already been the subject of other, official, inquiries. Criminal proceedings relating to charges of crimes committed during the disorders have now taken place in the courts, and we refer to these in para 4.24.5. The Police Complaints Authority (PCA), at the invitation of the West Yorkshire Police Force, has carried out an investigation into complaints made by nine individual members of the public against individual police officers. Such an investigation is supervised, and separately reviewed, by members of the PCA who are not, and never have been, police officers, but they are assisted in the investigation by police officers from another police force.

4.3.2.   Our Inquiry is different from these other inquiries, both the criminal proceedings and the PCA's, in two very important respects. First, we are concerned with the events as a whole, and not with the behaviour of individuals. Individuals have not had an adequate forensic opportunity to explain their situations to us. It would be most unfair, and improper, if our Report alone were to be used by anyone to condemn any individual.

4.3.3.   Secondly, in tracing the course of events we have adopted a less onerous burden of proof than that of the 'proof beyond reasonable doubt' which is required before identified individuals, whether police officers or members of the public, can be properly and formally condemned. Insofar as we have expressed judgements about these events in general terms we have proceeded on the basis of 'the balance of probabilities'. In making any comparisons between our Report and the results of these other inquiries it is important to bear these differences of approach in mind

4.4   The Police Complaints Authority's Inquiry

4.4.1.   Following completion of the PCA's investigation the Crown Prosecution Service decided that no criminal charges should be brought against any police officer. The PCA Inquiry has upheld one complaint on a technical ground, and agreed that the police officer concerned should receive advice and retraining. The other complaints were not upheld. The PCA's general conclusions were:

"Serious public disorder followed an initial confrontation between two officers and a number of young men on 9 June 1995. Allegations of police misconduct and assault in particular were of major concern to the public. The investigation has, however, found the allegations (with one exception) to have been entirely without foundation. An example is the allegation, originally the subject of complaint to the PCA but subsequently withdrawn that a police car drove over or onto the foot of a young man. This alleged incident fuelled the violence which followed. Careful examination of the evidence leads us to the conclusion that this incident simply never occurred. The stipendiary magistrate was of the same view."

4.4.2.   In their news release of 10 April 1996 the PCA went so far as to say:

"It is our conclusion that these allegations were without foundation.

The PCA has considerable experience of major public order incidents. We know how perceptions of events can become distorted when a person is caught up in violence and so we have placed particular emphasis on the evidence of independent witnesses and on objective evidence such as medical and forensic reports.

We have also painstakingly cross-referenced the many witness statements until we are satisfied that a true picture of the situation has emerged.

With the exception of one officer who wrongly exercised his power of arrest we have found no evidence of wrongdoing by any officer. In particular the medical evidence does not support the various allegations of assault.

Each complainant has been advised of the Authority's decision in their case by letter. They have received a detailed analysis of the evidence and an explanation of how the Authority has reached its conclusion."

4.4.3.   However, in an article in *Eastern Eye* of 10 May 1996, one of the members of the PCA directly involved in the investigation made it clear that:

"...we have not held a public inquiry into what happened last June.

We never pretended to. General issues about policing in Bradford, or its social problems, are for the Bradford Commission to report on.

..... we are looking at specific complaints and not the relationship between the police and the Asian community. So there is no 'report' clearing police of misconduct, as news articles suggest."

It is important to underline the limited nature of the PCA inquiry, as it was properly explained in this *Eastern Eye* article.

4.5   An Official Public Inquiry?

4.5.1.   In the House of Commons on 21 June 1995, at the conclusion of the debate on the disorders secured by the MP for Bradford West, the Parliamentary Under-Secretary of State for the

Home Department referred to the MP's call for the Government to set up a wide-ranging public inquiry. He rejected this suggestion, saying:

"The Government are satisfied that the inquiry by the Police Complaints Authority will investigate all the circumstances surrounding the complaints against the police over that weekend. We do not feel that any more detailed and lengthy inquiry is the best way to look at the root causes."

4.5.2.   Plainly, the Government's view of the scope of the PCA's role, as expressed in such a context, was wrong, and misleading. The inflated significance thus given to the PCA Inquiry, compounded by generalised presentation in the media, has led to widespread misunderstanding and disappointment amongst the Manningham public. Based on this misunderstanding, for far too many of those who spoke to us the PCA has become yet another example of a White establishment which ignores their wider concerns.

Part 2   Friday 9 June 1995

4.6   A Normal Day

4.6.1.   Friday 9 June was a normal day for the Toller Lane Police Division. There was no apprehension that major disorders were going to take place that evening. During that evening the Acting Superintendent, who was in charge of the division whilst the Superintendent was on annual leave, came in to the Divisional Police Station – Lawcroft House – specifically to oversee the initial stages of a murder investigation.

4.7   The 'Football Arrests'

Summary

4.7.1.   The events of this evening began when, according to many local reports, a "White neighbour" contacted the police about a noisy game of football being played by a group of youths. Despite making careful enquiries, we have found no evidence to this effect. At just before 9.25 pm two policemen, one of them fairly new to the job, were on their regular, normal patrol in a police car in Rosebery Road, Manningham (leading off Oak Lane) when they passed a noisy group of young men who were playing football at the junction of Rosebery Road with Garfield Avenue. They decided to intervene, and drove round the block to return to the scene down Garfield Avenue, officially a vehicular cul-de-sac at its junction with Rosebery Road, and arrested two young men, and then a third, in what was, by any account, a struggle in which one of the two policemen radioed for assistance. The first radio call was made at 9.25 pm, closely followed by others.

4.7.2.   The incident immediately caused considerable local interest. People emerged from their houses, attracted by the noise. The policeman again radioed for assistance, and the two used their batons to keep some of the assembled people at a distance. A fourth young man expressed his objection to the way the policemen had behaved, and was himself arrested. By 9.30 pm, the first police reinforcements had arrived (including, at 9.35 pm, a dog handler), and they sought to disperse the local people. The four arrested youths were taken to the Central Bridewell, where they arrived at 9.55 pm. All the policemen left the scene together rapidly, and without any explanation. The whole incident in Garfield Avenue had taken little more than ten minutes from start to finish.

4.7.3.   We now give two separate, and slightly more detailed, accounts, both of which **we** have constructed from the several accounts given to us.

The Police Version

4.7.4.   Approximately eight young men, playing football, shouted and swore provocatively at the police officers as they drove past them, with their vehicle's windows open. When the officers returned to the scene and approached the group, all except one of the youths moved out of the middle of the road. This individual was well known to the police as a trouble maker. He, A, and another young man in particular, B, were extremely abusive and threatening, so they were arrested. Both broke free, assisted by the others.

4.7.5.   A was rearrested immediately by one officer, but B ran into his house nearby, pursued by the other officer who then arrested him. In the house a young woman, B's sister, began pulling at the officer to interfere with the arrest, and B's brother, C, attacked the officer. The first officer handcuffed A to a wrought iron gate, and went to the assistance of his colleague, arresting C. At this stage, in the house, a radio call for assistance was made. Further radio calls for assistance were made, outside.

4.7.6.   The brothers, B and C, were placed in the policemen's car, but the policemen could not leave because of the third arrested youth, A, who, at this time, was still handcuffed to the iron gate. C left the car, having been inciting the gathering and aggressive group of about 20 hostile youths to attack the officers, but C did remain voluntarily at the scene.

4.7.7.   The officers had to wave their batons to keep the advancing crowd at bay. A fourth young man, D, then assaulted one of the officers and was arrested. C was rearrested and, as other officers arrived, A was placed with the other three youths in a police van. One of the newly arrived officers found, and took charge of, the original two officers' batons, which were actually lying **unattended** in the middle of the street.

4.7.8.   By this time there was a crowd of people in the street, about 100, the majority hostile and refusing to leave, and the newly arrived police officers dispersed them. All the police officers then left. Both of the original two officers were in fear for their own safety from the time of making the first arrests until assistance arrived.

The Onlookers' Version

4.7.9.   There was a loud noise of angry adult voices in the street, which caused people to go and look at what was happening outside. Two women, the mother and sister of the two brothers, B and C, who had been arrested, together with a small boy, were following the two policemen as they took the two brothers to their police car. The sister, in particular, was protesting **very** noisily in English and Punjabi, and claiming that the police had pushed her and hit her nine month old baby, whom she was holding. She reached out towards the police, and they brushed her aside. More people were coming out of their houses, including more relatives of the arrested brothers, shouting information to each other in Punjabi (which neither police officer understood), and in English, about what was happening.

4.7.10.   In particular, there were 12–15 people watching from the entrance to a back snicket near to the policemen's stationary car, consisting of curious local residents – men, youths aged around 17 to 18, women and children, predominantly but not exclusively Kashmiri people. Up to this point it had been a normal, if noisy, arrest so far as many of the onlookers were concerned.

4.7.11.   Then, one of the two policemen, very red in the face, shouted at those in the snicket entrance:

"Get back in your houses. If you don't get back you'll be arrested."

The policemen continued to ignore questions from several residents about why they were arresting the youths, and complaints about how they had treated the young woman and her baby in the house. The sister continued to be particularly noisy in her protests, and some youths were also noisily protesting. One of the police officers then produced his baton, and waved it aggressively and angrily at those at the entrance to the snicket, ordering them to move back into their houses. They moved back into the snicket. They could see no reason why they should go inside. One of them, a White witness, spoke to us about the witness's rebellious feelings and an increased determination to stay put in the face of the police officers' unnecessarily aggressive attitude.

4.7.12.   Meanwhile, still more residents were coming out onto the street, increasing the level of noise and confusion. The people moved forward onto the pavement of Garfield Avenue to listen to what one of the arrested brothers was saying through the window of the police car. Again, the two policemen waved their batons and forced them back. Someone said *"Get their numbers"*, and as some people went forward to read the policemen's numbers, again they were repulsed.

4.7.13.   Then, several more police vehicles and officers arrived. According to one onlooker, there were two plain clothes and four uniformed policemen, two policewomen, and a dog handler. One of the policemen was *"an Asian"*. Without any fresh assessment of the situation *"they came straight in"*. One White onlooker who had refused to go indoors was threatened with arrest. When the police officer was asked by this onlooker what he would be arrested for, the policeman replied *"Anything you like"*. Three police officers, including one of the original two, dealt with the fourth arrested youth, D, and in a manner whose roughness shocked the onlookers. His protest had, we were told, been verbal only, and not aggressive.

4.7.14.   The number of local residents outside in the street had now grown to 30–40. They were offended by the undoubted hostility, and in some cases, individual rudeness, of the police towards them. The only communication initiated by the police was the repeated shouted instruction to go back inside.

4.7.15.   Some angry youths, making a great noise, were then chased away by some police officers and a police dog. Other bystanders were told very roughly by policemen, who had their batons extended, to go indoors. An elderly man, standing nearby on his doorstep, was similarly dealt with by the police dog handler and, of course, was threatened by the dog. This man's son, Mr X, a much respected local figure, was later arrested whilst outside the local police station, where he had gone to make a protest about the treatment of his father.

All the police officers then left in convoy, driving over the pavement formed to make Garfield Avenue a cul de sac, with tyres squealing in their haste to get away.

4.8   Commentary

4.8.1.   We have not heard directly from any of the young men who were arrested, but we have been considerably assisted by a verbatim transcript of the proceedings when they were tried in the Bradford Magistrates' Court, during the period 25 September to 6 October 1995, for the alleged offences for which they had been arrested on 9 June. We have heard directly from two of the policemen involved, and from some of the onlookers. We approach our task of deciding which of two versions we prefer with considerable delicacy, limiting our task to what is strictly necessary for our purpose.

Background

4.8.2.   We are very conscious that we know next to nothing of any previous inter-relationships between those principally involved, all of whom were locally based. Some of the local people thought that one of the two original policemen had been *"winding up"* the local anti-prostitution patrols (see subsection 5.22); some were not surprised to see three of the four arrested youths in trouble with the police.

The Police Decision to Intervene

4.8.3.   On any view, the incidents we have just described were extremely rowdy, and the two policemen were originally facing a larger group of young men than just the ones arrested. These, or other youths who were soon on the scene, were obviously hostile to the policemen and resented their action in arresting the first three youths. We bear in mind that the Toller Police Division has to deal with a serious level of crime, including drugs and firearms offences, which makes it a very difficult area to police. We can therefore see a case for cautious police intervention, but whether the two police officers were wise to return to the footballers down a cul-de-sac, and with no obvious plan in mind, is another matter.

4.8.4.   We take very seriously the remarks made by the Stipendiary Magistrate, sitting as Chairman of the Bench which heard the cases against those arrested in Garfield Avenue, in giving the judgment of the court. The magistrates expressly made no criticism of the two police officers for approaching the group of young men in the first place, even though, as the Stipendiary Magistrate said,

" *two officers, striding out across the street in full kit – vests, batons attached, (unfortunately these days a sinister but necessary sight in many inner cities) – might in our view have inflamed a situation in what was clearly already a sensitive area."*

The Magistrates' Decision

4.8.5.   The Stipendiary Magistrate continued:

"There followed a series of unfortunate events which are much to be regretted, and we comment in passing that neither side frankly in this incident leave the court with any great credit."

4.8.6.   The Stipendiary Magistrate, after analysing carefully the conflicts of evidence, stated that the Magistrates found that the evidence of an independent witness

"... cast very significant doubt upon the reliability of the officers' evidence in the case of [D, one of the accused]. *That doubt must extend to the evidence of both officers...*

... We say here and now that we cannot pick and choose in the prosecution case those areas which are acceptable and those areas which are unacceptable ... and having found, as we do, that the prosecution based on the evidence of the two officers fails in one area it must inevitably follow, in our view, that the prosecution case falls round their ears like a pack of cards.

4.8.7   *Apart from the problems in the evidence against* [the accused D mentioned in the last paragraph] *we have firstly considered the evidence of* [one of the two policemen originally involved]. *His reliability fell apart and it fell apart at the seams under the withering fire of cross-examination. Significant discrepancies arose between the notebook, the first and the second statement. We might have accepted one or two omissions in those areas but there were so many in number. There was, in addition, a reluctance to come clean insofar as the second statement was concerned. Further, there was a problem highlighted by* [a second witness described by the Stipendiary Magistrate as "independent"]...

"A further problem was highlighted by [the first 'independent' witness]; *that was as to the attitude of the crowd. She accepted that they were noisy, but enquiring that that crowd contained men, women, and young children. The officers' description was entirely different: mainly men; violent; shouting; screaming and abusive.*

All of these points in our view go to the very heart of the evidence of [the first policeman] *and raise significant questions as to its reliability.*

4.8.8.   *We then considered in general the evidence of* [the other policeman], *and again problems as to his reliability along very similar lines.*

"Again we rejected his evidence against [the accused D]; *again we noted discrepancies and confusion as to his description of the crowd behaviour compared with that of* [the two witnesses described by the Stipendiary Magistrate as 'independent']; *again we noted important and significant failures to include in his notebook – the first and important* [sic] *document to be made up – matters which were significant. Not only that, but matters which at the time must have been clearly significant. For example, ... The list goes on. Suffice it at this stage to say that these issues raise, in our view, serious doubts again about the reliability of the Prosecution evidence in this case.*

In passing we would also comment that we rejected much of what was said by the defendants. We were not impressed by the way in which they gave evidence, nor convinced by what they said. In particular, for example, we rejected completely [one of the arrested youth's] *description of the* [police] *vehicle going over his foot, not only because of the impossibility of his own description of how that occurred but also because of the complete lack of any significant injury..."*

4.8.9.   The magistrates dismissed all the charges against the defendants. The magistrates had the opportunity of hearing all the available evidence relating to the charges, and the advantage of hearing professional argument on all sides. They certainly did not vindicate the defendants, but they did cast serious doubt on the evidence given by the police officers. We cannot, therefore, rely on the evidence given in court by any of the main participants as to the reasonableness of the arrests, but the medical evidence made available in open court did not support the rumoured claims of excessive violence in the making of these arrests which later fuelled the disorders.

4.8.10.   It is, to say the least, unfortunate if police evidence cannot be relied upon. The magistrates' findings, whilst reinforcing in local people's minds the independence of the courts, have added confirmation to the negative experiences of the police about which we heard so often from people in Manningham and elsewhere in Bradford.

The Police Attitude to Local People

4.8.11.   The magistrates expressly found that the first independent witness just referred to

"in particular gave ... evidence truthfully and particularly impressively."

As has just been quoted, the magistrates referred specifically to this witness's account of the attitude of the local people on the street, and the entirely different description of the two officers. We regard this as the most significant issue for us in this original event.

4.8.12.   It is quite clear that local residents became very angry at the way the police treated them. The explanation for the weekend's subsequent disorder is not, in our view, simply a case of alienated youths responding violently in disapproval of a minor policing incident. It is also the anger of the responsible, respectable and law-abiding adults which continued to express itself outside Lawcroft House later that evening in protest at what had happened to some of them, on their doorsteps, and which unintentionally encouraged many of the young men who expressed their anger violently to behave uncharacteristically for the community from which they came. It is clear to us that amongst the local residents there was very little sympathy for at least two, if not three, of the youths initially arrested. In considering what happened after these initial arrests took place we have to distinguish carefully between genuine protest (and exactly what the protest was about), the demands which followed the protests, and the criminal behaviour of violence.

The New Style of Police Equipment

4.8.13.   During 1994 there was a major change in the appearance of police officers in West Yorkshire, and the comment of the Stipendiary Magistrate in para 4.8.4 indicates a common public reaction to the sight. The wearing of protective vests, and the provision of side-handled batons and rigid handcuffs, instead of the former (and much less visible) traditional truncheons and folding handcuffs, has caused adverse comment from members of the public. It is seen as offensive, not defensive, and therefore provocative. Compared with the old style of equipment there is no doubt that it is an apparently threatening development. From the public's point of view, it appears that the police are expecting and provoking trouble in a particular situation when the new style batons are drawn, accompanied by a shouted command to keep back. To bystanders such a sight would be offensive.

4.8.14.   The police have good reason to protect themselves. In 1994, in West Yorkshire, 796 officers were assaulted whilst on duty, with the additional organisational consequence that 2,124 working days were lost to an overstretched force. Defensive training was introduced early in 1995 as a necessary precursor to the issue of the new equipment to any officer. We are satisfied that senior police officers are conscious of the need for a very strict discipline to be followed in the use of the equipment. There is no doubt in our minds that the officers using their batons to keep a crowd at bay were following their training in the defensive use of the batons. No one was injured by the batons. Our concern is that the use of the technique in the particular circumstances was unnecessary, and a provocation to anger.

Our Conclusion

4.8.15.   In our view, the two policemen, caught up in what for them appeared a difficult, fraught and dangerous situation which they had entered without any clear plan of what they intended to achieve, completely misread the behaviour of the majority of the gathering residents. The description by one of the policemen was of a crowd who were mainly men; violent, shouting, screaming, and abusive. We do not doubt that there were hostile youths present. Yet, according to several people whom we judge to be mature and responsible adults, the group which this policeman threatened with his baton comprised men, women, and young children; noisy, but enquiring, rather than hostile.

4.8.16.   Much of what was being shouted was in Punjabi. There was, too, some hostile element in the ever-increasing number of people. Two officers arresting three struggling young men in these circumstances probably did reasonably require further assistance. But, when the additional police officers arrived, they only had the urgent radioed requests for assistance as a basis on which to judge a complex situation. When they arrived, they, too, did not read it accurately.

4.8.17.   There was no differentiation made between curious local residents who later became protesters, responsible people trying to calm things down, and trouble-makers. All members of the public there were treated with equal hostility and contempt by the police. No attempt was made to explain what the police were doing, even when the arrests had been accomplished and all the activity of the other officers had ceased. Even the manner of exit, across the traffic barrier pavement, was unnecessarily provocative. The police swept in, and then swept out, having acted throughout as though the local residents were of no account, and incapable of understanding an explanation.

4.8.18.   It is difficult to understand how local officers should so misunderstand a local situation, and think it satisfactory that local residents could be so completely ignored for the purposes of intelligent conversation. How can such behaviour be regarded as policing with the consent of the community?

4.8.19.   The use of a dog handler is particularly telling. We can understand that all available support should rally to an emergency call for assistance by a police officer. We do not accept that all available support should be used without first checking that it is appropriate. The use of a dog where there is little evidence of violence, as was the case, we believe, with the people in Garfield Avenue, is questionable. The use of a dog against an elderly man on his own doorstep is even more questionable. The use of a dog in an area where the predominant culture regarded such an animal (with good reason in the culture's original setting) as unclean disclosed a lack of knowledge or of concern which is ominous.

4.8.20. The police activity in Garfield Avenue displayed all the signs of strangers caught up in circumstances they did not understand. A minor policing incident, because of the arrogance and ignorance which it disclosed to the local people, became a source of anger to a whole neighbourhood, and not only to people of Asian background, nor only to young people, as news of the incident rapidly spread.

4.8.21. We suggest that it was not entirely the individual fault of the policemen involved that they did not read the situation correctly. We have to question whether it is possible for White police officers to carry out their duties properly in an area so heavily settled by peoples of other languages and cultures, until the police force itself is much more a reflection of those cultures in its ethos, training, intelligence, and capacity to form constructive local relationships. We deal more generally with public concerns about policing in Section 6.

4.9 The Two Rumours

4.9.1. In the background of the disorders, from their commencement at about 10.00 pm on this Friday evening until the Sunday afternoon and beyond, there was considerable confusion about the causes of the indignation which so many local people were demonstrating. We have just described the anger of local people at the way they had been treated by the police in Garfield Avenue. It is also clear that individual experiences of racial insensitivities by the police, accumulated over many years, from crude offensiveness to complacent ignorance, provided a basis for the strength of feeling which was abroad in the local community, and that this indignation was widely felt by older, respected members of the local community. But it is also clear that some of the strongly and widely held views about what precisely had happened in Garfield Avenue during the original incident were wrong. We give the two examples of persistent allegations which have been repeatedly quoted to us, even by mature older people who were involved in persuading the youths to calm down.

4.9.2. They are clearly set out in the following quotations from contemporary newspapers:

1. An alleged police attack on an Asian woman.

"Three boys told [an older man] *who had remonstrated with them that they were protesting because an Asian woman had been manhandled by the police."*

"I think the trouble was started by a policeman attacking a girl – they also attacked a baby."

"We heard that two boys were playing football outside their neighbours; they were English neighbours and they called the police. When the police came the boys ran into their house. One of the boys' sisters tried to stop the police taking the two boys and one policeman pushed her and tore her clothes. That's why the trouble started."

2. An alleged outrageous assault by police.

"The story goes that a police van ran over the foot of an Asian teenager after a football match.

The two policemen got out of the car and, with intense amusement at what they had done, began laughing, eyewitnesses said. They began harassing the youth and, while his foot was still caught under their car, they decided to arrest him."

1. and 2. *"A fresh claim has emerged that a nine-month-old baby girl was hit on the side of her body with a truncheon...*

"Formal complaints have now been made against two police officers who were involved in the initial incident on Friday evening.

The first complaint alleged a police car was driven over the foot of an 18-year-old youth while he was playing football in the street.

The second complaint .... alleges that a 40-year-old mother, her three children and grandchild were allegedly assaulted with a police truncheon."

4.9.3.   The rumours continued to grow, and rapidly reached bizarre proportions. We were told by a very mature and widely experienced Asian professional man:

"What went through the community from household to household was that Muslim women were being attacked by the police".

A White man who met some young Asian friends late on the Friday evening was told that the baby was in intensive care, and the police had torn a lady's dress off. One mature woman, on enquiring in Oak Lane what had happened to cause the fire in Oak Lane, and the gathering crowds of people, was told:

"The police have knocked over and killed a little Asian girl."

By Saturday morning the rumour that the little girl had died in the Bradford Royal Infirmary was common!

4.9.4.   These two rumours appear to us to have little, or no, foundation in fact.

4.9.5.   In relation to the first, the PCA referred to:

'The baby who, along with her mother and grandmother, is alleged to have been assaulted. Two different accounts are given of this alleged assault but either would have caused obvious, if not catastrophic, injury.

Happily, the doctor found the baby well with no trace of injury. We can think of no reason why a mother should lie but we have not said that she has.

In the few minutes of chaos and excitement her perceptions may become distorted. We can also think of no reason why, or how, the doctor's evidence should or could lie."

No one has come forward to us to justify this rumour that a baby was assaulted.

4.9.6.   In relation to the second rumour, according to the article in *Eastern Eye* by the PCA member, referred to in para 4.4.3. above:

"The magistrate ... completely rejected the account of the police car running over the youth's foot, so did the two doctors who examined the youths, and so do we."

Although we have had to rely solely on the verbatim account of the evidence given in the magistrates' court to understand the detail of the allegation we, in turn, cannot comprehend how the police vehicle could possibly have run over the foot of someone who claimed he was unaware of the vehicle's approach because he had his back to it. We, too, cannot take this rumour seriously and, in the absence of any evidence given to us to the contrary, we firmly reject it.

4.10   Further 'Protest Arrests'

Background

4.10.1.   The Divisional Superintendent was on leave, and as a consequence there was an Acting Superintendent in charge, and an Acting Inspector on duty that night. When the Acting Inspector for the 10 pm night shift took over at the local divisional police station, Lawcroft House, he was briefed about the murder enquiry, and about the events in Garfield Avenue just described. He therefore decided that the officers going off duty should remain on duty in case of further trouble.

4.10.2.   A group of youths went to Lawcroft House, protesting about the arrest of their friends but, because Public Order offences and a juvenile were involved, the prisoners had actually been taken direct to the Central Bridewell. By this time, 10 pm, disorder in Oak Lane had already begun.

4.10.3.   A quite separate protest began when four of the residents who had seen the original incident went up to Lawcroft House, intending to protest to the officer in charge about what had happened. By 10.30 pm, less than an hour after the 'football arrests' in Garfield Avenue, about 60 local men, predominantly Kashmiri, had arrived outside Lawcroft House to protest at what had happened, as an example of inappropriate policing. As the news spread of their intended protest they were joined by others, but the purpose of the properly conducted older protesters was soon lost in a confusion of perceptions by both the police and community leaders called in to discuss the increasingly threatening situation.

The Demands, the Protests, and the Police Response

4.10.4.   There were demands from youths for the immediate release of the four who had been arrested. The crowds outside Lawcroft House were mainly teenagers and young men, but there were middle-aged men there too. For the older men, the concern was not for those who had been arrested, but the hostility and contempt shown to the local residents by the police when the arrests were made. Indeed, it is quite clear to us that many local residents had no sympathy at all for some of the arrested youths. It is, therefore, in our view, important throughout to distinguish between the broader based and proper concerns of the older residents (particularly those of the older protesters from Garfield Avenue), and the indignation of the younger men which was becoming more focused on the arrested youths and on getting them released.

4.10.5.   In the general anger the most vocal expressions were the demands for the release of all the prisoners coming from young men, who were concerned about how the prisoners might be being treated. In the shared anger and apprehensions, restraint of the young men by the older men was hardly possible at this time.

4.10.6.   The Acting Inspector wanted to get to the bottom of the protests, but as he approached the public exit he could see the size of the growing crowds outside, and the unruliness. A man pointed out to him a group of older men from the Garfield Avenue area and some of them were invited into an interview room for a discussion.

4.10.7.   Between 10.30 pm and 10.45 pm seven further arrests were made for public order offences in the vicinity of Lawcroft House, and unsuccessful attempts were made by local officers to disperse the crowds gathering there. Another public order arrest was made in Oak Lane. One of those arrested was Mr X, the son of the elderly man who had been affronted by the use of a police dog against him on his own doorstep, who was one of the original dignified small protest group from Garfield Avenue. He was awaiting a hernia operation, and did not move away sufficiently quickly when ordered by the police to move back. It would have involved him jumping 3–4 feet over an obstacle, he told us. Although not an old man he was, and is, a widely respected figure in the local community. We have not sought details of the other people arrested at this time, but we understand that they too had no previous convictions and were well regarded locally.

4.10.8.   The people arrested outside Lawcroft House were brought inside through the public entrance, and in the view of the older men who had been invited in for a discussion. The older men were further angered at the arrest of people they told us they respected.

4.10.9.   Tension increased amongst the crowds, as it became clear that the prisoners would not be released immediately in response to demands. Some people became increasingly abusive, and were throwing stones. The situation was plainly worsening, and could not be left by the police. On Friday evenings there are always a lot of people about on Oak Lane, and the crowds continued to grow – older protesters, excited youths, the curious, all mixed together. In addition, the groups of pickets from the anti-prostitution campaign were in their places on the nearby streets, and word was quickly spread of 'something happening in Oak Lane' by associates with cars and mobile phones.

4.10.10.   The Acting Inspector sensed the concern of the older residents from the Garfield Avenue area about the increasing tension outside, and their reluctance to be involved. Despite pressure to remain, they left Lawcroft House at about 10.45 pm. Those of their number to whom we spoke told us that they were not aware of the formal processes for making a complaint, nor were they told of them. They found the police unresponsive. Indeed, one told us he was himself told by a police officer at one point: *"Either go home, or you will be arrested".* Those who went home contacted councillors.

4.11   Commentary

Police Misreading

4.11.1.   Whilst the events in Garfield Avenue and the two rumours referred to in subsection 4.9 were the immediate occasion of the anger of many of the protesters, we have no doubt that the clinching factor in uniting young and old in openly expressing anger against the police was these further arrests of some of the protesters.

4.11.2.   Once more, the police officers outside Lawcroft House were being hostile and indiscriminate in dealing with the many residents who were there with no thought of creating public disorder, but with a determination to 'let the police know' that the unexplained hostility and contempt experienced by residents in Garfield Avenue earlier that evening was intolerable to them.

4.11.3.   We share the reaction of a White councillor who was told, by an outraged local resident, of the arrest of Mr X outside Lawcroft House:

"When I heard X had been arrested I got straight on to the police to make that point. For goodness sake, he's a member of the liaison committee just set up with the police over the issue of prostitution in Manningham. He just isn't the sort of person who'd be out here causing trouble."

4.11.4   We note the almost total absence of police explanation directly to the angry people on the streets, from the Friday night until the Sunday. To ignore repeatedly the very people who plainly are angry displays a distance from local people which is striking. We consider the police to have misread the local situation for a third time on this Friday evening. We have met, and spoken at length, with those of different backgrounds who know Mr X well. We have met, and spoken at length, with many of the people who were onlookers at the original incident in Garfield Avenue, and who went to Lawcroft House to protest at the contemptuous way they had been treated. This evidence, whilst very persuasive, might not be completely convincing of itself – it is open to the easy criticism 'these people would say that' in order to justify their involvement on that evening.

4.11.5.   What has finally persuaded us to accept the validity of this evidence is first, the consistency of the unfortunate police attitude displayed outside Lawcroft House with that, twice, in Garfield Avenue, as presented to us by reliable, independent evidence; secondly, the fact that this local Asian community in Manningham had never before been involved in such widespread collective protest against the police, or in widespread disorderly behaviour, and that by the Sunday evening (with limited success on the Saturday) the older men had actively and effectively imposed a local discipline on 'their' young men who had behaved so badly. Public disorder was not part of their intention or behaviour, at any stage from initial curiosity in Garfield Avenue to public protest outside Lawcroft House.

4.11.6.   We balance this criticism of the police against our understanding that intervention by the police to make people do what they are unwilling to do is often likely to meet with resistance, and is rarely going to be welcomed by those on the receiving end. It is understandable that police officers carrying out these difficult tasks should want to reduce the risk of crowd involvement in a police operation (as in Garfield Avenue) or of crowd violence (as in Oak Lane) to a minimum.

4.11.7   Almost any crowd with a common, generalised concern, can be used and misled by those with other agendas, and the apparent success of the patrols against the prostitutes (see subsection 5.22) had given some young men the idea that they could be stronger than the police. Yet the basis of sensible crowd control must be a reading of its intent and, where possible, careful discrimination between different elements in a crowd.

4.11.8.   We have concluded that there was a gap in understanding between police officers and the population of Manningham, and in these circumstances crowd control must be difficult to achieve, particularly in sudden, unplanned incidents such as happened when the two policemen made the original arrests on 9 June in Garfield Avenue, or when the hastily summoned support arrived in Garfield Avenue, or when the crowds of protesters appeared at Lawcroft House on the Friday evening. We consider this gap in mutual understanding to be a most serious matter, and can understand how it caused a succession of misunderstandings which became the pretexts for criminal disorders. It is an illustration of the necessity for policing by consent.

Concern for Those in Custody

4.11.9.   We are not aware of any direct basis for the concern which so many people in the crowds expressed about the well being of those held in custody, other than rumour, and the high profile cases of police mistreatment of those held in custody by other forces. But the concern was real enough. It provoked the demands for early release of the prisoners. It also provoked the concern of those public representatives who were discussing with the police ways of quietening down the crowds, that the representatives should be able to demonstrate that the arrested people had not been ill-treated by producing them.

4.11.10.   As with the affront involved in the use of a dog by the police, it is necessary to understand a set of culturally influenced perceptions which would not be as strongly present to a White crowd. It may well have been an influence for the older people that in their places of origin, there is, we were told, a strong likelihood that prisoners arrested in a confrontation with the police would be mistreated whilst in custody. The fact that the prisoners were kept in custody for, in the longest case, over six hours against an expectation of much earlier release, created another unfounded rumour which fuelled the violent behaviour. Unfortunately, many young people believe that prisoners are mistreated, particularly in the obscurity of being taken into custody, and especially if they happen to be non-White. We deal with the lengths of time the prisoners were actually held in custody at para 4.14.2.

Complaints Procedures

4.11.11.   People wished to complain about the actions of the police in Garfield Avenue. It is clear that the people wishing to complain were unfamiliar with the formal processes. This lack of familiarity showed again the following day. Complaints against the police are inevitable, irrespective of their validity. It is regrettable if there is not an effective process readily available for handling them.

The Anti-Prostitution Patrols

4.11.12.   We refer to the local campaign against prostitution in subsection 5.22. It was not directly linked to, or a cause of the disorders. But the existence of such an informal organisation, capable of disseminating information rapidly to young people already on the streets, undoubtedly set a precedent for such organisation as there was amongst the different groups of violent young men. We would be surprised if the success of the anti-prostitution campaign, in the eyes of the young people who had been involved, was not also a factor in encouraging some youths to believe that the restrained protests of their elders against the police would prove once more to be inadequate, and that their direct action would again be successful.

4.12   The First Night of Disorders

4.12.1.   In addition to the increasing crowds outside Lawcroft House, by shortly after 10 pm, youths were already committing criminal damage in the Oak Lane area, at a distance from Lawcroft House. At about 10.30 pm in Oak Lane, a shop window was smashed. There was a fire in the middle of the road, made from a nearby greengrocer's pallets. When Councillor A was driving along Oak Lane at about 10.30 pm there were already youths throwing empty bottles at the police. Those involved in this disorder were not indissolubly joined to the crowds assembling in protest outside Lawcroft House. Again, we have to distinguish between different groups of people. The local residents are no more a homogeneous bloc than in any other part of the Bradford Metropolitan District.

4.12.2.   At 10.45pm other officers were called from **nearby Divisions** under the standard police immediate response system which is used whenever assistance is required by one division for an unexpected situation. At first they were used to maintain order outside Lawcroft House. They, as well as the local officers, were met with bricks and bottles.

4.12.3.   In view of the bricks and bottles being thrown at the police officers the Acting Superintendent, at about 11 pm, decided that it would be necessary to deploy all available officers to prevent further crimes and to disperse people in the Oak Lane area, in full public order protective equipment, i.e. shields, helmets and flame-proof overalls, to prevent injuries from the missiles. This equipment is popularly called riot gear, and is used only exceptionally, as distinct from the equipment referred to in para 4.8.13 above. The first objective was to clear the area to the front of Lawcroft House, because of the size of, and the behaviour of some of the people in, the crowds, which was then estimated at 300.

4.12.4.   Before midnight there was more serious disorder in Oak Lane, leading eventually to an attack on a car saleroom and garage: vehicles in the forecourt were set on fire, and stones and petrol bombs were thrown, damaging cars and windows. A burning barricade was set up across Oak Lane. Because of the violence on the streets the Acting Superintendent, at shortly after midnight, asked for a **Force** emergency response, and over the next hour officers came from all over West Yorkshire.

4.12.5.   Later, as police cleared Oak Lane a group of young men went down St. Mary's Road and stoned other windows at the same garage premises. At 3.45 am a car was seen on a Lawcroft House video to pull up at the front of Lawcroft House. The boot was opened, and baseball bats and other weapons were removed by the occupants. Disorderly behaviour continued until nearly 4 am, with parading cars playing loud music.

4.12.6.   We have heard from several local residents of their amazement that the police did not concentrate on the relatively few trouble-makers, but treated all the people who were on the streets as potential trouble-makers. One mature Asian man, who is active in local affairs, told us he saw only the Community Police Constable walking round, talking and influencing people constructively. The police *"appeared like aliens"* was one description which encapsulates a general reaction. Several witnesses told us of the police restricting the movement of Asians, including an 11-year-old boy who had become stranded from his home by the suddenness of the events, but not of Whites. On the other hand, two White observers, both much involved in local affairs, thought that the police behaved *"impassively"* and *"quite properly"*. We note the differences in public expectations, based we were told, on experience of police behaviour.

4.12.7.   To the consternation of some of the onlookers who spoke to us, some of the police officers had no identification numbers evident on their protective overalls. The police accept that this may have been the case on the Friday night. The protective clothing, it is said, would have been hurriedly grabbed from the store room, and some officers may not have attached individual epaulettes in the hurried emergency response. It was an unfortunate circumstance which added to the indignation and anger felt by local residents. Once again, they felt that they were being treated as though they were unimportant, even to the extent of normal rules of proper conduct being ignored by the police.

4.12.8.   According to the police records, the disorders on this first night resulted in a White-owned chemist's shop being looted; a Sikh-owned supermarket being extensively damaged; a White-owned DIY store being damaged; 11 cars being damaged – these included two police cars which were hit by stones and five BMW saloons which were destroyed by fire on the forecourt of the White-owned Garage in Oak Lane; this garage's premises being damaged; and two windows in property owned by *"Muslim Asians"* being broken.

4.12.9.   It should, therefore, be clear that the extent of the disorder which erupted spontaneously on this Friday night was not extensive. However, a brief, factual recital of the damage caused does not convey the apprehension which many local residents felt as they saw the violence escalating. We heard of the terror of one mother (an Asian woman) alone in the house with her two children, as the firebombs were thrown at the nearby garage.

4.12.10. The instructions to the assembled police officers were to disperse the crowds in Oak Lane, but only to make arrests for serious crimes. This action took place without further arrests. By the time it was concluded all except one of the youths arrested in Garfield Avenue had been released from the Central Bridewell. The exception was a juvenile, who was released at 4.20 am. The disorder continued sporadically in the Oak Lane area until about 5.15 am.

4.13   The First Discussions

Background

4.13.1.   The discussions between the police and local representatives took place against a background of worsening disorder, and of considerable confusion about what had already happened. Those responsible for the disorder were not a cohesive force, and those on both sides of the discussions in Lawcroft House knew very little or nothing of the detailed background to the protests which underlay the disorders. The non-police participants gleaned much of their knowledge of the background from the leaders of a substantial group of youths who were near to Lawcroft House.

4.13.2.   We give both the police account and a generalised account of what happened based upon fairly widespread agreement about the discussion which took place. There is some understandable confusion in the recollections of people about the precise timings of different conversations, and different versions of precisely what was said. These variations are not important for our purposes.

The Police Initiative

4.13.3. As the crowds of protesters outside Lawcroft House grew, the police were contacting several people, recognised as 'leaders in the local community', to influence and calm the obviously deteriorating situation. The use of this informal mechanism is not unusual whenever the White dominated public services seek to communicate with Asians. The police were following a well-established convention. Shortly after the crowds began to gather, the Acting Inspector, on the instructions of the Acting Superintendent, sent for the sergeant in charge of community involvement, Sgt Z, who was off duty, and tried to contact Asian councillors.

4.13.4. One of the first local community leaders to arrive at Lawcroft House was Councillor A. He was a councillor whom the Acting Inspector had unsuccessfully tried to contact, and who had coincidentally come upon the protest and disorder on his way home. When Councillor A arrived in his car, youths were already throwing bottles in Oak Lane. At the top of Oak Lane, at the junction with Heaton Road, Councillor A spoke with a group of about 20 youths, who alleged that the police were arresting people unreasonably. He therefore went straight to Lawcroft House, and spoke with Sgt Z. Sgt Z had also collected Councillor D, and arranged for an influential youth leader to be collected.

4.13.5. At this time the sergeant did not know any background details, but shortly afterwards he was able to report to Councillor A that there had been some arrests, and that the people involved were being dealt with in accordance with normal procedures. Councillor A agreed to help try to calm things down. He asked about the releasing of the prisoners, and understood that the charges against them were not grave. He further understood that they would be released in about an hour, provided that order outside had been restored.

4.13.6. He advised that the police vans which were being stoned should be withdrawn. He thought that they were 'sitting ducks', and advised that their presence was a challenge, rather than a deterrent. Councillor A was constructive and reasonable, according to the police. He then left Lawcroft House, to find out more about the causes of the discontents.

4.13.7. Within ten minutes of the police vans being withdrawn, the serious attacks on properties in Oak Lane began.

The Protesters' Initiative

4.13.8. By 10.30 pm another councillor, Councillor B, had been contacted by a group of Manningham young men, who said that the police had arrested some of their friends, that other young people in the area were getting agitated, and that *"things might be kicked off at any time."* He telephoned Councillor C, who said she had already been contacted by a group from Skinner Lane, and she was going to Lawcroft House.

4.13.9. At 10.45–11.00 pm Councillor B, and some of the young men who had approached him, went to Skinner Lane, met Councillor C and her group, and the total group of 10–12 people walked to Lawcroft House. A street fire was burning in Oak Lane, where pallets had been set on fire, a group of young men were running towards Manningham Lane, the atmosphere was tense, and many people were watching from their houses as the councillors walked from Skinner Lane to Oak Lane on their way to Lawcroft House.

Information

4.13.10.   In Oak Lane councillors B and C's combined party met up with 20–25 people, mainly youths, talking to councillors A and D. Another 20–25 people were watching, but these were not involved in the *"commotion"*. They were onlookers. The young men complained of wrongful arrests and a police assault on a woman, and they were asking for the arrested youths to be released. Councillors A and D explained that they had already been contacted by the police and had had a discussion with them. As a result the police had withdrawn the vans from Oak Lane to Lawcroft House. The young men then focussed on the release of their friends who had, so they said, committed no crime, and complained generally of police heavy-handedness and racist remarks.

4.13.11.   Councillor A told them that since the police vans had gone back into the police station as agreed with him, youths should not go on damaging properties and lighting fires. He also gave to the youths the assurances he had understood from the police, that at least five of the prisoners would be released within the hour.

4.13.12.   The leaders of the youths accepted what Councillor A said, and by the use of whistles called a large number of the youths together to explain what they had just been told. This large group decided to stay on the open land known as Westbourne Green, near to Lawcroft House, until the five prisoners were released. This group was not, according to a police witness who should know, composed of youths who had been involved in the campaign against the prostitutes. Councillor B felt confident that, even though things were tense, something could be worked out, having regard to experience in handling difficult situations during the anti-prostitution campaign (see subsection 5.22). This confidence was shared by Councillor A, who thought that the situation was coming under control. After waiting a few minutes the Councillors went inside to see Sgt Z again.

The Police Account

4.13.13.   The police account to us of these discussions was:

"At about 11.45 pm, representations were made to the police by councillors A and D following dialogue with the group of youths, to the effect that the presence of police vans was exacerbating the situation. The supposed message from the streets was to the effect that if the increased presence of vans were withdrawn, the disorder would cease. In a gesture of good faith the police vans were recalled. Within ten minutes of that withdrawal, at midnight, a number of motor vehicles had been stolen and set on fire, burning barricades were set up across Oak Lane and a chemist shop had been broken into and looted...

By 12.30 am demands from the street relayed to the police by the councillors were to the effect that unless all prisoners were released immediately without charge the disorder would escalate. It was apparent from what Councillor A said to the police that the number of those arrested had been grossly exaggerated. ... An undertaking was given that the evidence would be reviewed by senior police officers in consultation with the Crown Prosecution Service prior to any individual being brought before the court. In the meantime facilities were offered, and accepted, for the community representatives to visit the cells at Lawcroft House and [the Central Bridewell] *to confirm the number of those arrested and to witness that all the prisoners concerned were well and not suffering from any form of maltreatment, as was being rumoured in the streets."*

4.13.14.   Sgt Z gave the police view to the councillors at just after midnight. The concerns of the senior police officers were to restore the streets to normality, and to deal with the complaints over time in an orderly manner.

Other Accounts

4.13.15.   Councillor A thought that there were at least 25 prisoners. Sgt Z said there were the four original prisoners, plus a further eight, but he would check – which he did. During the discussions Sgt Z pointed out that the prisoners could not be released until their papers had been properly processed, but they would eventually be bailed. It would probably take another hour. He told the councillors that the situation had deteriorated – fires had been lit, and properties in Oak Lane had been attacked. Some of the councillors said the situation would get much worse because of the strong feelings about the arrests. It was necessary to release the arrested youths to help calm things down. Sgt X said the police could not just release the prisoners, as they might face serious charges if the evidence justified such a course.

4.13.16.   It is not clear to us whether or not there was confusion in the discussions, about which prisoners were of concern to the youths with whom Councillor A had spoken, and how far these were distinguished from the men arrested outside Lawcroft House. There was, of course, an important difference in the constituencies of support for the two groups of prisoners, and those arrested in Garfield Avenue were held, not at Lawcroft House, but at the Central Bridewell because of requirements relating to the juvenile prisoner.

4.13.17.   The councillors asked, more than once, how long it would be before the prisoners would be released. Some of those representing concerns about the original prisoners appear to have thought that their release was more important than the processes which the police were required to follow, and pressed for the release of the prisoners without charge immediately. In view of the arrangement which they had made with the group of youths earlier one can at least understand their anxiety. The Acting Superintendent rightly maintained that the prisoners would have to be charged, but there would be no court proceedings until a senior police officer and the CPS had reviewed the evidence. Sgt Z pointed out the existence of the official complaints procedure to deal with any complaints.

4.13.18.   The councillors understood Sgt Z to say the releases were imminent. Twice the councillors went to the entrance, whilst waiting for the prisoners to be released, and could see the large group of people in front of Lawcroft House. They could also see the crowds from the window of the room in which they were talking with Sgt Z. Two of the youths who went into Lawcroft House with the councillors kept assessing the situation outside, and reported that the protesters were getting agitated at the delays in releasing the prisoners. The councillors refused to leave without the prisoners.

4.13.19.   Eventually, at about 1.00 am, Sgt Z asked for someone to go to the Central Bridewell, where the four people originally arrested were detained, because one of the prisoners there was a juvenile who would have to be released into the care of a responsible adult, and no relative was available. Councillor A and two youths agreed to go to the Bridewell. Councillor A had made the arrangement about these prisoners with the group of youths who were outside Lawcroft House. He was therefore the appropriate person to demonstrate that their friends had been released, and their demands fulfilled.

4.13.20.   At the Bridewell no prisoners were released, and it was difficult for Councillor A to find out what was happening to them. He waited 20 minutes and, in the end, told the constable with whom he was dealing that he would wait no longer than another five minutes. He then recollects being able to speak on the telephone to an inspector, who told him that he had been misinformed about the release of the prisoners.

"I told him of the potential for riots, but he said he was too busy and put the phone down."

4.13.21.   At 1.07 am, at Lawcroft House, the first prisoner was released after being charged and bailed. He was followed within 45 minutes by five others. The two remaining prisoners at Lawcroft House were released at 2.45 am and 3.09 am. Part of the time taken to complete the paper work was due to the time taken by the prisoners to obtain advice from the solicitor who had been called to Lawcroft House on their behalf.

4.13.22.   At just before 2.00 am Councillor A returned to Lawcroft House from the Bridewell, very angry at what had happened. He had been *"sent on a wild goose chase"*, and he had promised what he was not now able to deliver. He told Sgt Z that the police had let him down. Other councillors perceived the worsening situation, and that it would soon be out of control.

4.13.23.   Councillor B felt by this time that the police were using the councillors representing the group of youths to gain time in which to bring in reinforcements. These representatives had repeatedly had to send out messages that the assembled crowds should remain calm, because they would be out with those arrested in a few minutes, and their credibility was being eroded by what they regarded as repeated delays. They made it clear that, if the protesting youths lost confidence in the councillors to deliver what had been promised, it would be very difficult to control the youths.

4.13.24.   At about 2.20 am Councillor A had a very heated exchange with the Acting Superintendent, protesting that four hours had elapsed, and still the prisoners were not released, laid all responsibility for what was going to happen on the police, and walked off with the youth leaders who had been involved in the negotiations. He left Lawcroft House, but waited with the youths outside, making clear his anger and frustration to them.

4.13.25.   The three other councillors, B, C, and D, stayed, but conversation became meaningless and at 2.30 am they left. Councillor C went to the Bridewell with Sgt Z; councillors B and D stayed in front of the police Station, where Councillor A and some community elders were addressing the nearby people from the steps; Councillor D mingled with the crowds for 15 minutes and then went home.

4.13.26.   There were problems at the Bridewell. The officers there had independently to weigh not only the nature of the evidence on which the prisoners had been arrested, but also what was already known to the police about any of the prisoners, before agreeing to release them. Councillor C found the Sergeant there very reluctant to release the prisoners. Eventually they were released between 3.15 am and 4.20 am, the last a juvenile into Councillor C's care.

4.14   Commentary

The Trouble Makers

4.14.1.   It is clear, from the timing of the first outbreak of disorder, that there was no necessary connection between the disorder on Oak Lane and the discussions in Lawcroft House, and therefore with any delay in releasing the prisoners. By the time the most unfortunate lack of co-operation between the two police stations resulted in Councillor A having to make a pointless journey to the Bridewell, which was the most inflammatory stage of the discussions, most of the disorders on this first night had already taken place.

The Periods of Detention

4.14.2.   An official police explanation for the delays in releasing those arrested was given in a letter of 13 March 1996 to the MP for Bradford West:

"I have previously noted your concern regarding delays in releasing some of those arrested and each case has been examined by my investigating officers who were satisfied that the periods of detention were not unreasonable in the circumstances. It may help you to understand these delays by pointing out that the majority of those detained (both at the Bradford Bridewell and Lawcroft House police station) requested the services of the same solicitor which created logistical problems for the legal representative concerned and led to significant delays. Furthermore, following demands that released prisoners should be handed to members of the community, Councillor C attended the Bradford Bridewell and was present when those prisoners were released. Councillor C also acted as the 'appropriate adult' in respect of a juvenile prisoner whose parents could not be contacted at that time. The assistance of Councillor C was greatly appreciated by my staff and contributed to the expeditious but co-ordinated release of the Bridewell prisoners."

4.14.3.   We have no criticism to make of the time it took the police at Lawcroft House to process the prisoners held there. By contrast we note the much longer time taken at the Bridewell. The conduct of the police in dealing with prisoners is covered by an official code issued by the Home Secretary, dated 10 April 1995, *The detention, treatment and questioning of persons by police officers*. We have received no evidence that these requirements were not complied with.

4.14.4.   Taking a broad view of what we have been told about the circumstances, and advice from an experienced defence lawyer, we have not felt compelled to investigate further. Given the considerations which the officers at the Bridewell had to consider, the time taken may not have been unreasonable, though we wonder how far the serious concerns of the officers at Lawcroft House were allowed to influence progress. Even though we are surprised at the lack of understanding between the two police stations, we consider that it is too facile to ignore the circumstances in which the officers responsible for the treatment of the prisoners were placed and then to assume that all other considerations should have been overridden by the need to meet the situation outside Lawcroft House. That would be to employ tunnel vision as well as hindsight.

4.14.5.   Of much greater relevance is the failure to give an adequate explanation of the reasons for delay to the Councillors, and to Councillor A in particular.

Belief in the Rumours

4.14.6.   The cumulative recent experiences of local people by now included the indiscriminate hostility shown twice by the police in Garfield Avenue and again outside Lawcroft House, the pointless journey between the two police stations of Councillor A, the lack of direct conversation between the police and members of the public on the streets, and the failure to display identification numbers on the riot gear overalls. Given also the more general adverse experiences to which we refer in Section 6 it is understandable that the rumours of police misconduct should find such receptive ears on the streets. The only counters to these adverse experiences were the one Community Constable talking with people on the street outside Lawcroft House, and the efforts of Sgt Z inside.

Police "Heavy-handedness"

4.14.7.   We have heard from many local residents about the *"heavy-handedness"* of the police on the Friday and Saturday nights, by comparison with the Sunday. It has been said that the appearance of the police in riot gear on both occasions was provocative, and *"raised the temperature"*. We think that this is very likely, but we do not criticise the decision to wear riot gear. Given the hazards the police faced in confronting a crowd which included hostile, violent people, the decision to use riot gear was both justifiable and, in the event, justified on both evenings. Only when prospects of a settlement became apparent could the police take a chance with the safety of their officers, as happened on the Sunday. The instructions given by the officer in charge for the police vans to be withdrawn, and for arrests to be limited to serious crimes, clearly show his concern to avoid unnecessary confrontation.

4.14.8.   Our criticism is not of heavy-handedness, but of repeated organisational incapacity to police by consent. We criticise the underlying gap in understanding between the police and local residents. We think a much more communicative approach should have been selectively used before it became necessary to disperse the groups of violent young men. It is, however, comparatively easy for us to distinguish between different elements in the crowds of people who were on the streets near Lawcroft House, and in Oak Lane, on this evening. It must have been difficult for the senior police officers in Lawcroft House, already busy with a murder enquiry and all the routine of a normal shift, suddenly to have to deal with large crowds of angry people amongst which were determined troublemakers. It is naive to believe that in such circumstances the police can, in practice, clearly identify the 'goodies' and the 'baddies' when disorder actually takes place, and the police have to insist on dispersal, unless they have a very sound knowledge of the local people involved. So far as we can tell, no attempt was made, and it should have been, however incomplete the police' knowledge of the local people.

Local Residents' Responsibility

4.14.9.   We have criticised the institutional inability of the almost entirely White police force to read the local situation. We must now criticise those of the local population who, whilst not sympathetic at all to public disorder, were part of very large crowds which were alarming in their appearance, both to the police and to other members of the public. This criticism has to be balanced against our comments in paras 4.11.9 and 10, and the expectation of many in the crowds that the negotiations being carried out on their behalf by community leaders justified their presence and support. Some who had come to protest did leave the scene. Only some can justify their continued presence in the crowds by an active peace promoting role.

Part 3 Saturday 10 June 1995

4.15 Background

4.15.1. The following day, Saturday, some of the local shopkeepers were able to use the shutters on their premises as an insurance against further damage. Others boarded up, encouraged, we were told, by firms selling their services to cover the windows. Some extra security guards were employed at the Oak Lane Garage which had been attacked the previous night. There was widespread apprehension of more trouble to come. The police could not properly ignore the obvious tensions, nor the obvious fears of many local residents.

4.15.2. Apart from the time spent in a meeting held at Lawcroft House, Councillor A was on the streets in the vicinity of Oak Lane all day, indeed until 2.30 am next morning. He tried to calm the young men down but they would not listen to him. He was told that it was clear from the events of the previous night that Councillors had no power, and that they had lied about the releases of the prisoners. The young men therefore would take matters into their own hands. They were very angry.

4.15.3. Throughout the morning the police at Lawcroft House had to deal with the Press, and with those whose premises had been damaged in the events of the previous night. There were, of course, many other matters to attend to, including the murder inquiry, and the supervision of the anti-prostitution street patrols, at this tense time. The Divisional Vice Squad negotiated the suspension of the patrols through their usual contacts, and this established working relationship also helped to steer the anger of local people into a peaceful demonstration which some of the leaders of the patrols helped to organise for the following afternoon, Sunday.

4.15.4. There were many local people visiting Lawcroft House during the Saturday morning in connection with the events of the previous evening. There were those whose property had suffered damage, and those who wanted to protest at the actions of the police. We have heard several accounts of people who wished to complain not being helped to understand the proper process or the availability of relevant forms. It is said that at one point only the advice of a White councillor, who happened to be there, caused the appropriate forms to be located and made available – until they ran out.

4.16 The Second Discussions

4.16.1. Discussions with people who might influence the tense situation were again instituted by the police. The invitation met with a ready response from people apparently representative of the local residents, reflecting the widespread local concern at what had happened the previous evening. The Bradford Racial Equality Council was active from this day, and through the following weeks, in servicing what became a liaison committee representative of the city and of local communities.

4.16.2. In the afternoon, the meeting was begun at Lawcroft House at 2.00 pm, and lasted until early evening. There were two representatives from the Council for Mosques, a local vicar, the local MP, local councillors, and four young men who came on behalf of the crowd which was again growing outside Lawcroft House. The police were represented by the Divisional Commander, recalled from leave, and who chaired the meeting, an Assistant Chief Constable, and a Superintendent who was the head of the Force's Discipline and Complaints Department. For the police, the purpose of the meeting was to avoid a repetition of the previous night's disorders.

4.16.3.   Representatives from the residents actually involved in the protests at the original arrests (including Mr X who had been arrested outside Lawcroft House the previous evening) arrived at Lawcroft House **by coincidence**. They had a meeting to do with the prostitution campaign already arranged with a police officer, who told them that that meeting was cancelled. The residents asked the councillors why they, the councillors, were there. The councillors promised to get these residents included in the meeting.

4.16.4.   Even by Saturday afternoon the facts on which the protests were based were not at all clear to some of the representatives. One very vocal representative told us comparatively recently that those arrested in Garfield Avenue had not been bailed until 7.30 am, or later, on the Saturday morning!

4.16.5.   It was soon clear that there was an irreconcilable difference between the agenda of the police and the agenda of the representatives. The assurances given by the police, proper and relevant though they were, nonetheless were insufficient to meet the demands of those outside Lawcroft House and voiced by some of those in the meeting. Two of the other men present at the meeting, certainly not hotheads, told us that the attitude of the police was dogmatic, not co-operative; that they failed to use diplomacy in order to gain the confidence and understanding of the representatives, and thus failed to achieve a cooling down of the crowd. From the crowd's point of view they were able to achieve none of their specific demands.

4.16.6.   These demands were that the police should immediately drop all charges against those arrested the previous evening, i.e. the four arrested in Garfield Avenue, the seven arrested outside Lawcroft House, and the one arrested in Oak Lane; should suspend the two officers involved in the original incident in Garfield Avenue; and should apologise to the sister of the two arrested youths involved in the original incident in Garfield Avenue who was the basis of the rumour referred to in subsection 4.9. There was also, quite properly, complaint about Councillor A's unsuccessful journey to the Bridewell the previous evening.

4.16.7.   The police rejected these demands, explaining that since there had been no opportunity to review the evidence, it would be improper to make such decisions arbitrarily, even to avoid a serious threat of public disorder. However, the Assistant Chief Constable personally undertook to review the evidence, which he subsequently did in conjunction with the Crown Prosecution Service (see subsection 4.23).

4.16.8.   The police agreed that the Superintendent who was Head of Complaints would record and investigate any complaints made against the police with minimum delay, that the police would meet with representatives of Manningham youth, and that in view of the sensitivity of the situation the deployment of the two officers involved in the original incident would be reviewed. (In fact the Divisional Commander immediately redeployed the two officers to other duties away from Manningham, and they have since been transferred to another division at their own request.)

4.16.9.　At about 5.45 pm, Councillor A and two of the young men left the meeting, claiming that nothing had been achieved, and that they would go out and say so. The meeting ended. There was again a large crowd outside Lawcroft House, which some of those who had been in the meeting inside addressed. Shortly afterwards officers and vehicles entering or leaving Lawcroft House were attacked by stone throwers.

4.17　The Second Night of Disorders

4.17.1.　By Saturday afternoon, news of the previous night's limited disorders had spread widely. The publicity given by the media to the previous night's violence undoubtedly attracted many people to the area, and the obvious presence of reporters and photographers looking for trouble encouraged posturing. We were told that car loads of young men from outside the Manningham area, indeed from outside Bradford, came, eager to join their young relatives and friends in their protests, or to join in the excitement. One White man, in Oak Lane, was asked by a car load of youths from Leeds where Oak Lane was. A shopkeeper in Oak Lane had a similar experience. One of our informants told us he had met a group from Birmingham. During the day, as so often happens when the consequences of a natural or deliberate disturbance are having to be coped with by local people and the authorities, there were also many sightseers.

4.17.2.　One of the people who spoke to us, a mature Kashmiri professional man who was horrified at the disorders, told us that on the Saturday it was common knowledge in the Oak Lane area that the police were giving no explanation for their actions, and there were even more extreme versions of police intransigence being voiced.

4.17.3.　Outside Lawcroft House the crowd was large and growing. It again consisted predominantly of young men from the local Kashmiri community, but with many from elsewhere, and some from other ethnic backgrounds, and it appeared to be becoming more aggressive. At 3 pm the police had deployed officers outside Lawcroft House to control the crowd, who were obstructing the pedestrians and vehicles using Lilycroft Road and Oak Lane. The officers began to move the crowd down Lilycroft Road, towards Oak Lane. During the afternoon police cars in Oak Lane were stoned, and the police received reports of young men buying containers of petrol. One Kashmiri car driver described to us the tension that he felt around him *"in the early afternoon"*, as he saw *"police everywhere,"* and *"young men with scarves around their faces everywhere."*

4.17.4.　Outside Lawcroft House, we were told

"The crowd were uptight and aggressive, and the police were moving people down the road ... Some [in the crowd] *were watching. Some were ready for action. They were from all over Bradford."*

4.17.5.　Additional police foot patrols were deployed in the Oak Lane area, under instructions to maintain order without being heavy-handed. One witness contrasted the bottom end of

Oak Lane with the situation at the top, near to Lawcroft House. This witness said the bottom end of Oak Lane was full of older Asian men, the top was full of youngsters. Another witness said that people were there in their hundreds by tea time, but most of the people in Oak Lane were watching, rather than involved. Given the mobility of the groups, and the short distances involved, we are not able to give a snapshot picture of the situation. It is clear that there were crowds, mobile groups of youths, and an atmosphere of growing tension.

4.17.6.   One motorist wrote to the police that he was travelling down Oak Lane around 5 pm.

"There were several, separate, very large groups of Asian youths, with some police presence in the background."

and he felt the threat of violence. Others drove through the area, unaware that anything was amiss.

4.17.7.   The police were hoping that the discussions taking place in Lawcroft House would lead to an end of the crowd outside, and the potential for public disorder. As it became clearer that this was unlikely it was decided that a large force of police officers would be necessary to break up the crowd. The police therefore assembled outside Lawcroft House in riot gear, but did not advance immediately.

4.17.8.   The violence erupted shortly after 7 pm. It is not our intention to describe in detail what then happened; the following is intended to give a broad indication of the nature and scope of the violence, which was much greater than that on the previous evening.

4.17.9.   At about 7.10 pm there were about 300 people waiting outside Lawcroft House. Young men from the crowd broke up a wall behind the public house situated opposite to Lawcroft House slightly higher up Lilycroft Road, and began to throw the debris at the police.

4.17.10.   By 7.30 pm part of the crowd ran off into Oak Lane, then turned to face the line of police officers, throwing bottles, bricks and milk crates at them, as the police vehicles and officers moved very slowly down Oak Lane with the intention of dispersing the trouble-makers, who had erected a barricade across Oak Lane and set it on fire. Petrol bombs and stones were thrown at the police, and passing motorists were also hit. At this time a White woman, accompanied by a child and a dog, walked down Oak Lane without apparent hindrance.

4.17.11.   Given the events of the previous night, the police deployed their officers to concentrate on maintaining control of the Oak Lane area from Lawcroft House to Manningham Lane, to prevent a repetition of the disorders and damage of the kind experienced on the previous night.

4.17.12.   Shortly after 9 pm a group of about 60 young men broke away into Manningham Lane. The following account indicates the main sequences, but there were incidents in other locations too, of which perhaps the most serious was fire damage to cars on the forecourt of a garage at Frizinghall. In Manningham Lane the trouble-makers attacked passing vehicles and business premises with assorted missiles. Other groups of youths continued to inflict damage in the Oak Lane area, and near to Lawcroft House.

4.17.13.   Several young men came to Lawcroft House to offer to speak to young people on the streets, and they were then escorted through the police lines for this purpose.

4.17.14.   A family of three told us they were in a car which turned into Manningham Lane from Queen's Road at approximately 9.15 pm. They were aware of two or three large groups of Asian youths. As their car passed one group, *"a flaming bomb"* missed by a few inches and exploded behind the car. A split second later there was a loud thud on the rear near side window and a strong smell of petrol. They pulled up further along Keighley Road and found the window glass chipped. They were indignant at lack of adequate police follow up to their complaint, as the police helicopter was overhead and the incident, in their view, should have been observed.

4.17.15.   The police helicopter, a substitute not so well equipped as the normal one, was following the group in Manningham Lane. Someone in the group threw a petrol bomb at a retail store near the junction with Drewton Road, and then the group made its way along back streets to Lumb Lane. In Lumb Lane they attacked a club, cars, a garage, and the windows of public houses. They then travelled via Green Lane and Salt Street into Carlisle Road where they attacked the Carlisle Hotel. The shops and offices which were damaged were unoccupied, but the pubs were full of customers, many of whom were, naturally, terrified. By this time it was about 9.45 pm.

4.17.16.   The group then split into two; one sub-group went via St. Mary's Road back to Oak Lane and threw missiles at police officers. The other went in the other direction along Carlisle Road to Whetley Hill, and then turned down towards the city centre. Sections of this sub-group committed several acts of damage and violence and, as the sub-group went down Whetley Hill, they set fire to seven cars on the forecourt of a garage (often referred to as the Citroen garage). The fire spread to the garage itself, destroying it and a vehicle inside, and extensively damaging 11 other cars. The large Kashmiri-owned garage immediately opposite was left undamaged, but the conclusion drawn by many people that this distinction denoted the racist nature of the disorders has to be balanced against the fact that the garage which was attacked was undefended; the garage opposite which escaped attack was heavily defended by its owner and his locally-based extended family.

4.17.17.   This group then ran down Whetley Hill into Westgate, causing considerable damage. Five, out of six, public houses were attacked. Some of the young men then went further into the city centre, smashing windows and looting shops. By 10.50 pm they had reached Westgate. Young men in cars, including taxis and private hire vehicles according to one reliable report, followed the looters, and received looted property into their cars. One restaurant had its large plate glass windows smashed, whilst customers and staff tried to escape the flying glass. Passing vehicles were attacked, and their occupants and pedestrians were threatened and intimidated.

4.17.18.   In Oak Lane at about 9.30 pm a group attacked the garage which had also been attacked the previous evening. The showroom windows were stoned and firebombed, but stayed intact. Office and workshop windows there which had survived the previous night's attack were stoned and broken, damaging equipment and cars inside. The security men on duty there felt obliged to leave, such was the ferocity of the attack. After ten minutes they were able to return, as police cleared the gang from that area. As on the previous evening there followed a parade of cars with noisy radios. At 12.30 am there was a second firebomb attack on this garage, and at 12.45 am the police returned and set up roadblocks.

4.17.19.   Sporadic disorders continued until 2 am.

4.17.20.   One *Telegraph and Argus* journalist described to a trade journal his four hour duty that night in Manningham as *"the most frightening experience I have ever had as a journalist."* His colleague, a photographer, was threatened with death twice by the same group, who tore the film from his camera on the first occasion at knifepoint. Another observer described to us the most violent language being used by some of the youths in relation to the police.

4.17.21.   Some estimates were of 700 youths on the rampage, but official police figures are less than half that. There were 300 police officers deployed to restore order.

4.18   Commentary

Why did the disorders continue?

4.18.1.   Several shopkeepers and residents in the Oak Lane area told us that the alarmist attitudes of both the window protection firms and of the media were influential in hyping up the atmosphere of tension during Saturday. The prospect shopkeepers were given of £1,000 worth of damage, and other consequences, if all windows were smashed, against a precautionary cost of £100 to board up, proved irresistible for many. Although we can understand the effect which boarded and shuttered windows must have had on passers-by, we cannot accept that this was a **cause** of the Saturday disorders.

4.18.2.   The second subsidiary reason we were given was the role of the media. Certainly the publicity about the events of the previous night drew attention to the tensions in Manningham, but we cannot accept this as a **cause** of the Saturday disorders. The Friday disorders had begun without publicity, and the following day, Sunday, ended peacefully after a greater blaze of publicity than had appeared on the Saturday. The media may have sparked a response from people predisposed to join in the disorders, and the media may have exaggerated, or wrongly analysed the causes of, the disorders, but the media were not themselves a cause.

4.18.3.   In our view the disorders took place again on the Saturday night because the police were unable to convince the local representatives that their concerns were understood and would be taken seriously (though we do not suggest that the representatives' formulated demands should have been accepted), and because the police failed to relate to the aggrieved residents themselves. The general indignation which therefore continued provided the occasion for youths motivated by distrust of the police, or attracted by the potential excitement, to follow a very small number bent on confrontation with the police.

Official Discussions

4.18.4.   Where there had previously been an opportunity to plan a response to local concerns, the police in the Toller Division had successfully used the services of local councillors and other community leaders to help explain what was happening, and why. The police did so again when the crowds assembled outside Lawcroft House on the night of 9–10 June 1995, and during the following day, but not with success. We understand that similar methods had been successfully used in another Division in which several outbreaks of violence by young men had occurred.

4.18.5.   On the Friday night the police were suddenly faced with a substantial and growing protest, accompanied by criminal disorder, from the local Asian communities. In the absence of other means, the device of talking with seemingly representative figures was obviously attractive. One Asian councillor wondered aloud why talks with a variety of representative figures would not have seemed appropriate on Holmewood (a White housing estate). Answering his own question, he said it was because the police regarded the Asian community as aliens, and did not know how to handle them.

4.18.6.   The large Asian communities also have had some expectation that official dealings are for 'community leaders'. We doubt if it can be regarded as a permanent substitute for speaking directly and confidently with the local people involved in a tense situation. An increasing number of Bradford born and bred British citizens of Asian parentage rightly look to be treated as capable of being involved directly in any discussions, and many local people unflatteringly suspected the agendas being pursued by some of the community leaders.

4.18.7.   However, such an approach can be a useful shortcut to achieve mutual understanding quickly if the people involved in the negotiations carry sufficient weight with the people with the concerns. But the task must be one of mutual explanation, not of position taking.

4.18.8.   By Saturday morning the prisoners had all been released, with no suggestion of improper treatment. The representatives included people who must have understood the inability of the police to drop all charges, or to punish the two officers originally involved, or to apologise to the woman alleged to have been assaulted, without carefully following detailed procedures laid down formally for everyone's benefit. To insist that decisions should be made without regard to the evidence was unacceptable. Influenced by our view that the events of the weekend revealed a habitual inability to relate adequately to the Asian population, we are driven to accept that the police, however correct their responses, were insufficiently convincing in explaining their proposals to the community representatives.

4.18.9.   We are also far from convinced that the representatives looked sufficiently carefully at what the police were saying. The concerns of local residents were well founded, and needed following up, but the demands formulated by the young leaders amongst the crowds were impractical and unlawful, and should not have been allowed to dominate the discussions as they did.

4.18.10.   Both sides must take some responsibility for the failure of these discussions, irrespective of whether the discussions could have been alone sufficient to deal with widely and long held grievances.

4.18.11.   What, then, is the proper role of councillors (or other community leaders) who become caught up in an intermediary role? For so long as the police cannot deal with insight directly with individuals or public crowds themselves, it seems to us important that the limits of the intermediary role should be clearly established through mutual discussion between the senior police officers and the leaders likely to be involved. However successful such exploration of the intermediary role might be, we remain of the view that direct discussion with the people primarily concerned is much to be preferred.

Lack of Direct Contact with Local Residents

4.18.12.   It is unfortunate that the police failed to establish the causes of the local residents' indignation by direct contact, but that is not so surprising since the indignation was about the repeated failure of the police to understand them and their concerns. We have already drawn attention to the failure of the police to engage with the local residents over the Friday evening and throughout the Saturday. That the residents from near Garfield Avenue should have become involved in the Saturday discussions only by co-incidence is yet another example.

4.18.13.   We think there are useful lessons to be drawn from the many local people who found the policemen drafted into the area from elsewhere to be particularly distant, and even hostile, and from the contrast between the unsuccessful local policing strategy used on the Friday and Saturday nights and the successful strategy employed on the Sunday. Local people, the overwhelming majority of whom had no intention of actively causing trouble, could not understand why the police officers on duty during the Friday night and the Saturday would not talk directly with them about what was happening.

The Complaints Procedure

4.18.14.   One of the comments often made to us by people who do not live in the area, and who learnt of the events through versions in the media, was that protests should be made through the official procedures which have been established by law, and that crowd protests are very likely to produce disorderly behaviour. We agree, and given that the message of the police in the discussions was that protests should be channelled through the normal official procedures, rather than by crowd scenes, there should certainly have been a very clear, purposeful police organisation made available to support the fulfilment of that message.

4.18.15.   We have to conclude that this was not done on the Saturday morning, when the incidents of the previous night were fresh, and that the officers dealing with enquiries at Lawcroft House were overwhelmed. Once more, the local residents were not dealt with face to face in a way that is the entitlement of any citizen. The lack of assistance in understanding how to make a complaint confirmed once more the local residents' view that the police were contemptuous of them. We can perhaps understand that there was a lack of time to deal adequately with complaints on the Friday evening, but there should have been arrangements made to meet the foreseeable needs of the Saturday morning.

Police Operations

4.18.16.   It is easy, with hindsight, to criticise the police operation which dealt with violence on the Saturday, and we have heard such criticism. There are three main complaints. First, the assemblage of a large, single force was, it is said, provocative to those who were looking for a physical battle; secondly, the police officers' impassive, impersonal attitude offended or frightened the large number of local people who felt helpless and who wanted protection and an end to the threats of further violence; thirdly, the relative inflexibility of the assembled force made it impossible to deal with individual crimes, or to protect people and property.

4.18.17.   One of our informants, a local Kashmiri man, said:

> *"Up to that point* [when the police line began to move forward] *the police were very restrained and disciplined. Then the order came to move. The dogs started going at the kids. They just went for people. One man on the floor was mentally abnormal. I went over there. I was shouting to the police to get off the streets very loudly and call the community leaders."*

4.18.18.   It is, in our view, almost inevitable that police officers drafted in to an unfamiliar area to deal with disorder will themselves be tense, and have no understanding of the locality and its people. Once again, we heard descriptions of them in phrases such as *"they were behaving like aliens"*; or *"the Sergeant told me to piss off"*. One father, whose son was injured, told us that he asked a policeman to call for an ambulance, and the officer replied *"Take him to the graveyard"*.

4.18.19.   We have been able to follow the course of the police dispersal of the crowd outside Lawcroft House and down Oak Lane on the unedited video film taken from the police helicopter. As with the Friday night's operation we do not criticise the general conduct of the police operation in terms of it being heavy-handed or provocative. Because we have not been able to pursue individual situations in detail, we can only note with concern that some allegations of unnecessary police violence, of which an attack on a person with Down's syndrome is one, have been made. In this particular case we understand that legal proceedings are being pursued. In general terms the dispersal operation was undertaken slowly and cautiously, with some freedom of movement for some members of the public. To that extent the police did, on this occasion, choose between the different members of the public.

4.18.20.   We have already commented sufficiently about the second complaint made to us, the police failure to relate to local people.

4.18.21.   The third complaint made of the police operation is of its inflexibility and consequent incapacity to do more than disperse the trouble makers from Oak Lane. One witness claimed that a non-local officer told his colleagues, in the hearing of the witness, not to interfere when the attack on the 'Citroen Garage' began. We cannot say whether this specific allegation is true. We have no reason to doubt the sincerity of the witness.

4.18.22.   A question we have been asked several times about the Saturday evening is:

> "Why did the police protect Lawcroft House and chase the violent groups towards the City Centre?"

To these people it seemed that the only concern of the police was to preserve Lawcroft House from attack, rather than to maintain public order elsewhere. Putting a similar point, some people have asked us why it was that the city centre was not better protected on the Saturday evening, given that there was a clear likelihood of further trouble, with the city centre a vulnerable target. On the Saturday, the police did institute arrangements to deal with a potential Bradford emergency from 6 pm onwards. Traffic on the approach roads to the city centre was vetted, but the centre itself was policed in a normal way to minimise disruption.

4.18.23.   According to the police, the first pressure on police deployment on the Saturday evening was the local crowd outside Lawcroft House, which had been the focus of the previous night's protest, and which clearly contained potential trouble-makers. Threats that Lister's Mill, opposite, was to be burnt, and Lawcroft House bombed, were taken seriously by the police, and the majority of available police officers were therefore concentrated there. We were told that a further drain on police resources during the evening was made by the many calls from distressed members of the public who had suffered from, or witnessed, the disorders, so that officers had to be deployed in immediate response. In the event, the greatest number of trouble-makers did remain in the relative vicinity of Lawcroft House, but the sub-group which went into the city centre were able to cause considerable damage without restraint.

4.18.24. It is easy to be wise after the event. We therefore do not criticise the decisions which led to the lack of adequate police deployment to protect the city centre, given the difficult situation the police faced. We do, however, think that the vulnerability of the city centre, and the unpredictability of violent gangs and looters, should be specifically considered by the police in the event of future threats of disorders, particularly when the build-up of trouble indicates that some of the trouble-makers are not very local, but from a wide area of the city and beyond.

Part 4   Sunday 11 June 1995

4.19   Calming Measures

4.19.1. The shock to citizens which the events of the previous two nights had inflicted, on older members of the local Kashmiri community particularly, caused increased and more effective intervention to prevent another repetition. *"Elders were incensed at what had happened"*, according to one local Kashmiri professional man who spoke to us. Representatives of the Council for Mosques were particularly active in encouraging parents to keep their sons under control. We have also received persuasive evidence of young men working hard, and with courage, to counter aggressive agitators in the crowds.

4.19.2. Messages of support for the police were left at Lawcroft House. But the potential for another night of serious disorders remained. This time the police strategy, under wider, more senior, leadership, was much less openly confrontational than on the previous day, and discussions between senior police officers and local representatives were much more constructive. Unlike the previous day, police officers were widely but strategically dispersed, were not in riot gear, and were able to interact in a pleasant and direct way with the many members of the local public who were concerned at what had happened.

4.19.3. In the event disorder was confined to some stone throwing at policemen, from the crowd which gathered in the evening outside Lawcroft House. A White councillor who was in the area that day knew of a planned peaceful protest meeting by older people that afternoon, and was struck by the disparate, uncoordinated groups of youths on the streets. Those who, on behalf of the police and of the local Kashmiri community, took part in non-confrontational and successful discussions, and those in the crowd, including the Bishop of Bradford and other leading figures from several backgrounds in the city, who asserted some common sense in the face of agitators, deserve commendation. The relatively low toll taken by the 'Manningham Riots' is due to the effectiveness of these Sunday discussions and assertions. Once more, the relatively sensible and decent values for which Bradford has a deserved reputation became dominant.

4.20   The Crowds

4.20.1.   The following two newspaper extracts encapsulate the differing emphases in the accounts we have heard of the nature of the crowd outside Lawcroft House during the evening. What is very clear is that the potential for further trouble was still present.

4.20.2.   One newspaper of 12 June 1995 described how

"... a shifting crowd of 600 roared their approval as a ringleader called for violence... Across Heaton Road stood the policemen, shifting nervously from foot to foot as they waited for the hail of stones that had flown on the two previous nights to begin again ... but elders urged peaceful dispersal. Shortly before 11 pm the crowd began to move in groups towards the police station."

4.20.3.   The description in another newspaper of the same day was:

"Last night several hundred young people gathered peacefully on a clearance site close to Manningham police station after calls for orderly protest. Police said that other groups were also in the area.. Youths with their faces veiled Palestinian-style carried placards attacking alleged police racism, and in the only moment of violence, two stones were hurled at the high wall... After local Labour councillor N had read out four requests for an apology and inquiry, a younger speaker briefly took the microphone and demanded more direct action, to applause from a section of the crowd... The meeting was attended by the Bishop... who urged that grievances behind the community's evident anger should be carefully examined. "I understand your frustration and anger. But you have expressed your hurt and now is the time to discuss what can be done. You won't get anywhere with violence."...Officers were last night out on patrol without riot gear, but equipped with the body armour and longer truncheons which have become standard issue."

4.20.4.   The *"local Labour councillor"* referred to also appealed to the crowd to calm down, we should add, as did another councillor, both to some vocal dissent, but the atmosphere generally was more open and constructive than on the previous day.

4.21   The 'Peace Women'

4.21.1.   At about 11.30 pm a group of eight members of Interfaith Women for Peace set out from a member's home in Manningham for Lawcroft House. The IWP had begun in Bradford in March 1994 as an informal gathering, mainly of Muslim and Christian women, meeting monthly on a Sunday afternoon in each other's homes to share news and ideas. The eight women members met on this evening at the initiative of one of them. There were four Asian women and four White women, and they carried candles and a makeshift banner saying 'Peace' in Urdu, English and Arabic. Women had not been involved in the disorders or the protests, and this very public intervention was particularly striking. It marked the end of the crowd scenes.

Part 5   The Sequel

4.22   No Further Disorders

4.22.1.   On the following Wednesday, 14 June 1995, a meeting was held at the Grosvenor Centre, organised by the Racial Equality Council, at which local people called on the police to *"stop the apparent intimidation, harassment and arrests of Asian youths"*, and reiterated previous demands for the suspension of the two officers alleged to have handled roughly the young woman and her baby, and for charges to be dropped against the people arrested on the Friday whilst making protests.

4.22.2.   The following weekend passed peacefully, despite fears of the extremist activities which often batten onto such a situation. The police made discreet arrangements to be available in case of trouble, and some shopkeepers in the Manningham area again boarded up their windows. Some workers in the Manningham area left work early on the Friday afternoon, amidst a build up of rumours about further troubles.

4.22.3.   A rumoured coach invasion of extremist right wing groups did not materialise. Members of the Socialist Worker Party distributed anti-police leaflets, but appear to have made little impression. They advertised a meeting at the Grosvenor Centre for Sunday 18 June 1995, which was immediately followed there by another meeting organised by Hisb ut-Tahrir (see para 5.25.1), in which the disorders were blamed on democracy and the capitalist system of the West.

4.22.4.   Both meetings were condemned by local leaders, who ensured that the meetings' organisers were *"given short shrift"*, in the words of one White observer. The very existence of such meetings, however, sent shivers down the spines of some White citizens, and the Hisb ut-Tahrir meeting reinforced their indiscriminate views about the extremism of all Muslims. Because the existence of the Hisb ut-Tahrir meeting gave such offence to some people, we should stress that the management of the centre were misled by the information in the application to hold the meeting. The decision not to cancel it, when its true nature became known a few days beforehand, but to ensure that the audience included respected elders, was a commendable response, and the city council immediately revised the booking arrangements for holding future meetings in locations for which it has responsibility.

4.22.5.   The Mela is a two-day multi-cultural festival usually held in Lister Park, Manningham, on the central weekend of the Bradford Festival. In 1995 it was held three weeks after the disorders, and was peaceful and successful, with attendances of 40,000 on the Saturday and 60,000 on the Sunday. Some of the young people who contributed to its success had also been directly involved in the disorders.

4.22.6.   At the time of writing this Report the first anniversary of the disorders has passed, and there have been no serious disorders during the intervening time in the Manningham area.

4.23   Discontinued Prosecutions

4.23.1.   As a result of the review promised by the Assistant Chief Constable at the Saturday afternoon meeting on 10 June 1995, the Crown Prosecution Service for West Yorkshire, on

20 June, advised the police, in relation to the seven people arrested outside Lawcroft House and the one in Oak Lane, that in their view

"the arrests were justified in order to prevent the escalation of serious public disorder. The public interest does not require continuation of these prosecutions."

4.23.2.   This view, from an independent official body, is expressly contrary to the view taken by many of the protesters that the arrests of all the people who were arrested outside Lawcroft House were not justified. The statement appears to us to contain its own inherent contradiction. The discontinuance of prosecutions was stated to be not on grounds of lack of evidence, but because of *"The public interest"*. If the arrests *"were justified in order to prevent the escalation of serious public disorder"* it is difficult to understand what public interest was being served in not continuing with the prosecutions, assuming there was sufficient evidence.

4.24   Police Investigations

4.24.1.   There was, and is, much indignation amongst some of the White population of the city that the Asian population should protest at all at any of the arrests. Such a response would, it is said, be unlikely if the arrested person were White. This indignation was partly fuelled in the days following the disorders by the public announcement that charges against the eight arrested during the Friday evening protests were to be discontinued. There was unfortunate confusion that this announcement meant that no proceedings were going to take place against those who had first been arrested, or, indeed, against those violently involved in the disorders. We have tried to clarify, through this Report, this and other misleading generalisations that have abounded in our enquiries.

4.24.2.   According to the *Telegraph and Argus* of 12 July 1995 a local Asian councillor said that the local Asian community wanted to see those who had committed violent acts in the disorders punished. He said:

"our main concern was over the people arrested initially for disorder and the police have now met our demands for charges to be dropped."

Even in this quotation there is some ambiguity but, as has been shown, the concern of the older protesters had been about the seven arrested outside Lawcroft House and the one in Oak Lane, and it was these charges which had been dropped.

4.24.3.   There is also indignation amongst many people that more criminal charges were not pursued against those involved in the disorders. We have to draw attention to the very proper requirement that before any individual can be convicted of a criminal offence it is necessary to produce evidence which proves guilt beyond any reasonable doubt. The task of the police, therefore, was to obtain and examine available evidence which would clearly identify those committing criminal actions as quickly as possible. A specific enquiry team was set up for this purpose.

4.24.4.   The police reported to us:

"During the course of the three month long enquiry ... a total of 41 arrests were made for offences arising out of the riots."

4.24.5.   Arising from the disorders, 16 people have been punished by the criminal courts on charges of arson, assault, breach of the peace, conspiracy to cause explosion, disorderly conduct, possessing an offensive weapon, and offences against the Public Order Act 1986. The last of these cases was dealt with by the courts in June 1996. The courts dismissed a number of cases, and the police or the Crown Prosecutor discontinued some cases. The only custodial sentences were one of 12 months imprisonment for robbery, and three of detention in a Young Offenders' Institution.

4.24.6.   There has been criticism by some young Asian men that the police were being vindictive in seeking the culprits responsible for the disorders. This is not our view. The police were right to pursue the crimes committed, just as they seek to pursue other reported crimes. That is their duty, a duty owed to the general public in the interests of public order, and especially to those who were put in fear, or were attacked, or whose property was damaged, by unacceptable behaviour.

4.25   The Extent and Cost of the Violence

4.25.1.   The police record, based on complaints made to them, is that over the two nights of disorders 102 premises were attacked, varying from a broken window to substantial fire damage. There was also some looting. Of the 102 premises, three were owned by African Caribbeans, three by Sikhs, and one by a *"Pakistani Muslim"*. The remainder were White owned. However, we have become aware of two other buildings which were damaged, one owned by a Pakistani, though the name of the business there would not indicate this, and the other owned by a Sikh. Sixty-six vehicles were damaged, four of which were owned by Asians. 10 members of the public were personally attacked, all White. Nine policemen received injuries classified by the police as *"not serious"*, this being a relative term, since one policeman required stitches to a head wound.

4.25.2.   There were no attacks on places of worship, nor, with the exception of one violent attack on a householder followed by theft (which may have been opportunist), on houses.

4.25.3.   Numbers cannot convey the violence of which many of those in the crowds of disorderly youths were guilty. The violence to buildings, especially to occupied buildings, was bad enough, but the following descriptions of what it was like to be personally on the receiving end of this kind of behaviour give some indication of the extent to which some of the young men lost control of themselves. This was shameful violence, without any regard for other people who happened to be there. Insofar as it is explained as a 'protest' it is an unjust way of protesting against real or imagined injustices.

4.25.4.   The following words are from a police account which we have checked against the relevant witness statements.

"One victim was attacked and beaten by four men who stole his van, which was later found abandoned, having been set on fire, and the tools of his trade stolen."

"a man and his wife were in their car and surrounded by [about 50] rioters. Every window in the vehicle was smashed before one of the rioters reached in and ... hit her [head] with a stone. The lady sustained ... cuts to the back of her head which required stitches."

"Three of the victims were white females. One was racially abused before being thrown to the floor and robbed of her handbag. Another was insulted in racial terms before being indecently manhandled."

4.25.5. It is not necessary, even if it were possible, for us to give an accurate figure of the cost of putting right all damage that was done on the two nights of disorders. Our very approximate estimate is a little over £0.5m. The Police Authority, under its statutory liability to compensate those who suffer financially from the consequences of rioting, has estimated a much smaller financial cost to the authority than the £1M estimate that was circulating in the media immediately after the disorders. The extra policing cost was £214,000.

4.25.6. There may, of course, be losses for which claims to the Police Authority have not been made within the very short time allowed. In addition there may be extra security and insurance costs for the future, and there were certainly some serious adverse effects on trade – and therefore on employment and prosperity – in the particular area in which the protests originated, as well as more generally in Bradford. It is quite impossible for us to estimate the cost of lost trade for the businesses affected by damage, or for those businesses affected indirectly as a result of the extensive adverse publicity on the neighbourhood, and on Bradford generally. For as long as can be remembered Bradford has attracted bad publicity from outside media, and here was one more opportunity for the media to exaggerate Bradford's problems.

4.25.7. The violent young men caused a substantial loss to the very community whose indignation they claimed to protest. There is, too, a cost in human relationships within the City, which cannot be quantified, but which must be redeemed by conscious effort.

4.25.8. The above record is a sorry one. Those involved in the violence have undoubtedly brought great shame on their families, on their communities, and on Bradford. But it would be wrong to leave the assessment there. In no way do we wish to minimise the fear, injury or trouble that these actions caused, but even taken together they were not a major, crippling, event for the city, or anything like as serious as many of the contemporary accounts made out.

4.25.9. Much of the life of the city continued normally throughout the weekend. Many people, even people who lived quite close to the scene, were unaware of the disorders, other than the presence of the police helicopter. One very responsible White observer, who was closely involved with monitoring the events, said:

"On the Sunday, elders of the Asian community were magnificent. There was a large number of people with vision, and a small number of trouble makers."

4.26   What was the Local Reaction?

4.26.1. At most, it is estimated that there were about 300 youths involved in the violence on the Saturday night, many less on the Friday evening. Given that they were predominantly

Kashmiri, 300 is a very small proportion of even just the local Kashmiri population under, say, the age of 25, and the folly of treating them as representative becomes clear.

4.26.2. A group of mainly Pakistani businessmen which met shortly afterwards was appalled at the events, and angry with 'their' politicians for being inflammatory or ineffective. Only a wish to avoid raising tensions deterred them from immediately issuing a press release to this effect.

4.26.3. Several White, and Asian Bradfordians from other than Kashmiri communities, have expressed to us their regret that no apology for, or sufficient condemnation of, *"the Manningham riots"* was made by the local Asian community. In fact several such apologies were made, and we republish this one by the mainly Pakistani group of businessmen just referred to, dated 16 June 1995, in full:

"We strongly condemn wanton destruction and regret what has happened to innocent citizens and businesses.

Appreciate those businesses which are staying in the affected area indicating that confidence built over a generation or more cannot be shaken by one weekend.

Accept that the proper way to deal with grievances against the police is through lawful means."

4.26.4. One very experienced observer spoke to us of *"a massive sense of deep regret"* amongst the people he saw on the streets on the Sunday evening.

4.26.5. A prominent local Asian councillor apologised to the Manningham shopkeepers whose businesses had been affected by the disorders – and was criticised by some young people for doing so. According to the Daily Telegraph of 12 June 1995:

"Mr F said: 'I absolutely condemn the behaviour of the Asian youths involved in violence. That cannot be excused irrespective of police behaviour.' "

4.26.6. According to the Telegraph and Argus of 14 June 1995:

"Councillor F said: 'I can publicly say that I strongly condemn the violence and the damage to property which took place on Saturday night. I extend my sincere apologies to those business people who have suffered as a result, through no fault of their own.' "

4.26.7. We have heard directly from many local adults of their shame and concern. In a letter we have seen, written on 15 June 1996, one of them wrote:

"the behaviour of the Asian youths was utterly deplorable and there can be no acceptable excuse for the damage that was done to local businesses.

These youths are unruly, uncouth and a disgrace to their community and so too are the so-called 'community leaders' who have supported them. It is time the police were allowed to do their job properly and stop having to pussyfoot around these thugs who are destroying the society that the original hardworking immigrants to this country strove to create along with the indigenous population...

In the Asian community with whoever I have discussed the weekend incidents they have all expressed their utter horror and shock. Our sympathies lie with the police, particularly with those who have been injured in the course of their duties.

I would like to add that I am not alone in my expression of these opinions but there are significant numbers of Asian community members who would also like to express their wholehearted support for the police and condemnation of those responsible for the weekend riots.

We sincerely hope there is no longlasting damage to community and police relations."

4.26.8.   On the Friday following the disorders, there were calls for peace made in mosques, accompanied by strong condemnation of the violence.

4.26.9.   An Asian councillor, who was in no doubt that the violence was wrong, and had spent much time trying to calm things down over the weekend, told us his great difficulty had been to get at the true facts of the original policing incidents. Because of this it had been hard to argue with the violent protesters, and to balance condemnation of the disorders with understanding of the particular injustices which were said to be the cause.

4.26.10. Another Asian business organisation wrote in July 1995 to all the businesses which had been damaged of which they were aware, expressing their concern.

4.26.11. Police Officers had many meetings with local people in the days and weeks which followed the disorders. In the words of the police:

"The common theme was condemnation of the violence, the prevention of further outbreaks of disorder, and a desire to re-build relationships."

4.26.12. A Pakistani women's English class in the Manningham area expressed great concern about the disorders and, as a group, expressed shame for what had happened. Several had been challenged by Whites in racially abusive terms following the disorders, and were concerned lest this signalled a violent White backlash. They rightly regarded this unintelligently indiscriminate response as very unfair. 172 mainly Kashmiri women meeting in Manningham signed a simple and clear note:

"As women we feel sad about what happened at the weekend.
We want everybody to listen to each other.
We want peace."

4.26.13. Almost all of the girls and young women to whom we spoke, or about whom we heard, expressed shame and concern.

4.26.14. We draw attention both to the limited publicity given to the apologies and condemnation, and to the considerable extent of the apologetic feelings which undoubtedly existed, and which were frequently expressed. This contrast can be understood first by reference to the confusion of motivations which were the particular causes of the disorders. Those many people who were angry at the police were determined to pursue their protest about the alienation between the police and the local community despite the distraction caused by the disorders. It can also be understood by reference to the myth amongst many in the White communities that the local Asian community is an organised unity whose monolithic views can be clearly and authoritatively expressed. If the publicity was deficient, we are nevertheless satisfied that the attitudes of condemnation and shame were very extensively present within the local communities, and that many local people worked extremely hard to minimise the extent and duration of the disorders.

4.27 What was the Reaction of Others?

4.27.1.   For some regular visitors the events undoubtedly caused Oak Lane to be regarded for a time as a place to avoid. During this time some businesses closed, and some lost customers.

4.27.2.   A non-'Pakistani' Asian group wrote to us:

"In our opinion the community elders and leaders should accept part of blame. Unfortunately, they have failed to condemn the bad behaviour of the rebellious youths and instead condemn the police."

4.27.3.   One White woman with many years involvement in constructive bridgebuilding with families from other cultural groups in Manningham represented a viewpoint held by others when she wrote:

"I have had to confront negative thoughts which contradict my long held beliefs and attitudes. Living as I do so close to the Manningham area I know the area very well and pass through it on a daily basis. Seeing the devastation left by the riots made me both very sad but also very angry. Now whilst Bradford could never be called a thriving metropolis (not this century anyway), this deliberate wrecking spree has made me resentful. My roots in Bradford go back a long time and I have always been fond of it. I feel despair at its demise in the present economic climate but also anger that youngsters, many of whose loyalties are divided, can feel it is right to systematically destroy property specifically owned by white people. I personally know the owner of the ... shop in ... Since the riots her business has been completely dead. Not only that, but the insurance on her windows has increased to £6 per week. I also know the owner of ... He and his father have worked very hard to build up and maintain the business. Bad publicity doesn't do these businesses any good at all, though I must say I am surprised that no Asian people are employed there, as many customers are Pakistani."

4.27.4.   Her closing comment is also important. We dealt with the employment situation in subsection 3.8.

4.28 Were Disorders Expected?

4.28.1.   We have carefully looked for any evidence which might suggest that the disorders were preplanned. Inevitably, we have heard of general apprehensions of trouble, based upon perceptions and experiences of the general lawlessness which afflicts modern life, but we are not aware of any firm insight that this particular weekend would be any different to any other. It is worth commenting, however, that, given the evidence of tensions to which we refer throughout this Report, people in Bradford ought not to have been as complacent, and then surprised, as they obviously were when the disorders took place.

4.28.2.   We fully accept the genuineness of those who told us that they sensed trouble was brewing, and we did hear indirectly of two youths who had been caught with cans of petrol a few days prior to the disorders, and of youths who were angrily determined to fight the police. These may have been straws in the wind, but we think they were no more than straws. We have heard no direct evidence that the disorders were pre-planned but, not surprisingly, none of those who took part in the violence have spoken directly and openly to us about their activities.

4.28.3. We accept that there was a longstanding and increasingly obvious sense of grievance amongst young men particularly, but we doubt if its manifestations reliably indicated that there would be disorders on that specific weekend. On the Friday night there had been no knowledge in another part of the nearby inner city, amongst young people to whom we spoke, of the events then taking place in Manningham. There was widespread surprise there about them afterwards. We also accept that some of those involved in the violence used mobile phones, but we do not regard this as strong evidence of a pre-planned, thoroughly organised, co-ordinated, event, even on the second night. Young people have always had informal grapevines, and they unsurprisingly now use modern technology, as they had in the anti-prostitution 'vigilante' patrols (see subsection 5.22).

4.28.4. Given the sequence we have traced from the chance event of the 'football arrests', an event which was not itself pre-planned, we are convinced that the Friday disorders were a spontaneous Manningham event by local young men who acted on the back of the anger felt, and verbally expressed, by their elders.

4.28.5. We regard the Saturday disorders as resulting from organisation by local young people that day, with miscellaneous and mainly Bradfordian extras, attracted through family, school and social networks, plus some outsiders alerted by the publicity in the media.

4.29   The Violent Protesters

4.29.1. Some older representatives of the local community cannot accept that youngsters could possibly carry out the highly selective targeting which the violent youths achieved, without some highly organised leadership. It is only slightly easier to accept that those who led the violence and looting were *"a bunch of unstable drifters"*, or *"not normal boys, but drunkards and thieves"*, to quote from two of our older informants. Even if this were the case, there was widespread uncritical acceptance of their leadership by many local youths until the local community imposed order by the Sunday evening. There is some evidence that extremists battened onto the anti-prostitute campaign, and it is possible that the events of the Saturday night were similarly influenced.

4.29.2. There were leaders of the violence, but there was no central direction, although the leaders of the groups appear to have drawn on the well-known organisational procedures of the vigilante patrols, and the Saturday disorders were certainly prepared for during that day. There were, too, pre-existing gangs, who took the opportunity to join in a contest with the police, and to express their antisocial feelings, for once being all on the same side instead of against each other.

4.29.3. The violent protesters on the Friday, and those associated with them, were overwhelmingly local Kashmiri youths, and we are confident that many parents in Manningham whose children were involved in the previous night's disorders took action to prevent a repetition on the Saturday; we also know that their action was not always effective!

4.29.4.   On the Saturday those involved in the violence came from several, but mainly Asian, backgrounds. The overwhelming majority were aged from mid teens to mid twenties, but many were very young, we were frequently informed. One local classroom assistant told us she had recognised one on the TV who was an eight year old.

4.29.5.   We have been reliably informed that, once reports of the Friday disorders in Manningham were known, trouble-makers and excitement seekers from other areas of Bradford and beyond, and to a very limited extent, from White and other ethnic groups, joined in on the Saturday. Indeed, four of the youths arrested by the police in connection with events during the Saturday disorders were White youths from Barnsley who had travelled to Bradford with assorted offensive weapons. All the remainder of the 41 arrested in connection with the Friday and Saturday disorders were, according to the police, *"Muslim Asian males"* aged between 15 and 37, the majority in their late teens or early twenties. Each of them lived in Bradford, the majority in Manningham, Heaton or Girlington.

4.29.6.   Two experienced Manningham based police officers told us that their examination of video records of the Saturday night events had identified only a very small number of youths known to them. We are confident, however, that most of the youths who came into Manningham on the Saturday were from other parts of Bradford. We think it unlikely that complete outsiders could have moved in the way many of those involved in the violence did without significant local knowledge or contacts.

4.29.7.   No girls or young women took part in the disorders.

4.29.8.   It is unfair to attach blame indiscriminately to everyone from the communities from which the majority of the comparatively small number of violent protesters came. We express dismay at the hostile verbal White backlash against Asians generally, which followed the disorders. It is, moreover, grossly unfair to other communities from south Asia even to call the disorders Asian.

4.30   The Violent Protesters' Purpose

4.30.1.   There were several distinct groups of violent protesters, and since we have not met most of them it is only possible to deduce any common purpose from their observed behaviour. We note two distinctive features: first, the antagonism towards the police, to which we have already referred in describing the events which took place.

4.30.2.   Secondly we note the picking out of non-Pakistani business premises for wilful damage. Some Asian non-Muslim businessmen told us that they feared that the Muslims were trying to drive them out of Manningham, and Indian sub-continental rivalries may have been present to motivate some of the violent protesters. The very firm opinion of many of the people who spoke to us was that there was a racist element in the motivation of **some** of the violent protesters.

4.30.3.   A non-Muslim Asian group wrote to us:

"We would like to bring to your attention that the majority of the shop owners in this area are from the Pakistani community, but the damages were inflicted mainly upon the white and non Pakistani businesses.

This reflects the attitudes of the youths towards the non Pakistanis."

4.30.4.   There is no doubt that, in general, Pakistani business premises, i.e. belonging to the largest section of the Asian communities, were not attacked, but White and Sikh-owned business premises were. Personal violence was directed against Whites, but by only a very small minority even within the groups of violent young men. We have met several White residents of Manningham who moved about freely during the disorders.

4.30.5.   There are two factors to be borne in mind when evaluating this situation. The first is the fact that almost all the local Pakistani businesses premises are owned by occupiers whose families also live there or nearby, whereas the attacked premises, but not the pubs, were mainly vacant at night. The second is that the mainly local young men involved in the violence would be known to the Pakistani families in the vicinity. These two factors must have had some influence on the behaviour of many of them. However, our own conclusion is that, despite the influence of these two limiting factors, the predispositions to violence which we discuss in the subsequent parts of this Report exercised a considerable influence on the choice of targets.

4.30.6.   For those leading the groups involved in the violence there was an opportunity to take on the police, and also to express frustrations at other, more prosperous, sections of the Bradford population. They chose the premises to be attacked. For many of those involved in the violence, however, there was probably no more involved than an opportunity for excitement, apparently legitimated by the protests of older people against the police.

4.30.7.   It is impossible to find a rational or constructive reason for these disorders, which were unprecedented in Bradford. Certainly no one has gained anything from them.

4.31   The Media

4.31.1.   We have mentioned the media in several places in this report and do not wish to overstress its significance in relation to the disorders. But we were told of some incidents which require both recording and comment.

4.31.2.   According to the Report by Foundation 2000, *"The Voices **Must** Be Heard"*:

"Media manipulation was self evident. One young man was asked to put a scarf over his head to portray the image of 'jihad' against the west."

4.31.3.   A mature Kashmiri professional man told us how he and a policeman to whom he was talking on the Sunday evening had to keep turning away from a provocative photographer.

"I joked with the policeman 'Hit me'. 'I wish you would', said the photographer. Then an eight year old child appeared carrying a banner 'No Justice'. The photographer told the child to shout, but the first shot was not good enough, so he encouraged the child to snarl and shout louder."

4.31.4. We have not examined contemporary TV, apart from one programme which was specifically drawn to our attention. In that case we read a transcript, which had confused events of the Friday with those of the Saturday, leading to a false conclusion.

4.31.5. Perhaps in these days enough people are wise to the deceptive ways of some of the media, and discerning in their appreciation of the likely truth, or otherwise, of what they see and read. We think, however, that the conduct we have just described is unprofessional, and to be deplored. Such standards, and much of the instant commentaries on the situation, caused great local anger. Several local people involved in calming things down over the weekend told us that they had refused to co-operate with the media, even though they had held strong views about what had happened.

4.31.6. The *Telegraph and Argus* received professional recognition for its coverage of the disorders. Even in this case, however, there is much local disappointment at the way the accounts of the violence are seen to have obscured the widespread anger at the police.

4.32   The Implications

4.32.1. We have already commented on the sequence of events at appropriate stages in this Section. We consider the wider implications of these events in the following Sections of the Report.

Section 5

Shared Problems; Perceived Divisions

5.1   Limits of Ethnic Relevance

5.1.1.   In this Section of our Report we address some of the general background to the disorders. The problems which face Bradford, in coming to terms with the decline of its former staple industry, the wool trade, affect most of its citizens adversely, irrespective of their ethnic or cultural background. It is, however, obvious that the effects vary in intensity from severe to marginal, depending on ... what? We have seen, in Section 3, how disproportionately the effects are experienced in the different ethnic groups. A similar message is given in the recently published report *'Race' and Housing in Bradford*.

5.1.2.   We think that it is important, when considering the problems of this multi-ethnic city and how best to respond, not to confuse the nature of problems which have other than ethnic roots with their ethnic incidence. Poverty is widespread in Bradford. People from various ethnic backgrounds are poor, unskilled, and unemployed, and the socio-economic outcomes are similar to those which affect so large a proportion of people from some of the ethnic minorities. The grossly different levels of deprivation suffered by different ethnic groups raises very serious doubts about the fairness and effectiveness of political and organisational programmes, but the problems may not necessarily stem from ethnic causes.

5.1.3.   In a letter we received the writer, a White person, makes this point very clearly:

"In the aftermath of the riots the Pakistani community has had the spotlight focussed upon it. Unfortunately this has provoked some negative responses from the White community (many of whom I'm sorry to say have succumbed to the 'White flight' syndrome). Some commute daily through the inner city areas in order to get to work in town. What do they see? Boarded up buildings, decaying and neglected housing, and rubbish-strewn streets. There is no point in saying that similar conditions prevail in many of the housing estates on the fringes of the city – these commuters do not have to drive through them and are thus blissfully unaware. So they see this degeneration as an Asian problem rather than one of poverty, despair or apathy."

5.1.4.   Many White families share with many Pakistani or Bangladeshi families a poor educational background, with the result that they all experience high unemployment. This is aggravated in the case of the Pakistani and Bangladeshi groups by shortsighted racial discrimination by some local employers against well qualified applicants, but only the discrimination is **necessarily** racial in origin. 'What are the special educational factors which have caused the poor educational background?' is the question which should be asked in this example, irrespective of the ethnic identity involved. Only then can appropriate responses be framed.

5.1.5.   But although it is often more appropriate to undertake a class, rather than an ethnic, analysis to understand problems that are associated with deprivation, there are differences of culture, religion and history which do affect people individually and as distinct groups. Insofar as these have a bearing on a problem they have to be identified, and taken into account. It is therefore necessary to avoid superficial judgements, and generalised allegations about problems, and to plot the root causes with differentiating care, if those causes are to be dealt with effectively. The remaining part of our Report seeks to assist such an approach.

5.1.6.   Guided by the information volunteered to us, we explore in this Section the ways in which the city is perceived to be divided, and we follow through with a closer look at some of the circumstances of the young people growing up in Manningham.

Part 1   The Perceived Divisions

5.2   The Challenge of Immigration

5.2.1.   The local historic traditions of Bradford as a city have developed from different sources, including significant immigration from Ireland, Germany, and Eastern Europe over the last hundred or so years. These traditions began to be increasingly challenged over thirty years ago by substantial immigration from the Indian sub-continent.

5.2.2.   Learning the appropriate ways of behaving in accordance with the values and beliefs of parents and grandparents is an experience common to all ethnic groups. For minorities, cultural symbols affirming these are more pressing than for the settled majority, whose ways of life are constantly confirmed by, and intertwined with, the taken for granted institutional structures and processes of the society which they have inherited. We have heard from many sources of the time warp in which social customs are conserved by those who migrated to Bradford.

5.2.3.   Where discrimination is practised against minorities the push towards encapsulation, and the stressing of difference, by members of the minorities increases. Their reaction may then be one which stereotypes the majority as immoral, lax, irreligious and so on. The same pressures operate on many White Bradfordians who find themselves in a minority in their traditional locality, no doubt aided in both cases by nostalgia. In these circumstances, unless effective counter measures are taken, there will be tensions based on mutual ignorance, with potentially disastrous consequences for all.

5.2.4.   This was put very clearly in a letter which we received:

"If people believe that they have suffered racism or discrimination either by the police or anyone else then this will determine their attitudes and subsequent behaviour. I will cite my own case as an example... A few years ago when my younger son was about 13, he and a friend went to the park to play. Whilst there they were approached by about five Asian youngsters who demanded to know what they were doing there as this was their park. They then attacked my son's friend and my son, being no hero, ran off. Now my husband and I reasoned with him that this was not a racist attack as he believed, but simply a group of boys establishing territory as gangs have always done. This didn't convince my son and he's not been there since... No matter what I think, my son's attitude towards Pakistanis has been affected by his experiences despite the fact that he shares our deep affection for our Pakistani friends. Of course, these may seem like minor incidents compared with the day to day abuse that many black and Asian people have to contend with. We are all degraded by it."

5.2.5.   The disorders, in the expressions of opinion which followed, did release some of the pent up feelings of anger and frustration held by many people, but we have been shocked at the need for absolute assurances of confidentiality expressed by many people who came to give us their general views or experiences, at the extent of the separation from other groups practised by so many citizens, and at the sense of embarrassment at the political sensitivity of some of the important subjects which citizens, officials, and politicians alike felt they could not pursue openly. A further consequence of the lack of intelligent mutual understanding which is so widespread in Bradford is the increasing extent of monocultural communities in which young people are being trapped, foreshadowing increasing tensions in the future.

5.3   A Manningham Focus, but ...

5.3.1.   In an Inquiry into disorders which began in a part of Manningham where the majority of the population is by ethnic background from rural Kashmir, though born here, it is inevitable that we – and those who spoke or wrote to us – should concentrate on their circumstances. We wish to make it clear, however, that we have been at pains to balance our work with investigation of the circumstances of other groups within Bradford, though the main focus of our work remained on Manningham throughout. This very local frame is of great importance for decision makers. The themes we have prioritised relate to large parts of Bradford, but the appropriateness of any practical solutions will depend heavily on very local conditions.

5.3.2.   For example, one professional worker, with considerable experience of working in Manningham and Girlington and other parts of the city, emphasised the importance of distinctive local features and common problems in this way:

"I have seen a lot of changes in Manningham over the last fifteen years. There is lots of hope there, more so than on the Council estates. Lots of wanting to do the best for the children, but not knowing how to achieve it...

The different natures of Manningham and Girlington give rise to differences in key community issues. The broad priorities in both neighbourhoods are the same: housing and the environment; crime and safety; employment, training and economic development."

Although we express the broad priorities slightly differently, we touch on all these subjects in our Report.

5.4   The Asian Communities in Bradford

5.4.1.   We have shown a statistical analysis of Bradford's present population in Section 3 above. Although there are many different ethnic backgrounds represented in that population, and a continuing inflow and outflow of migrants, the majority of the Asian population are either Bradford born or received most of their upbringing here. As the Asians settled they increasingly formed distinct groups around cultural and religious identities, groups increasingly reflected in formal representative organisations.

5.4.2.   Some Asian groups are very small and have adapted more successfully to the traditional life of Bradford, and to its changed economic fortunes since the first of their group arrived here, although their individual educational and social backgrounds were often more advantageous than those of others. Because they are small in number, they also have the means of ready discussion about issues of common concern, and an organised capacity for mutual reinforcement despite their greater individuality of lifestyles and dispersed settlement.

5.4.3.   There is a considerable contrast between the general situation of the people from these smaller groups and those from the much larger group from Pakistan. The larger group is sometimes seen as a threat to the smaller groups because of its potential political weight, but the larger group is not a monolithic bloc, any more than are the Whites.

5.4.4.   The Asian population of Bradford first began to arrive in significant numbers in the 1950s and 1960s. To a large extent this movement arose as a result of the need of the textile industry for workers to undertake jobs that were increasingly unattractive to the indigenous population, but which maximised returns on new investment. Many people were recruited in India, in Pakistan, and in what was then East Pakistan and is now Bangladesh, by Bradford firms.

5.4.5.   The first people to arrive were men, who tended to live in communal residences. It was a number of years before families became re-united here in significant numbers, as women and children joined their husbands and fathers. The nature of extended family links means that this process is still not seen as complete by many families, so that strong family ties with the Indian sub-continent continue to be promoted.

5.4.6.   The first arrivals came with the intention of staying for a number of years in order to earn enough money to establish themselves in relative affluence on returning home. First they had to pay off the loans which they had taken out in order to purchase air tickets, then they had to pay the agent who had recruited them, before they could begin to save.

5.4.7.   A major reason that the first immigrants often did not return, but brought their families here, was a result of British immigration controls on those from the Commonwealth, first introduced in 1962, and tightened in 1965, 1968, 1971, and 1981. When fathers wanted to bring their sons over to work here the mother had to come too. The result was the establishment of families born and educated here. The other reason was that dependants (women and children) were allowed in, but not 'primary migrants' i.e. those of working age, except in very restricted numbers – first on vouchers, then only if they had scarce skills, eg doctors. This meant that those adult men who were already here found it almost impossible to come and go. According to one respected elder, it is the wives and children who insisted on remaining here, despite the obvious deterioration in the availability of work.

5.4.8.   We are informed that the original migrants tended to have a strong view that they were wanted by the community to which they came – they had a place within it, and made a contribution to it. The history of the last 30 years for many of them can be seen as a continuous erosion of this initial feeling, and its replacement by increasing feelings of alienation, frustration and rejection.

5.5   The Different Asian Groups

5.5.1.   Map D (Appendix 5) shows the locations from which migrant groups have come to Bradford from the Indian sub-Continent, and Map B (Appendix 3) shows the ethnic group information within each electoral ward in Bradford.

Descriptions

5.5.2.   As with all attempts to describe groups of people, there is a danger of over-simplification. The following brief paragraphs are only a very general introduction. Even though we are conscious of the danger of causing offence by superficial descriptions we have become aware of such a widespread lack of knowledge about the different groups of people whose background is in the Indian sub-continent that we are risking this attempt. Part of Bradford's problem is that the information was not readily available.

The Pakistanis

1.   A General Description

5.5.3.   The largest group of Asian immigrants, with some of the poorest economic and educational backgrounds in the settlements from which they came, and with ways of life deriving from rural areas as they were thirty or more years ago, are the Pakistani Kashmiris and Pathans. The first generation who settled in Bradford usually did so in close geographical proximity to their fellows. Their very numbers provided a protective barrier against the pressures of living in a quite different society.

5.5.4.   Although the Kashmiri and Pathan groups who have settled in Bradford are, for many purposes, properly described as Pakistani, there are other families settled here whose origins are in other parts of Pakistan, including people with a much more cosmopolitan culture from the major cities.

2.   The Kashmiris

5.5.5.   The territory of Kashmir is partly in India, and partly in Pakistan, and has been the subject of hostilities. The Bradford Kashmiri families are almost entirely from that part of Kashmir which is part of Pakistan (many being also referred to as Mirpuris because of the proximity of their ancestral villages to the old city of Mirpur in Kashmir), and, as a generalisation, they have found it difficult to adapt to life in Bradford. This is the largest sub-group to have settled in Bradford.

5.5.6.   There are many factors which contribute to large scale population movement, but one of the most important for those Kashmiris who came to Bradford was the poverty of their existing situation, and their hope for improvements in their families' living standards. The Mirpuris were displaced from their traditional land tenure by the Mangla Dam project, which created a massive artificial lake, and flooded the ancestral homes of thousands of people. Whilst compensation was paid to them, it was not adequate to maintain living standards.

5.5.7.   For many Kashmiris the status of Kashmir is of great importance, and it cannot be entirely ignored in the understanding of political pressures from the Indian sub-continent which are of concern to older people here.

5.5.8.   We were told that the Kashmiris are rarely found in senior positions of authority in Bradford, and studies of their circumstances emphasise their relative disadvantage. There is a feeling amongst many Kashmiris that they are the majority of the Asian community, but get the minority of what opportunities there are. Unlike the Bangladeshis, whose distinct cultural background is **officially** recognised within the UK because of the officially recognised country from which they originated, the Kashmiris are not separately recognised officially. It is a matter for careful consideration whether their distinctiveness should be so recognised.

3.   The Pathans

5.5.9.   This group is invisible for almost all official Bradford purposes, according to several well informed observers of the Bradford scene. Their number in Bradford is not officially recorded, but has been estimated currently at approximately 2,000.

The Bangladeshis

5.5.10.   After the partition of India in 1947 into the separate countries of Pakistan and India, East Pakistan subsequently separated from Pakistan, and is known as Bangladesh. The Bangladeshis settled in Bradford rather later than the Pakistanis, in the 1970s. The Bangladeshis are not a large group in Bradford, especially when compared with the Pakistanis, but the group suffers by far the highest proportionate levels of stress (see para 3.4.13).

The Gujaratis

5.5.11.   A small group in Bradford are the Gujaratis and, again, we have been told that they have to struggle hard to ensure that their distinctiveness is recognised. Gujarat is a state in India. We were told that the people described as Gujarati in Bradford were mainly Muslim people.

East Africa

5.5.12.   There is a small number of Asian people, of different original backgrounds, many of whom came to Britain from Kenya in 1968 and from Uganda in 1982. They are the descendants of workers who moved to East Africa from the Indian Empire in the days of the Raj, and who were often displaced as a result of racist attitudes adopted by the post-colonial Governments in East Africa. In East Africa they tended to be a middle class interposed between White and Black, and they were usually fluent in English. They therefore tended to be well educated, and those that came to Bradford have, in general, achieved a measure of prosperity.

Religious Groups

The Hindus

5.5.13.   Religion, rather than a specific geographical base within the Indian sub-continent, is the determining factor. One estimate of current numbers of Hindus in Bradford we have seen is 6,000, of whom many are from India. They are not settled together in one place, and many appear relatively prosperous.

The Muslims

5.5.14.   The largest group of recent settlers in Bradford, defined by religion, is Muslim, mainly from Bangladesh and Pakistan. As with Christians and those of other religions, the orthodox Sunni Muslim population of Bradford is sub-divided into religious groups with different histories and emphases, each tradition having its own Mosques and Imams. The Bradford Council for Mosques brings together many of these groups, and seeks to speak for and represent their interests. We are not aware of any tensions between these groups which might threaten the peace of the city. There is, however, one very small group, the Ahmadiyyans, whose claim to be Muslims has been challenged by the much more numerous orthodox Muslims of all kinds. This claim has recently been the subject of a protest by orthodox Muslims because the Ahmadiyyans requested that they should be described in an official council publication as Muslims.

5.5.15.   When referring to religious or other groups there can be no other proper basis than self chosen ascription for a secular authority to adopt, in our view. We have heard evidence of Muslim leaders taking offence at an official recognition of the Ahmadiyyan Mosque, and also of the nervousness of public officials whenever this question of recognition of Ahmadiyyans arises. We, of course, express no view on the religious arguments, but firmly propose that toleration of difference should be practised by those who seek it for themselves. In secular affairs this ought never to be an issue.

The Sikhs

5.5.16.   Religion is the determining factor in this group description, but the geographical origin of Sikhs is in the Punjab in India. Their social circumstances in Bradford are similar to those of the Hindus. As with the Hindus, the current estimate is that there are approximately 6,000 in Bradford, and they too are not settled in one place.

Hindus, Muslims, and Sikhs

5.5.17.   We were conscious of a great deal of concern amongst Hindu, Muslim, and Sikh leaders that the historic religious rivalries and strife of the Indian sub-continent should not be replicated here. In 1993, following the attack by Hindus on the Ayodhya Mosque in India in December 1992, 24 Hindu places of worship in Britain were, we were told, attacked by arsonists, including five in Bradford. Hindus believe that Muslims were responsible, but told us that there had been few arrests. Hindu and Sikh representatives have spoken to us very strongly about their apprehension and experiences of Muslim aggression, and were disappointed at the lack of police responses to particular situations. Some Muslims believe that

"Hindu extremists from Bradford took part in the demolition of the [Ayodhya] mosque and that one businessman exported bricks to India to help lay the foundations of a temple on the site of the mosque."

5.5.18.   In a development of this, we heard from a Muslim leader that Bradford Hindus had sent a gold brick for the new temple there.

5.5.19.   The Council for Mosques acted to negotiate constructively with local Hindu leaders after the Ayodhya mosque incident in India in 1992. Such tensions are rightly said to be a diversion from the issues that urgently confront all Bradford's citizens, and attempts to re-create them here are increasingly recognised as no more than inflammatory escapism, though they do exist in Bradford and are dangerous. It would, however, be naive to think that what has, and is, happening on the sub-continent will have no effect on Bradford inter-relationships, unless it is openly discussed and constructively managed. This has happened in the past in Bradford, as representatives of the different religious loyalties have shown valuable leadership. It is the responsibility of all the groups concerned to continue to do so, assisted by the teaching of shared history, and by the pursuit of the common goals and interests which exist here.

5.6   The African Caribbeans

5.6.1.   Migrants from the Caribbean, both men and women, came to Bradford in the 1950s to jobs in a range of industries and public services, including engineering, chemicals, and the health service. Many of them were from the smaller islands. Some were from Jamaica. They were of many different Christian denominations – Catholics, Protestants, Seventh Day Adventists and members of Pentecostal churches.

5.6.2.   Some had served in the British Armed Forces and at least one had been a 'Bevin boy' working in the coal mines. These had spent time in Britain during World War II. Others came from rural areas or towns in what was then the West Indies, straight to Bradford, and yet others went first to other areas of Britain before settling in Bradford. The majority of this group now in Bradford, which is estimated currently at approximately 6,000, were born here.

5.6.3.   These Bradford citizens do not feature elsewhere in our Report because we received little information from them, though what we were told was impressively well prepared, and carefully presented. We deal at this point with the information we have relating to them, for convenience.

5.6.4.   They are no longer heavily concentrated in the Lumb Lane – Manningham area, following housing clearance and redevelopment schemes, and families choosing to move to other areas. We were told that many of the younger people still regard Lumb Lane as their cultural centre, even though there were only two places left there in which they could meet.

5.6.5.   Some people have commented that racism in Bradford concentrates on Asian people, and that the racism experienced by African Caribbeans is thereby reduced. This may be so, but there is no place for complacency. Like many of the smaller minorities they feel ignored by public authorities. We were given the example of an advert for a public sector job involving liaison with members of the African Caribbean and Asian communities, which stated that *"the ability to speak Urdu and Punjabi would be an advantage"*. We can understand the pressures which might have forced such an advertisement (which we did not see), but we can also understand the anger from African Caribbeans because it effectively excluded them from consideration.

5.6.6.   Those African Caribbeans who spoke to us appeared to have lost confidence in the established race relations arrangements in the city, and to have abandoned them. Some of those who spoke to us were particularly angry at the common assumption that young black men *"were all muggers, drug dealers and pimps"*. The comments we make in this Report about the disproportionate adverse impact of the local economy, the public services and local democracy on some Asian groups apply also to African Caribbeans.

5.6.7.   There are tensions here, too, which cannot easily be solved. To us, the use of cannabis, but not hard drugs, was openly promoted as a cultural entitlement by some younger people, as was a noisy, late night life-style in Lumb Lane. By contrast, we heard from older African Caribbean women, in a semi-public meeting, views which were the same as we had heard from women from White and Asian communities.

5.6.8.   One example of good practice which came to our attention was The Frontline Initiative. A study in 1993, by the newly founded African Caribbean Economic Establishment (ACEE), highlighted a lack of awareness of, and access to, enterprise support services, including training, for members of this minority group. It referred to

"alarmingly high levels of exclusion from schools and disproportionate unemployment."

5.6.9.   In July 1995, at a public meeting attended by over 40 people to discuss the work of ACEE, it became clear that action was needed to deal with the immediate economic and social problems of African Caribbeans, particularly those of young people. The Frontline Initiative was the result, supported by the city council's Social Services Department and The Joseph Rowntree Charitable Trust. Although its objectives were intended to relate to the particular needs of African Caribbeans, they usefully reflect some of the major problems for people in the inner city more generally.

5.6.10.   The objectives are to:

- *"enable socially excluded people to move towards employability through their involvement in self-help initiatives;*
- *work with other organisations to promote and improve the employability of young African Caribbeans;*
- *promote responsible citizenship and local democracy in a multi-cultural society;*
- *establish an overview of what successful good practice is available locally and nationally;*
- *re-vitalise social integration in Lumb Lane and Manningham;*
- *reduce incidents of racist violence and youth delinquency;*
- *establish links between youth and other services and local police to improve the information flows and facilitate preventative intervention."*

5.7   Other Ethnic Groups

5.7.1.   Although, judging by their names or accents, we have heard from individuals whose origins were outside the UK, particularly from Ireland and Eastern Europe, we have not received any representations on their behalf as minorities, and the African Caribbeans only made their views known after our express and repeated invitations. This reticence probably reflects the starting point of our Inquiry. 'The Manningham Riots' were widely perceived as being the product of attitudes in the local Pakistani population and therefore not to be the concern of other groups. The briefness of this paragraph reflects this background.

5.8   An Asian Historical Perspective

5.8.1.   We were told that if one examined the issues in Bradford which have been seen as important within the Asian communities a significant trend could be discerned. Initially, few protests were made by the migrant workers, but this changed to resentment which then manifested itself in traditional forms of lawful democratic protest. As time went by this protest became increasingly strident, and began to take forms nearer and nearer to the boundary between what is legal and acceptable and what is illegal and unacceptable. The disorders in Manningham could be seen as a crossing of this boundary line.

5.8.2.   Whilst it is clearly important to understand the nature of individual flashpoints, they should not be divorced from underlying movements in attitudes and changes in cultural assumptions taking place within the communities concerned. We were given some notes to indicate some of the most public past events which were seen as points where attitudes and responses in the Asian communities were clearly changing, and we now set out a shortened version of them, with some added comments.

Anti-Fascist Activity in the Seventies

5.8.3.   In the late 1960s, and the 1970s, the presence of so many people from the New Commonwealth in Bradford increasingly attracted right wing elements on the fringe of politics. A number of candidates stood on an anti-immigration programme in local elections and there was an upsurge of extreme right wing activity.

5.8.4.   There was a widespread response and reaction to this, which was led by elements of the White establishment, particularly from within the Labour and Trade Union Movements. There were large numbers of Asian people involved in these campaigns, but generally they were seen as foot soldiers supporting, and being led by, White opinion formers. It was also clear during this period that the Asian communities were keen to be seen as adhering strictly to acceptable British patterns of protest and behaviour. There was no suggestion of law breaking by Asian people; indeed, the whole purpose of these campaigns was to show the Asians as victims in need of support and assistance.

5.8.5.   These campaigns were seen as successful, and Asians were portrayed as law abiding people resisting unreasonable and improper attacks upon them. It was sometimes said that they were 'more English' than the indigenous population, in terms of their adherence to lawful, non-violent protest, and respect for democratic processes.

5.8.6.   It must be stressed that throughout this period the majority of young people were seen as completely within the control of the older generation of Asians and, with the exception of one or two small groups of young activists, they had no identifiable agenda of their own.

5.8.7.   One of the most significant of the groups which became active in Bradford at this time was the Asian Youth Movement, which increasingly came to be seen as the voice of young people from the several Asian communities, working together. It was not able to continue in this way, as succeeding generations of young people were not attracted to it, and its strength dissipated as its activists grew older, and pursued their careers.

5.8.8.   This reliance on traditional action and 'White liberal' support created expectations which later led to tensions and disillusionment.

'Bussing'

5.8.9.   One of the first real stress points was the question of 'bussing'. This involved the Council, as the Local Education Authority, in transferring 'immigrant pupils' on a daily basis by bus from the inner city to suburban schools, in order – it was claimed – to assist acquisition of English, to maintain 'ethnic balance' in the schools, and to ensure some social contact with White children. There was increasing resistance within the Asian communities, which led to a campaign to end the policy. There was a strong feeling that the whole process was racist in effect, and tended to isolate children from the communities of which they were a part.

5.8.10.   There was an underlying feeling that, in reality, the White establishment was trying to distance children from their ethnic, cultural and religious backgrounds in order to destroy their own culture and assimilate them into White society. It was also a fact that many of the children were spending up to an hour a day on buses, to the detriment of their education.

5.8.11.   The campaign continued until the policy was revoked by the council in 1979 and was, at the time, seen as a successful use of traditional methods of protest. We suspect that financial considerations weighed more heavily on the council in 1979 than was realised by the protesters.

The Recession of the Late 1970s and Early 1980s

5.8.12.   Unemployment was not seen as a problem for the first 15 or so years of Asian presence within Bradford, though the threat was obvious to those prepared to look ahead. By the end of the 1970s, and into the 1980s, there was a massive increase in unemployment in Bradford which began seriously to affect the Asian population, as those with jobs began to lose them, particularly as a result of the decline in traditional industries such as textiles and engineering. This process meant that the younger generation began to have rapidly decreasing prospects of obtaining employment. The absence of work encouraged a trend of using a distinctive religious faith as an open expression of personal identity within the Asian communities. This was, and is, particularly noticeable in relation to the Muslim community, because it is by far the largest minority community, but it is by no means unique.

Representative Bodies

5.8.13.   In 1981 the Bradford Council for Mosques was set up to represent to public bodies the common concerns of the different Muslim traditions within Bradford. It has often played a significant role in arriving at a resolution of tensions, and has been matched by the activities of other minority group representative bodies. It now has 44 organisations and 28 mosques formally affiliated to it.

The Bradford 12

5.8.14.   The first significant occasion when young Asian people were seen to come into conflict with the law was the case of the 'Bradford 12' in 1982. The 12 were a group of people accused of making petrol bombs. They claimed their actions were *"to confront Fascists and defend their community".* A strong campaign was launched to defend them. They were seen by many young Asian people as the first group who were prepared to contemplate unlawful actions. They were acquitted by the court, but this made little difference to the urban myth which surrounded them. A consequence for many young Asian men was distrust of the police, and a feeling that the police would not support the rights of citizens from the ethnic minorities.

Halal Meat

5.8.15.   The demand for the provision of Halal meat in schools was the first issue which could be seen as an attempt to link demands with a clear expression that the Muslim community was distinct from any other. This, of course, was a religious matter, but it arose because of the very large number of people from Pakistan and Bangladesh who were, almost by definition, Muslim. For the first time Muslims had the self-confidence to assert their religion publicly, in a way which openly challenged the traditional culture.

5.8.16.   There was a strong reaction against the demand for Halal provision, ostensibly based on animal rights issues, but which many Muslims firmly believed to be racist and anti-Muslim in origin.

5.8.17.   In 1983 the council granted Halal provision, but it was seen by many Muslims as having been granted reluctantly, with no real commitment to the stance it might have represented. This further strengthened the perception that people of Asian origin within Bradford would have to fight for their distinctive cultures against a resistant and unsympathetic establishment. By this time the Muslim view was increasingly differentiated from those of other Asian communities within the city.

The Honeyford Affair

5.8.18.   Another manifestation of changing attitudes and increasing tensions during the mid-1980s was the controversy surrounding Mr Honeyford, who was the Headteacher of Drummond Middle School in the heart of Manningham. In this particular matter we can see no point in making the principal character in the story anonymous. Mr Honeyford wrote an article, initially for a small circulation right wing magazine, which was critical of the effect which large numbers of pupils with an ethnic minority background had upon educational standards. He articulated a view that the preservation of social identity was being given priority over social integration. This article was then quoted in the national press, and was almost immediately the subject of enormous local and, indeed, national controversy.

5.8.19.   An intensive campaign was waged against Mr Honeyford, and he was soon seen as a symbol of unacceptable White attitudes to the Asian communities. There was a widespread belief that he had shown unacceptable racism and, even more significantly, that the initial official response was dismissive and unsympathetic to the feelings of Asian people. By the time that he left his post there had been a significant effect upon Asian community attitudes, which had hardened against what was increasingly seen as an extensive racist White reaction.

5.8.20.   The view became more widespread that if the Asian people were to succeed in gaining respect for their distinctive identities, they would have to do so by the weight of their own action rather than through the willingness of the political establishment. It was also clear to many that adopting a White liberal agenda had not been successful, and so there was from this point increasing support for an alternative agenda. It was also a turning point for many in the older generation, who had previously held the view that the appropriate engine of change was the political mechanism of the White population, and they began to demonstrate that their opinions were changing. For the first time television and newspaper pictures showed older members of the community demonstrating anger and frustration in public.

The Rushdie Affair

5.8.21.   Throughout the period from the first migrant settlement onwards, the factors affecting community relations had been mainly very local. This began to change in the 1980s. National British politics, and the politics of international Muslim resurgence and of the Indian sub-continent became involved, and began to have an effect within Bradford.

5.8.22.   From the Iranian Revolution in 1979/80 there came a burgeoning sense of Islamic identity among Muslims, particularly amongst the young. The identification with Iran's assertions of an Islamic state was unaffected by the fact that the large majority of Muslims in Bradford are Sunni Muslims, whilst the Iranian Revolution was clearly located in Shi'ite theology. The effect of this was that, just as people in Bradford began to assert their Muslim identity, this was the time when it became unacceptable and threatening to others.

5.8.23.   An obvious example is the Salman Rushdie controversy in the winter of 1988/89, when the Iranian Leader, Ayatollah Khomeini, issued a death threat in the form of a fatwah, against the author Salman Rushdie, as a result of what was perceived by many Muslims to be a blasphemous portrayal of revered figures in his book *Satanic Verses*. The international condemnation of this death threat was seen by many Muslims in Bradford simply in terms of it being anti-Islamic. Similar feelings were aroused later, in the international response to the Gulf War, to the destruction of the Ayodhya Mosque by Hindu extremists in India in December 1992 and to the Bosnian situation.

5.8.24.   The first Bradford event relating to *Satanic Verses* which gained national prominence, was the public burning of a copy of *Satanic Verses* in January 1989. This occurred before the fatwah. The people involved were almost certainly ignorant of the tremendously emotive effect this would have on those brought up in the dominant Western culture, with its memories of Nazi Germany, and a deeply held belief in free speech. In India and Pakistan the burning of flags, books, effigies etc. are quite common events, and are seen as more or less acceptable forms of protest. There is still little understanding, within large sections of the Muslim communities, of the effect this incident had on White opinion of them.

5.8.25.   This event was followed by a large demonstration and rally in the Tyrls in central Bradford, which degenerated into disorder. This was probably the first occasion when people of Asian origin were involved in large scale public action where there was no significant involvement of Whites in support and/or leadership of the events. It was also the first occasion when large numbers of young Muslim men and youths were involved in street action. The scale of the event was unexpected. The Council for Mosques was caught off guard, and suspended the use of public demonstrations as being too vulnerable to trouble makers.

5.8.26.   The police, too, were caught off guard and there were many Muslim people unhappy at their response. This increased the belief that the police were anti-Muslim. Towards the end of the afternoon a number of White youths were seen to direct aggression towards some of the young Muslim people involved in the demonstration. There is a strongly held belief amongst many Muslim young men that the police response to these people was, because they were White, much less aggressive than it had been to the original demonstrators. Many of the young Muslim people who were in the crowd that day still remember the anger they felt at the actions of the police, and at what was, in their view, a different response. This had a major impact in alienating young Muslim culture from the White establishment, and particularly from the police.

The Race for the Parliamentary Labour Vacancy

5.8.27.   The internal political agenda within the local Labour Party has been destabilised over a number of years by the competition to be selected as the Labour parliamentary candidate for Bradford West. In April 1993, the sitting MP announced his intention to stand down at the next general election and therefore, by 1995, there had already been two years of uncertainty and conflict. The controversy which flowed from the member's suggestion that the next candidate should be a woman spread far beyond the local Labour Party members who would normally make the selection of parliamentary candidate, and predictably became a topic of concern throughout the substantial Asian communities in the constituency.

5.8.28.   Many local political actions over this prolonged period were seen by local people who spoke to us as being affected by the selection race. We have heard locally of many suspicious allegations that the politicians seeking candidature have had an axe to grind. As we write this Report we understand that the present MP intends to seek re-election.

The Local Election Campaign of 1995

5.8.29.   The campaign for the city council elections occurred shortly before the disorders of June 1995. For the first time in Toller Ward, which includes part of the area involved in the disorders, candidates were fielded by the two main political Parties, who both emphasised and concentrated on loyalties within the Muslim community. The Conservative candidate was a Muslim from the Jat Clan, which had a very large association in the area, and the Labour candidate was a Muslim from the Bains Clan, which had a much smaller presence in Toller Ward. Two of the existing Labour councillors were from the Jat Clan, which led to divided loyalties and conflict.

5.8.30.   The Labour councillors were asking people to vote for party loyalty and against clan loyalty. A further complication was that the Labour Bains candidate had caused the deselection of a sitting, highly respected, White councillor. This latter factor meant, we were told, that some White members of the Labour Party were unhappy and disaffected. In the light of national party political forecasts, the Conservatives were only likely to win the election if they could persuade large numbers of Asians to vote for their candidate. In the face of a massive anti-government swing the Conservative Party made one of its rare gains in the whole country.

5.8.31.   During the local election campaign many Asian community divisions and loyalties were highlighted, and many young men roamed the streets for several weeks with the enthusiastic support of their elders. *"Jat or Bains"* was the frequent cry on the streets.

5.8.32.   The whole election came to be seen as between warring clans. The Asian people in the area were subjected to immense conflicts of loyalty, whilst the White people felt marginalised and threatened by a conflict which they did not understand. Both political parties had released forces which the party hierarchies did not understand, and could not control.

5.8.33.   Who won is not our concern. We were told that one effect was to grant apparent approval for public disorder from the older Asian generation to the younger. There is no doubt that many of the young men involved had a most exciting time. They were allowed to vent anger and aggression publicly.

Labour Ward Party Suspensions

5.8.34.   The University Ward Labour Party, which also includes part of the area involved in the disorders, had at the time of the disorders in June 1995 already been suspended by the National Executive Council of the Labour Party, as a result of alleged violence at the selection meeting in late 1994 for a council candidate. There was a strong feeling that this was generated by an earlier attempt to deselect a sitting councillor because of his Bangladeshi origin.

5.8.35.   In 1995, shortly after the disorders, Toller Ward Labour Party and Bradford Moor Ward Labour Party were also suspended by the Labour Party NEC. The suspension of Toller Ward was on the ground of the alleged involvement of Labour Party members in supporting the Conservative candidate for the Toller Ward Council seat in the circumstances we have just described.

5.8.36.   The suspension of the Bradford Moor Party was a result of the 1995 local election campaign, where there was a suggestion that many members of the Labour Party had supported, and voted for, the Conservative candidate, who was a Muslim, against the Labour candidate, who was a Sikh. There was some inflammatory anonymous literature distributed, making reference to the non-Muslim origin of the Labour candidate, and the Jewish origin of one of the sitting Labour councillors. The Labour candidate had a majority of under 100, in comparison to previous years when the majority had usually been in four figures.

5.8.37.   The University and Bradford Moor Ward suspensions were lifted in the middle of 1996, but there is still a strong local resentment against what took place. We have been told that a very large number of the local Asian community viewed this sequence of suspensions as racist, which inevitably has led to further alienation from, and anger at, the party political hierarchies and the orthodox British political system. It should also be understood that many of the local political conflicts are, for many older Muslims, related to the current political situation in India and Pakistan. Even the most knowledgeable White politicians have little understanding of these issues.

5.8.38.   It is clear that the increasing involvement of Asians in local party politics has highlighted and exploited differences within the Asian communities in a way which has brought them to the notice of others in Bradford, and in particular to the White political establishment of the city. There had been a widely held view within the White population that the Asian community was homogenous, with needs, aspirations and assumptions which were similar throughout the whole community. These events destroyed the validity of these assumptions. There is no doubt that this false preconception had been very comfortable, and its destruction leaves many White people involved in politics confused and alienated. It is a potentially dangerous situation, requiring responsible discussion.

The 'Vigilante' Anti-Prostitution Campaign

5.8.39   We refer to this campaign, which was in being at the time of the disorders, in some detail in subsection 5.22.

5.9   The Consequences of Division

Tensions

5.9.1.   Tensions between different assumptions about ways of living, often unquestioned on all sides, are likely to arise in a city divided as we have described, particularly when discussed in the abstract, and with no attempt to hear explanations. Traditional ways of dealing with other people, whether in the home, in the wider family, in work, or in public places, may conflict. The very uncertainties which people understandably have about those from a different background may encourage stand-offishness and superficial correctness at the expense of real communication between individuals.

5.9.2.   To these have to be added the divisions, often invisible to the outsider, relating to religious, social, or political divisions within the seemingly monolithic blocs of the other communities. The effect of the extremely complex matrix of clan and family loyalties in Kashmiri communities, which has recently caused such an upset to the traditional party political culture of Bradford, is a clear example. The traditions governing marriage in some Muslim cultures, for example the caste system which is deeply ingrained in Pakistani culture, and which strongly affects the choice of a son- or daughter-in-law, are not widely understood in the White population. Similarly, the vast majority of older Muslim people have no understanding of what they see as a lack of loyalty and support within most White families, or of the place of the public house and of alcohol in the White culture, which they view with distaste.

Ignorance Breeds Fear.

5.9.3.   The mutual ignorance which is so common in Bradford between people of different ethnic groups (we are all 'ethnic'!), when coupled with unfortunate experiences of the behaviour of members of another group, quickly extends the particular experiences to cover all people from that group. The logical fallacy of converting a particular into a general proposition underlies so many people's attitudes. 'Groups of Asian young men' all quickly become 'Gangs of Asian youth' to those White people who experience rudeness and harassment from some Asian young men. Experience by Asians of disrespectful comments from some policemen becomes evidence of a racist police force. Only the confidence which comes from greater individual familiarity can counter this destructive tendency, which is worryingly frequent.

5.9.4.   Unfortunately, there is a well advanced isolationism which is actually reducing important opportunities for mutual learning. There are several pressures within the schools system in Bradford, which we discuss in Section 6, which are leading or have already led, to schools with virtually no White children in attendance. One Kashmiri man, already taking a responsible lead in civic affairs, told us:

> *"I was schooled where there were only a few 'blacks'. I can relate to indigenous ways and culture. But now, too many blacks come into contact only with blacks. This inevitably obstructs communication and understanding."*

5.9.5.   At a public meeting held in Manningham a young Asian man carefully distinguished between racism and ignorance.

> *"We never got a chance to learn about English people and they haven't had a chance to learn about us."*

Another Asian member of the public at the meeting asserted that

> *"there is simply not enough mutual learning about each other's culture and behaviour".*

5.9.6.   We agree. We suggest that the themes we have identified in our Report, coming as they do from the concerns expressed by many people from a variety of backgrounds, are worthy subjects for urgent **mutual** exploration. The extent to which this challenge is accepted will identify the bridge builders. Only in this way can the solutions be developed to the problems which are shared.

Racism

5.9.7.   Racism is a common term to many Bradfordians. We use the term to mean not only negative judgements about others seen as racially different, but the practice of discriminating against them, intentionally or unintentionally. Many explanations of its causes are put forward, but it is the consequences of the practice of racism which are of concern in a multi-ethnic city. In one school we visited an 11 year old, after detailing his ambition to be a soldier, told us:

> *"About two years ago, some Asians moved next door, everyone tormented them, broke their windows and stuff. Everyone was nasty to them, even my Mum and Dad. I felt bad about that. Real bad. They were nice people to me, but they had to move out."*

5.9.8.   The experiences of racism suffered by members of the non-White ethnic minorities are too well documented to need cataloguing here, and the existence of only a few paragraphs on this topic should not be taken as an indicator of the extent or importance of the subject-matter. Racism is as widespread as it is dangerous and hurtful. In many White areas of the city and metropolitan district Asian people hesitate to go. For many job seekers there are preliminary hurdles, often subtle, to exclude them from further consideration on racial grounds. In many social settings exclusion is practiced. The requirements of the law to prevent racial discrimination are evaded in many instances.

5.9.9.   These practices are not just regrettable and rather stupid; they injure the life of the whole city. Perhaps even more importantly, they obstruct a proper **enjoyment** of Bradford's unique ethnic population mix.

5.9.10.   Racism is usually regarded as experienced by members of minority groups at the hands (or mouths) of the majority, but it is an attitude which can be learned and practised by any group, however irrational it may be, and however unfortunate its consequences. We have heard from several White people that, in some streets of inner Bradford where they are in a minority, they have experienced objections to their presence from Asian young men and boys on racist grounds, whether as residents, sharers of facilities, or simply as passers by.

5.10   The Term 'The Community'

5.10.1.   A phrase that has been used so frequently in our investigations that it has become tedious is: '**the** Community'. Its meaning appears to depend entirely on the context, and when the phrase '**the** Community' is used it can be difficult to know just what is meant, since most people belong to more than one community. Similar popular imprecision occurs from the influence of the Arabic word "Umma", of particular significance to Muslims.

5.10.2.   The word 'community' can be used to describe the people living in a local geographically defined area, e.g. the Girlington community; or those of a particular, and geographically dispersed, religious group, e.g. the Hindu community; or those of a particular ethnic group, e.g. the Polish community; or a combination of geography and one of the other defining bases, e.g. the local Muslim community of Manningham. When the defining words are added, the problems decrease. However, its use obscures differences within an identified community, notably those of gender and of class, and fails to recognise the range of opinions held in a 'community'.

5.10.3.   We tested the use of the word community by considering the communities to which one of our informants told us he belonged. He told us:

"I would view myself as a member of the following communities, depending on the context and in no particular order:

Black, Asian, Azad Kashmiri, Kashmiri, Mirpuri, Jat, Maril'ail, Kungriwalay, Pakistani, English, British, Yorkshireman, Bradfordian, from Bradford Moor."

Then followed his work and social communities:

"I could use the term 'community' in any of these contexts and it would have meaning. Any attempt to define me only as one of these would be meaningless."

5.10.4.   The moral seems to be that the unity of a community on an issue, as alleged by its representatives, should never be extended beyond its obvious, explicit base without careful enquiry.

5.11   Local Communities

5.11.1.   Although there is one city, and one metropolitan district, we consider it misleading to think of either of these geographical and administrative groupings as a community for more than very limited purposes. Very rarely do people think of Bradford as one community, even as historically defined before amalgamation with other areas, like Keighley for example, for the purposes of a single local government unit.

Geographical Definitions

5.11.2.   Inner city communities can be defined geographically as well as ethnically. We were impressed by work carried out in West Bowling to identify the precise limits of that community. We were told that it was a disadvantage to the local community that it straddled three Parliamentary constituencies and three City Council Wards.

Strong Local links

5.11.3.   The attachment of people, and especially of immigrant groups, to a particular locality with which they are very familiar ought not to cause surprise. For the insecure it represents the security of familiarity in which the chances of being humiliated, or excluded, are much reduced because of the presence of relatives, friends, and familiar associates. One example which occurred during our investigations was that of the city council's proposal to demolish Salt Street, which had been home to Pakistanis from the earliest days of their settlement. (We express no view on the merits of this proposal). The following quotations are taken from the *Telegraph & Argus* of 25 March 1996.

> *"We want to stay here. This is an established community where everyone knows everyone. This is the heart of the community. People here have all their amenities close by such as mosques, schools and GPs. Some of the residents have lived here for 30 years or more.*
>
> *One of the oldest residents .... ,69, said: 'I have lived here since 1962. My children and grandchildren live in this street. I couldn't settle anywhere else.' "*

5.11.4.   As the social and economic confidence of individuals or families increases, the security of familiar territory can be left behind. We have come across some instances of this in the larger ethnic minority settlements but it is, as yet, exceptional because of conservative cultural influences exercised by some of the older generation, as well as by lack of clarity in legal home ownership within some families and the poverty of many families. We sense that some of these factors are beginning to change; we have heard some assertions that familiar territory is not important. Plainly, the abstract question "would you like to move?" can lead to no conclusion. Familiarity is only one influential factor amongst many others when deciding to remove.

5.11.5.   We have tried to trace the trends of movement by different ethnic groups from one part of Bradford to another, and from Bradford altogether. We have not succeeded, but we believe there is strong anecdotal evidence to support the conclusion that the dispersal of the ethnic groups from particular localities is following a similar pattern to that of the migrants who came to Bradford in the middle of the last century. If this is right, it has profound messages for those who are planning for the Bradford of the future, its City centre, its housing, its schools, and its other public Services. Fortunately, the *'Race' and Housing in Bradford* Report deals in depth with this subject.

Town Cramming

5.11.6.   We were told that the pressures on land use in West Bowling, within the period 1991 to 1995, resulted in the net loss of open space of just over 16 hectares. It was described as *"the art of Town Cramming"!* We have seen similar problems in Girlington and Manningham. The tension between the expanding population of Asian communities staying in the locality in which they first settled, and of finding adequate land for recreation, new housing and industry there, is one which it is very difficult to resolve. We were disappointed at the general lack of appreciation of this problem amongst the public, and the amount of strident argument, rather than constructive discussion, created in relation to the proposals for Housing on Westbourne Green in Manningham, which were prominent during our investigations.

5.11.7.   Yet the strength of local links cannot be underestimated. We can appreciate the financial and practical problems which would be involved in converting redundant industrial premises to residential and other uses. Some local people do not.

5.12   Individuals

5.12.1.   Each citizen is an individual. In dealing with each other, stereotyping as a means of understanding is unsatisfactory. A person's family, class, education, job, race, culture, religion, and many other features, will all be part of a complex and unique mix. The person you are dealing with is never adequately described as, in typical Bradfordspeak, a "Paki". It is almost always more important to know that he is, for example, a Pathan, and a leading member of a particular Mosque, or that his grandfather came from near Mirpur, and that he is an industrial chemist. Similarly, it is will never be adequate to describe the person you are dealing with as a "Gori", just because she is a White woman. She may well be herself the descendant of Irish forebears with a very similar family experience of painful adjustment and acceptance, and active in promoting better relationships, or any one of a thousand other possible variations.

5.12.2.   Inappropriate descriptions of this kind are commonplace and, as a constant feature of the language of many children, they do not bode well for the future.

5.12.3.   So, in Bradford, in addition to all the White people of various religious and cultural backgrounds, geographical loyalties, and social and economic status, we have many other groups, similarly divided. For example, the geographical background of some may be in India, but they are Muslim. There may be Hindus whose family roots are in Pakistan, and there are people whose claim to be Muslim is rejected by others who claim to speak for Islam. Orthodox Muslims themselves belong to different traditions.

5.12.4.   We have people who relate to, say, Girlington (where they were born and have grown up), who are related to people in Mirpur, Kashmir, who may not attend the Mosque for Friday prayers, yet who value the traditional Mirpuri culture of their relatives, and would be properly affronted if that culture were to be insulted. There are people whose immediate forebears lived in East Africa, but whose roots go back to the Indian sub-continent. All this should cause no surprise, but it is not reflected in many of the conversations one hears in Bradford, where untested assumptions govern many thoughts.

5.13   Young People

5.13.1.   In the circumstances we have described, young people from ethnic minority families growing up here face considerable insecurity, particularly as they leave the relative shelter of school, and have to find their place in the wider world of work, and of society generally. Increasingly there are, too, young people of mixed race, often unaccepted by either of the communities from which their parents come, and whose insecurity may therefore be the greatest in the midst of Bradford's cultural divisions. For the younger people, Bradford is home, and their future is here. In contrast, for the older people who came with an intention to return, strong personal links are retained with their place of origin.

5.13.2.   This has led to a situation where the generations can fail to communicate with each other. Many young people do not believe that their parents understand their situation. The interface, between the relatively closed world of many families and the wider world in which young people being brought up here actually move, can be very limited.

Part 2 The Response So Far

5.14   Bridge Building

Bradford's Record

5.14.1.   Tensions are likely to arise between groups of people who want to be treated as identifiably separate, and keeping a balance between the right to be different and the demands of equal citizenship requires constant attention if those tensions are to be accommodated. We wish to counterbalance our description of the City's divisions by referring to the very many instances we have noted of people making determined efforts to overcome the apparent barriers between them. We are also quite confident that far more people wish to cross these barriers than to maintain them, but they often have little opportunity.

5.14.2.   There is a long history of bridge building in Bradford, across ethnic, religious, and other divides. Indeed, the history is so rich that we could not possibly do justice to all those who are, or have been, involved. Some major, and very many minor, sources of friction between different groups and with public organisations have been negotiated over the last twenty years, because of the robustness of ad hoc bridges made at an official level. We have already mentioned some examples, and in later sections of our Report dealing with public services we will indicate others.

Informal Examples of Bridge Building

5.14.3.   We have come across many examples of informal bridge building, both conscious and coincidental, organised and individual. Some Asian women at one meeting told of encountering prejudice when they had first come to live in Bradford, but eventually the barriers were broken down. In one case a woman had been very moved to know that people at the local church had prayed for her seriously ill daughter. Another had offered support to an elderly White woman whose husband had been taken ill. A third had started helping at the local school.

5.14.4.   Another woman made the suggestion that it always helps to smile at people when you are dealing with them! As a White health worker who had tried to learn Urdu told us:

"They laugh at our Urdu, but it helps to break barriers".

5.14.5.   In one area of Manningham older people had organised a successful community bonfire party for youngsters of all races, and were planning a multi-cultural party for the Christmas holidays at the local church hall. Even in these circumstances there were problems from threats by gangs towards those young people who mixed with other communities.

5.14.6.   One White woman teacher who has experience of visiting the homes of pupils in the Manningham area, in an attempt to build bridges between school and home, wrote of her visits:

"I have always been given a warm welcome and feel privileged to have had this opportunity to meet families informally. I have observed that despite cultural and religious ties there are as many types of Asian family as there are English or European. Some households are very strict whilst others are more liberal. Some children are also very spoiled, as they may be in English homes."

A Workplace Example

5.14.7.   Evidence of effective bridge building is given in the T&GWU Paper also referred to in paras 5.21.8 and 6.20.9.

"The optimum example of integration is that of our workplace, where there is a wide range of Culture, Religions and Origins, working together in an environment which is a perfect example of how racial harmony can be achieved.

Tolerance, and an understanding of each others needs, enable the work place to be a friendly, comradely and welcoming place to be.

Many new employees have come along with quite alternative and right wing views, however, these are quickly overcome by the harmony which is clearly in existence within the workplace.

Many activities ranging from sport, social to political are always encouraged, to promote the good practice which is achievable in any community, be it in a factory or residential area."

A Joint Charity

5.14.8.   Another example is the Curry Project

"through which Sikhs, Hindus, Muslims and Christians provide evening meals for homeless people. It was a Sikh whose concern for social justice gave birth to the scheme, and he invited other people of faith and goodwill to join him. The number of helpers continues to grow."

The Churches

5.14.9.   We were most encouraged by the Bishop of Bradford as he spelt out the strategy of the Anglican Church, which deliberately maintains congregations and resident clergy in parishes which are not economically viable, in order to provide a helpful, active presence in the inner city. In Church of England schools there are up to 93% Asian children. A large proportion of the Bishop's, and of other senior clergy's time, is spent in working across religious and sectarian divides. We also came across the important initiatives of other churches seeking to value people of other faiths, and to build up mutual understanding and respect. As an example, in para 5.26.11, we refer to the insights derived from the experiences of "Touchstone". More locally, the Girlington, Heaton & Manningham Council of Churches

Community Relations Group has published a leaflet on *Ways Forward ... for Churches and Individuals*, containing ideas for encouraging good community relations.

The Inter Faith Centre

5.14.10.　We have already referred briefly to the Council for Mosques, and the representative bodies for other Asian religious groups, and their successful management of several difficult issues. Many of the 'Faith Communities' of Bradford have created excellent mutual relationships, despite historic rivalries, and the work of the Inter Faith Centre on a schools' religious education curriculum is a national model.

Building More Bridges

5.14.11.　It is inevitable that much of our Report should make challenging, even depressing, reading. Yet so much of the quality of life in Bradford seems to depend on people's attitudes. It is easy enough for people to find some examples with which to justify sweeping ethnic generalisations, and we heard such attitudes from people of all backgrounds. The result is that some citizens have to endure some very harsh treatment at the hands of people who exercise their power in an offensive way.

5.14.12.　Fortunately, it is also true that an increasing number of citizens are learning to value people of other cultures, going way beyond the narrow limits of polite correctness. For them, stereotypical fallacies are no longer allowing differences to overcome common values and problems. Examples of individual good neighbourliness are frequent. There is a growing number of informal meetings across the ethnic boundaries. There is certainly an expressed desire for more opportunities to learn about each other from many people of all ages and backgrounds. We doubt if these healthy and stimulating trends can be best developed by official, top down, means, but we do suggest that all formal and informal organisations should have openly on their agenda their willingness to build bridges across the divisions.

5.14.13.　The topics for discussion are not all one way. The White majority of the population need to be more aware of their often thoughtless indifference, but minority communities need to face up to the critical views reasonably held by others, in robust dialogue. Their members, too, have an equal responsibility, as citizens, to help solve their own undoubted problems in adjusting to life in Bradford and to contribute to the solution of the city's wider problems.

5.14.14.　We intend the contents of this Report to stimulate more open and honest discussion; to overcome the nervousness which prevents people from squaring up to the tensions which arise in an ethnically diverse city. Almost everywhere we have looked there is a need for more mature discussion, uninhibited by racism or timid tokenism. As one of those whom we interviewed told us, echoing others, people are *"fed up with tokenism and palliatives"*. Others are horrified at the entrenched views held by people with no real experience of meeting those whom they defame.

5.14.15.　Only by open and sensible discussion will problems which have been created between people of different backgrounds be understood and solved. One would have thought that Bradford, of all places, could rise to this challenge! Over and over again we were impressed by the directness of the people who spoke to us. Weasel words are culturally inappropriate in Bradford, in all its main ethnic traditions.

5.15   Bradford City Council's Race Relations Policy

5.15.1.   The history of race relations in Bradford was analysed for us by one of our interviewees, based upon his close involvement for some years, and we broadly adopt this analysis because it has been supported anecdotally by others to an extent we cannot ignore. In short, we observe a process of initial indifference, followed by official response to agitation, followed by meaningful activity, followed by tokenism, which in turn appears to mask indifference. In what follows we refer specifically to the city council, but the council is only one agency amongst many influential bodies in the city. Its record far outshines those of many of them, and any criticism should not detract from its achievements. Its democratic significance, however, determines its prime importance in such a subject.

5.15.2.   As jobs and prospects disappeared within the private sector, there was an increasing concentration of interest by members of the minority communities upon large public sector employers, particularly Bradford Council, which were increasingly seen as the most viable alternative sources of jobs. This was particularly true for the better educated, more articulate and young members of the Asian communities, who increasingly moved to employment by the city council and other public agencies. Several leaders of the Asian Youth Movement thus became involved in advising the council.

5.15.3.   Initially there was much concentration on Race Equality procedures in appointments. The city council then adopted an all-party approach in which the emphasis was on appropriateness of service provision. The council began to change its organisational practices, and to acknowledge the presence of citizens with different cultural and religious backgrounds than those of the traditional White majority.

5.15.4.   It is impossible for us to appraise the success of the council in detail, but it is clear to us that significant changes did result. For example, there was a measured increase of ethnic minority employees from 2% in 1985/86 to 8.8% in 1995/96, with the proportion of white collar staff now standing at 13%. It has also been clear to us that many changes in the appropriateness of the council's services have been made, not least in the several schools we have visited.

5.15.5.   From the mid-1980s the open political drive for achieving the benefits of a more equal citizenship was lost, and has never been recovered. One explanation we have been given is that, because the initial discussions with the city council were inevitably centred on adaptations to fit minority values and practices, with a resulting controversy of articulate opposition or envy from some in the White majority, a reaction against making further concessions has set in, and the result is evasion of the many tensions which now need discussion. Fear of, or hopes of benefit from, an electoral backlash has caused a pusillanimous attitude, in failing to open up further deliberations, failing to redistribute existing allocations of resources, or failing to promote new ventures, according to many informants. We consider these allegations in Sections 6 and 7. Another explanation is that the heat generated by the Honeyford Affair (see para 5.8.18) caused many White people to avoid discussing openly what might be racially sensitive issues.

5.15.6.   The February 1993 Carr Report *Alibis for Inaction*, dealing with the council's procedures for handling complaints of discrimination, showed the ease with which a difficult challenge like racial discrimination, however clear the formal policy may be, can slip away from proper implementation if there is a lack of committed direction. Regrettably, there appears to us to be a lack of commitment to meaningful discussion of ethnically involved issues within the present political processes of Bradford, though there is still a strong bureaucratic control of the correct formalities.

5.16 Racial Equality Council

5.16.1.   The Bradford Racial Equality Council, which was formerly the Community Relations Council, is the oldest official body in Bradford involved in race relations. It is funded from public funds, and has recently survived the creation and demise of the West Yorkshire Racial Equality Council. Over the years it has done valuable work and it is still the only body with the role of bringing together representatives of the majority of the diverse ethnic and cultural groups within Bradford. There is no doubt, however, that to many of the younger people it is now seen as part of the establishment, and its role and potential is undervalued by them. Nor does it presently command the confidence of those members of the African Caribbean community whom we met. We have been told that rivalries within the organisation impede its effectiveness.

5.16.2.   As with any individual agency with a specialised remit, there is a danger that it is regarded as the box into which race relations issues should be placed and dealt with, leaving other organisations free to get on with their business without having to bother about such matters. But, in Bradford at any rate, dealing with racial tensions and their relevance to the life of the city should be part of the mainstream activity of all organisations.

5.16.3.   Whilst it clearly could have a role to play as an inter-agency facilitator, the REC does not currently influence mainstream activities in the city significantly. It is our view that it should concentrate its efforts and limited resources on achievable priorities.

5.17 Local Leadership

5.17.1.   In addition to the considerable time we spent in Manningham we spent several days visiting, and learning about the situation in both West Bowling and Girlington, the latter a geographical community adjacent to Manningham. We were favourably impressed by local leadership and its potential in all these communities. Our experiences in other communities which we visited reinforced our view that leadership and potential leadership at the local level can be strong enough to undertake demanding tasks, and gain local support.

5.17.2.   Training in leadership skills is being organised to meet current challenges. Only a small amount of financial support would be needed to build on established good practice. It seems to us that many of the priority challenges we have identified could be tackled in this way, in implementation of an approved strategy, though we do not pretend that such a course will be easy, consistent, or rapidly successful.

Part 3 Young Men in the Manningham Area

5.18 Social Conditions which create a Predisposition to Violent Protest

5.18.1.   Lord Scarman's Report on the Brixton Riots, after outlining the social conditions in that area, many of which were repeated in Manningham in 1995, and which are found in many parts of Bradford at the present time, wrote of the rioters in Brixton:

"2.37 The accumulation of these anxieties and frustrations and the limited opportunities of airing their grievances at national level in British society encourage them to protest on the streets. ... They live their lives on the street, having often nothing better to do: they make their protest there: and some of them live off street crime. The recipe for a clash with the police is therefore ready-mixed: and it takes little, or nothing, to persuade them that the police, representing an establishment which they see as insensitive to their plight, are their enemies...

2.38 None of these features can perhaps usefully be described as a cause of the disorders... But taken together, they provide a set of social conditions which create a predisposition to violent protest..."

5.18.2.   We were frequently told by expert field workers that the circumstances of life in Manningham created widespread low self-esteem amongst young men which encouraged antisocial reactions. We, and many of our informants, regard these circumstances as *"a set of social conditions which create a predisposition to violent protest."*

5.18.3.   Some have tried to argue that, because the social conditions apply equally to many people who did not violently protest, they are irrelevant to our remit. That is to misunderstand the nature of a predisposition, and its distinction from a cause, but even if we are wrong to regard these themes as relevant to the disorders, there is still an acute need to deal with them.

5.19 Untypical Behaviour

5.19.1.   We explained in Section 4 of this Report that the disorders were not typical of the Asian boys and young men of Manningham, nor of the local community (however defined) as a whole.

5.19.2.   We think it is worth reflecting on the truths contained in the following quotes:

"there were those [rioters] *who have never had a criminal record but they were committing some of the violence... some of those young people throwing the bricks were helping the police on Sunday calming the situation down, even to the extent that some of them were getting harassed by their peer group from other areas."*

"there were no fights at the Mela this year [ie. 1995], *like there were before, because we* [some Manningham young men] *were helping to steward it and knew who the trouble-makers were and kept them from causing any trouble."*

5.19.3.   From Foundation 2000s report *The Voices **Must** Be Heard*:

"Young people themselves have not been given the credit they deserve in terms of playing a valuable part in their communities. They are often seen as delinquents or social misfits and not

as the decision making adults of tomorrow. They have a very important role to play and need to be heard, taken seriously and given a stake in deciding their own destiny."

"Talking to groups of young people and individuals, one can clearly see the wasted talent and wasted potential in our community. It is not only in Manningham but elsewhere in Bradford, black and white alike..."

"These are the same young people being congratulated by Bradford commuters (mostly white) for assisting them and their cars up and down Oak Lane when the whole region suffered from a severe fall of snow this year [1995] *which left many motorists stranded in their cars."*

5.19.4.   We therefore look at the social circumstances of young men in Manningham, to try to understand better why some of them and their associates from other parts of the city should have behaved as they did on the two nights of disorders in June 1995.

5.20   Space at Home

Poor Condition

5.20.1.   We are dealing with conditions which affect many more people than just young men, but our reason for dealing with them here is the limited nature of our remit. A large percentage of the housing in the Asian settlements, which is usually owner occupied by a family, is not just overcrowded, but is physically in a poor state. The vast majority of the housing in Manningham is Victorian and Edwardian terraced property. The expectation was created in the 1960s and 1970s that city council renovation grants would provide assistance to repair these properties and bring them up to a modern standard. The expectation is still there, but the money is not, and the extensive incidence of unemployment means that private money is not often available for this purpose. The result is that much of the stock continues to deteriorate.

Overcrowding

5.20.2.   We have not pursued the topic of housing as a main theme because it was rarely raised with us directly as being of major relevance to our work, but the nature of the housing conditions within the Manningham area do have a profound effect upon the young people who live there. On this subject, reference should be made to *'Race' and Housing in Bradford*, which has just been published and which we welcome.

5.20.3.   Severe overcrowding amongst Asian families is common. The number of new household creations, as large young families grow up, is considerable, but there is no possibility that the aspirations of these incipient family units will be met, unless there are changes in housing policy.

5.20.4.   There is a strong tradition that young people do not leave home until, or even when, they marry, and so they do not have the option of leaving home which is available to many young White people in similar circumstances. This, again, leaves no space for adolescent children and means that much of their development, particularly of young men, takes place outside the home. There is also some evidence of young men having to leave home and sleeping rough, despite cultural resistance to the very idea. All this means that there is a strong imperative for street culture to develop and dominate the lives of young men. This culture is, by its nature, not subject to close scrutiny by the older generation.

5.21   Street Behaviour

A Distinct Culture

5.21.1.   In an area like Manningham the majority of the Asian boys and young men will go, or will have gone, to schools where the vast majority of their peers are from the same background. When they leave school, being mainly unemployed, or employed in family businesses, they carry on within their existing social matrix. This leads to the development of a culture with its own values and customs, which is quite distinct and in many ways hidden.

5.21.2.   There is one important factor relevant here, according to one of our Asian informants, that differentiates many young Asian people from many young White people. In adolescence there is greater freedom for the latter to meet socially without supervision. This is not formally permitted in Asian cultures, although young men have much more leeway than young women in sexual matters.

5.21.3   It is no accident that all of those involved in the disorders were male. Boys are openly allowed much more freedom, whereas girls are expected to live tightly prescribed lives. This leads to a situation where the public street culture is exclusively masculine. This then leads to a concentration on masculine elements of development. Groups of young men roaming the streets are an obvious manifestation of this tendency.

Antisocial Behaviour

5.21.4.   We received very strong testimony from people who live in many parts of Bradford about the extent of the antisocial behaviour of boys and young men **of many different ethnic backgrounds**. They spoke of intolerable levels of harassment, vandalism and street crime. This is a problem which is widespread, and is certainly not confined to one geographical area, such as Manningham, nor to one ethnic group, even though some variation in the type of crime can, we are told, be statistically discerned between ethnic groups.

5.21.5.   We heard, from different parts of Bradford, of several families, White and Asian, whose children never played outside because of the lawlessness on the surrounding streets; of one Bangladeshi family whose children were subjected to considerable harassment by their Mirpuri neighbours' children; of repeatedly broken house windows; of a school wall whose rebuilding was eventually abandoned after its repeated destruction by local children before the mortar could set; of a White boy who never went out without an iron bar and chain with which to defend himself, to prevent repetition of previous attacks by Asian youths; of Asian bus drivers who were surprised when a White colleague wanted to take proceedings against Asian youths who had verbally abused him – it was part of their normal day to endure racial abuse from White youths.

5.21.6.   One man, a resident in the inner city, told us that since he came to live there in 1985 his car had been stolen once, and vandalised eight times. His property had been burgled three times, with four attempted burglaries in addition.

5.21.7.   One of the most disturbing expressions of concern at current levels of antisocial behaviour came from a meeting we held with elderly people, from several ethnic backgrounds, in another part of the inner city than Manningham. It was an all too familiar set of allegations, towards the end of our Inquiry's consultations, of harassment, vandalism, minor crime, reprisals against complainants, and police indifference. The sense of suppressed anger, and of despair, was most marked. In the church hall in which we met, evening meetings had been abandoned, and a security firm was employed to safeguard the parked cars of the congregation on Sundays. Friends were reluctant to visit the area, people were afraid to go out at night. Windows in sheltered accommodation for the elderly were broken so regularly that the council ran out of glass, we were told.

5.21.8.   A more precise evaluation concerns violence on buses. We are indebted to the local branch of the Transport and General Workers Union for a copy of a paper which they prepared in early 1996 on *Violence on Public Transport*, and from which the following quotations about Bradford are taken:

"1995 saw the highest level of assaults against Bus Workers ever recorded in the region. A 27% rise brought the total for the year to 124, compared with 98 in 1994 and 44 in 1993. ... There is clearly a problem in Bradford as the assaults in other Yorkshire Rider Districts are only a fraction of this total.

There is no clear pattern for the assaults situation in Bradford, except that an assault is much more likely to take place when the Schools come out, rather than the historical theory of when the pubs come out...

Acts of vandalism are more common than those of assault, and happen in just about every corner of our city."

5.21.9.   We did analyse the assaults on bus drivers over the six months January to June 1996, and can confirm the absence of any obvious racial pattern in the criminals or the victims.

5.21.10.   Although the levels of vandalism, theft and assault are all unacceptably high, only some young men are determinedly antisocial; but many are easily led, and deceive their parents. The overwhelming majority are decent young people who, in our experience, responded to courtesy with courtesy.

5.21.11.   Nonetheless, the present scale of antisocial behaviour is sufficiently large to make the consequences intolerable for a large number of people of all ages, and many people believe it to be increasing noticeably year by year. One particularly incensed Asian woman probably spoke for a lot of people in her scathing contempt for those Whites who excused, or failed to condemn, wrongdoing when the culprits were not White. It was, she rightly said, patronising, as well as stupid.

Gangs and Groups

5.21.12.   In our investigations we heard from many White people, especially the elderly, about the threat of Asian gangs. There is no doubt that in an area like Manningham, where the vast majority of young people are Asian, the older White residents tend to perceive the misbehaviour we have just described in ethnic terms. This is to ignore the fact that the threat from gangs and from antisocial behaviour, is similar in the estates which have largely White youngsters.

5.21.13.   Asian gangs do exist, and they do threaten White people in public places. But they also threaten people of all kinds; this, and inter-gang hostility, at least shows that the motivation is by no means exclusively racial. On the other hand, the presence of youth gangs looking for excitement in a multicultural community does frequently lead to racial difference being used as a pretext for both victimisation and gang fighting. We are sceptical as to the depth of the racial motivation which is involved in many of these cases, beyond the desire to express anger at representatives of a seemingly hostile culture.

5.21.14.   We are concerned to put this very real problem of Asian gangs into perspective. Many White people are unable to distinguish between an Asian gang and 'a group of Asian youths'. Even when the term 'gang' is clearly inappropriate, as when groups of Asian youths helped motorists passing through their area in the snow, a group of unknown young men from an unfamiliar culture can seem menacing to the inexperienced. Often, people feel threatened even where no threat has been intended. It is important to differentiate between groups of young people who congregate on street corners for normal social interaction, and the groups organised for antisocial purposes.

5.22   The "Vigilante"/Prostitution Campaign

A "Red Light" Area

5.22.1.   For many years the Lumb Lane area of Bradford had been the red light area of the City. This had been tolerated by the local community, which had, over many years, been increasingly settled by Muslims but, when the prostitution spread to nearby areas where the residents were unused to the trade and its consequences, a campaign was launched to use street patrols, or pickets, or vigilantes (the choice of description varies) to displace this activity from the area, after local people heard of a successful similar campaign in Birmingham.

5.22.2.   The adverse effect of the reputation of the area was pointed out by one of our informants:

"When our lads went for jobs and gave their address, they were regarded as coming from a red light district."

5.22.3.   The pre-existing situation is graphically described by two quotes, the first from an African Caribbean source:

"Lumb Lane and Manningham is an infamous area which acts as a focal point for the district's hardened and very long-term unemployed. It boasts a history of a vibrant illegal drugs and prostitution industry, and from time to time, cases of extreme violence and gunfare."

The other is from a newspaper:

"Sick of finding used condoms and hypos in their front gardens, and of having their women harassed by kerbcrawlers, and even sicker of hearing the police saying that they could do nothing to clean things up, they'd taken matters into their own hands, and formed themselves into vigilante groups."

5.22.4.   There were several television programmes screened, both fictional and factual, which highlighted and brought to national attention the problems of prostitution in the area. In particular, the *Band of Gold* programme before Easter 1995 increased the publicity about the area, and is considered to have greatly increased the number of kerb-crawling men.

5.22.5.   There is no doubt that local people felt that the area was being portrayed in a way which represented a slur on them. This inevitably led to resentment, not just about the direct nuisance value of prostitution, but also about the effect it had upon the local image of the area. This feeling was sufficiently articulated to be discussed as a problem affecting the image of the whole of Bradford by several agencies, including the city council and the Bradford Congress.

The Patrols

5.22.6.   The anti-prostitution patrols began during the Easter holidays in mid-April 1995. The campaign itself eventually consisted of groups of mainly young men who, in theory, were supposed to maintain a fixed presence at strategic places, but in practice often roamed the area, 'persuading' prostitutes to go elsewhere. The young men believed that they were cleaning up their own community's area. The prostitutes, however, believed they were being harassed, as some undoubtedly were.

5.22.7.   We have attached particular importance to understanding this campaign because of its overlap in time with the disorders in Manningham of June 1995, its geographical proximity to the disorders, and some features common to both on which we have commented in Section 4.

The Extension of the Red Light area

5.22.8.   We heard about the anti-prostitution campaign in particular from a group of local residents adjacent to Lumb Lane, and from some of the police officers directly involved. What they told us coincided with most of what we have been told by others, both officials and private citizens. It seems there had been mounting concern about new territory being used as a red light area, after traffic calming measures in 1991 began to displace the prostitutes from Lumb Lane itself. Streets which had never known the problem found the presence of prostitutes brought the circumstances described in the newspaper article above. There had also been an increase in the number of younger women involved, mainly due to a need to feed their drugs habit. A substantial petition was organised, and local councillors were involved.

Police Action

5.22.9.   As a result of repeated protests from residents the police adopted new tactics, and began to focus on the male clients, rather than on the prostitutes. This was explained at a meeting with local people in November 1994, and implemented between November 1994 and January 1995. Fifty-two prostitutes, 368 kerb-crawlers, and three males importuning for an immoral purpose, were arrested. As a result, there was a considerable reduction in both the number of kerb crawlers and of prostitutes, but the police action was not sustained. When the picketing began at Easter 1995, both the police vice squad and the older people organising the picketing worked hard to ensure that the picketing was peaceful. Many of the prostitutes understood the protest being made about areas near mosques, and thought they had complied.

The Local Activists

5.22.10.   In the group of local residents who spoke to us there were White and Asian residents involved, and some of the middle aged and elderly men who spoke to us had themselves been out peacefully patrolling their streets. They had deliberately begun a quiet campaign of patrolling their local streets, hoping that their constant presence would deter prostitution.

5.22.11.   One White woman from this group told us how she broke down and cried on reaching home after the walk from the bus, because kerbcrawlers assumed she was a prostitute. The group told us:

> *"The media have painted a picture of vigilantes but we started it to counter the movement of prostitutes here. After 5 pm each day life for women* [ie local residents] *was intolerable."*

5.22.12.   Within this group there was residual indignation at what they thought had been police reluctance to accept the scale of the problem for local residents. They felt that there was police resentment at local people interfering in a professional matter, and that there was injured police pride when the local residents succeeded in clearing 'their' streets. There were widespread suspicions of attempts by the police to provoke incidents of misbehaviour by the patrols, including that the police had given cassettes to prostitutes to record harassment which some police officers then sought to provoke.

> *"Our community was boiling over about it, but the young lads were under the control of the elders. We were scared of clashes occurring between the lads, the pimps and the police. So we got to know the lads. There were 500 lads out on the streets for over eight weeks. The whole community was behind them. The police were trying to hassle and to tempt them, but we knew the police were waiting."*

5.22.13.   We asked where the 500 lads came from, as we were interested in possible parallels to the disorders. The answer was that much of the campaign took place during the Easter holidays, and that school friends and young relatives came from all over Bradford.

> *"The lads found self-esteem doing this."*

We also heard that youths came from as far afield as Birmingham.

Trouble

5.22.14.   The description so far represents the intentions of many residents who supported the patrols. Unfortunately the initial intention of peaceful picketing was overtaken by roving gangs of young men, some as young as 11 we were told, not following the local organised arrangements of continuous peaceful presence in an allotted place. This younger element bragged about clearing the problem completely, and ignored the police. Extremists tried to make it an Islamic cause, and said English law was irrelevant. *"We will police this part of the city",* was their claim, we were told. These developments exposed women to apprehension and, in some cases, violence.

The Police View

5.22.15.   The police told us that they thought that the problems were mainly caused by incomers from other parts of Bradford, particularly by the end of May, and by a "younger end" who hid behind the elders and then tried to take over. The police view was that the campaign was well organised at one level by 20–30 year olds. There was constant liaison between the police and an ad hoc committee of local activists. The view of the police was that

"these street patrols were, in the main, peaceful, organised, and responsible but there were isolated incidents of abuse directed towards prostitutes and innocent members of the public. The outcome of these patrols was that they effectively displaced the prostitution problem from the residential areas of Manningham to other, sparsely populated areas in the city centre division."

A Big Issue

5.22.16. Although we sympathise with the indignation of the residents who found the consequences of prostitution on their doorsteps intolerable, we also share the concern of those who seek to protect girls and young women from serious maltreatment, and of the police that there is no real solution to the problem within the existing law. Merely to remove it from one area to another solves nothing except, of course, for the residents from whose area removal is achieved. However, there is no doubt that Lumb Lane and its nearby streets no longer have a red light trade, and the campaign has been seen locally as successful. Direct and, at least technically, illegal, action was seen to work.

5.22.17. Prostitution is not a non-Asian activity. *"Prostitution is racially integrated!"* was a striking comment from a professional person very familiar with the problems and the people involved. So far as we could understand from several very different but authoritative sources, there are few Asian prostitutes, but many Asian pimps, and many Asian clients.

5.22.18. There are many difficult issues involved in this situation, issues which cannot be satisfactorily dealt with under existing law, and which are well beyond our terms of reference. The related facts are ones which many people do not want to face up to. The police are left to sort out the situation as best they can, and are criticised from all sides. We cannot help commenting that the Chief Constable of West Yorkshire's recent attempt to raise the subject for intelligent public discussion deserves support. We also commend for public understanding and political interest the excellent "Streets and Lanes" multi-agency project involving Barnardos. This presents the unacceptable and illegal conditions of some of the girls and young women, which should engage the responsibilities of the police and social services in particular.

5.23 Drugs

5.23.1. Because Bradford is, according to official information, a major centre for illegal drugs, and because the related crimes are often so much more serious than those to which we have just referred, we deal with the subject separately. For many disillusioned young people drugs are increasingly seen as the easy way out from unpleasant realities, and the drug culture is having an intensifying influence upon the young. The fact that this culture is illegal makes it even less open to scrutiny by parents than the street culture we have just described. In the Asian communities particularly there is a very strong element of denial of the problem, which means that even close family members will not acknowledge that a relative has a drug problem when they do become aware of it.

5.23.2.   The police informed us:

"Despite [Toller] *being one of the smallest of the 17 divisions in the force, arrests in connection with the possession or supply of heroin, cocaine and crack represented 19%, 25%, and 23%, respectively, of the total arrests for the* [West Yorkshire] *Force during 1994. Possibly as a consequence of the nature of the division's problems, the number of firearms related incidents are also among the highest in the force."*

5.23.3.   According to the *Yorkshire Post* of 12 July 1995, after disorders in Leeds involving drugs (public disorders do occur elsewhere, even in Leeds!) the Chief Constable of West Yorkshire said:

"50% of all property crime in our region is as a direct or indirect result of drugs. The statistics also do not reveal the violence caused by drugs... we can expect 30% of today's youngsters will be involved in drugs by the age of 13, and 50% by 16."

5.23.4.   According to a doctor who has pioneered the rehabilitation of addicts in the inner city, his successful work has resulted in a reduction in the criminality of his patients by over 90%. Like so many much needed initiatives in Bradford, it is limited in scope mainly by a shortage of cash. Some other health workers in this area of the city emphasised to us the impact of drugs on their work.

"Hard drugs have a major influence; it is a huge problem for the city. Bradford is a major centre, and it has escalated in the last two years. There is a lot of brown heroin coming in. We only see the tip of the iceberg."

5.23.5.   We were particularly impressed with the frankness and conversational abilities of one small group of first year pupils at an upper school who, without any lead from us, gave us some impression of their developing outlook. According to the notes we made of various contributions in the class discussion, they were frightened of the

"gangs of bad boys in Lister Park. Drugs is a big problem. They grab your money, Asians and Whites. They give our religion a bad name. They swear at White men. We feel bad about it. We all feel bad."

5.23.6.   The prevalence, and rapid recent growth of both drugs dealing and usage in the inner city areas, and on the largely White council estates, has frequently been drawn to our attention. These are areas to which we have paid particular attention, but we certainly do not dismiss the probability that the drugs problem is much more widely distributed than in just these areas. Because of Bradford's frequent connections with Pakistan there is an obvious potential for heroin importation. The unfortunate consequences of this problem are manifold; we draw attention to two.

5.23.7.   First, successful drug dealers, of whom there are said to be many, present a role model of economic success in communities where such success is seldom seen. There is no lack of envy, we were told, amongst many young men for the expensive lifestyle of *"fast cars, mobile telephones and posh houses"* enjoyed, with apparent impunity, by known drug dealers. Such people are alleged to be well known locally, but apparently beyond the reach of the law, because of limited police resources, lack of evidence volunteered by the public, and the violent stifling of potential witnesses by the criminals.

5.23.8.   Secondly, the distribution of addictive drugs is so great that very young children are being hooked in ever increasing numbers, often by being offered their first supplies free. No child is safely beyond the scope of this evil. In recent years we understand that there has actually been a price war in Bradford between rival drug suppliers, and the price of drugs has been continually dropping at the same time as the availability has been ever more easy.

5.23.9.   There is now a co-ordinated multi-agency response to this threatening situation in the recent formation of the Bradford Drugs Action Team. But parents cannot afford to leave it to an underfunded police force and an ineffective system of criminal justice, as though it were society at large's problem, but not theirs individually. As with so many of Bradford's current problems a more determined and less supine citizenry is called for, in all parts of the city. We applaud the Chief Constable of West Yorkshire's recent initiative in pressing for consideration of the virtues of regulation rather than prohibition. The present regime is not effective, the funding of treatment is inadequate, and intelligent public support is needed for alternatives.

5.24   The Need for Discipline

5.24.1.   There is a large number of citizens, of all ethnic backgrounds, who are very angry at the lack of an adequate system of criminal justice to catch and punish known wrongdoers. Whilst their short cuts to the treatment of very summarily convicted offenders rarely went beyond the 'lock them up and throw away the key' stage, there appears to be a great need for unsocial behaviour by youths to be noted, checked, and dealt with.

5.24.2.   Unfortunately, and probably not only in Bradford, ordinary people are very uncertain how to intervene when faced with misbehaviour by young people, even at home. In public places, White adults hesitate to intervene where Asian children or youths are concerned, in case they are accused of being "racist", a not uncommon response. Asian adults hesitate to intervene where White children are concerned, in case they excite a bigoted response. Some Asian parents who spoke to us regretted the current antipathy to corporal punishment, and expressed their fear that "Social Services" would remove their children from them if they punished them in this way.

5.24.3.   Responsibility for improving youth discipline was often unfairly placed on schools – where sanctions for disciplining unacceptable behaviour are very limited, and where class sizes are very large and increasing at a time when other stresses are common – and the professional law enforcers are under resourced.

5.24.4.   We doubt if this serious problem can be resolved solely by official means, though there is some evidence from American experience that multi-agency approaches to the prevention of criminality (as distinct from crime) can be successful. Parents and members of the public must be prepared to learn in what ways they can actively and properly co-operate with schools, the police, and other agencies. Equally, the official bodies must learn to engage public co-operation if counterproductive self help is to be avoided. It is a problem amongst Asian and White communities, and all communities therefore need to square up to it. We return to this subject in Section 6, Part 2.

5.25   Extremist Factions

Hizb ut-Tahrir

5.25.1.   One experienced Asian Councillor wrote to us:

"a very dangerous current of 'counter racism' is developing among the Asian youth. It is a combination of religious bigotry and intolerance on one hand and challenging of White racists on the other hand... High on rhetoric, attacking anything that moves, seeing Zionists/ Christians/sold out Muslims conspiracy in everything, unfortunately this is gaining ground among Asian youth. These fringe religious groups have been agitating the youth for some time and played a significant role in the disturbance."

5.25.2.   The use of the word Asian in this quotation means Muslim. The only extremist group specifically mentioned to us was Hizb ut-Tahrir, which appears to provide a simple solution to current problems, allowing young Muslim men to value their own traditions at the same time as striking back at an unwelcoming mainstream society. They can even criticise their elders for 'not being Muslim enough'.

5.25.3.   Such groups exist in many religions and societies; the existence of overzealous, strongly motivated groups of people with totalitarian views is not confined to nominally Islamic groups. A false triumphalistic hope is both common, and especially attractive, amongst the disadvantaged. Popularly, these groups are often referred to as extremists, or fundamentalists. The inappropriate phrase 'Muslim fundamentalist' is now, like the word 'Asian', so much a part of common speech in Britain that it is difficult to avoid. Yet it is offensive to Muslims who take their faith seriously. They are the ones who are fundamentally Muslim, and those of their number who have spoken with us join with decent people of all backgrounds in condemning the naive, text chopping heterodoxy of those who promote violent totalitarianism as a tool of their religion.

5.25.4.   We give a useful quotation from *The Independent* of 13 June 1995, in an interview immediately after the disorders with a White Bradfordian concerned with inter-faith issues:

"Yet another [option] *is Islam. Which explains the slogans for Hamas. 'It looks like Islamic fundamentalism... It's a reactive identity – it is one thing they perceive the Whites do not have. So they become assertively Muslim.' But it is a DIY Islam, an Islam of slogans rather than of substance. And it is fed by the Islamophobia which it in turn generates."*

5.25.5.   We referred to a meeting organised by Hizb ut-Tahrir immediately after the disorders, in para 4.22.3, in which the local, mainly Muslim, community had ensured an unsympathetic response. The Telegraph & Argus on 26 July 1995 reported:

"Bradford Muslims have condemned a radical Islamic group which aims to recruit the city's youngsters in the wake of last month's riots. Activists from Hizb ut-Tahrir, or Party of Liberation, flooded the Manningham area during the disturbances and have held recruitment rallies at college campuses, community centres and mosques ... But the Bradford community has moved to distance itself from the extremists, saying that they are breeding racial and religious tension. Some mosques have already banned the activists."

5.25.6.   We were interested to hear of another occasion in Bradford, when an hotel was misled into making facilities available to Hizb ut-Tahrir, and that at the 1996 Mela, which occurred as we were writing our Report, there was again an attempt by this organisation to use the occasion for propaganda by taking over vacated stalls. It is reassuring to know that the organisers moved rapidly and effectively to stop this happening.

Leaflets

5.25.7. We have also been given copies of objectionable posters and leaflets, and told of objectionable grafitti and rhetoric, which caused great apprehension to many people, and which certainly revealed a capacity for callous and organised hatred in the name of a spurious religious zeal. One particular leaflet encouraged young Muslim men to seduce Sikh girls, in order to shame them in the eyes of their Sikh community and capture them for the Muslim faith. At one meeting we were told by representatives that, in the previous six weeks, at least six girls from the Bradford Sikh and Hindu communities, aged 16–25, had been taken, by this means, into Muslim families in Pakistan. We need hardly emphasise the tensions which such leaflets, and even just rumours of any associated incidents, cause.

BNP and NF

5.25.8. During 1984 to 1986 the British National Party and the National Front targeted Bradford for recruitment. They stood in elections but failed to make any impact. Although there appeared to be little activity during our Inquiry it would be foolish to assume that they have disappeared for ever. They, too, can create fears of violence, and can be the cause of civil unrest. We certainly do not dismiss their potential for causing trouble in Bradford, but we are not aware of any present reason to regard them as other than a part of the extremist fringe of politics in British society.

Fascism

5.25.9. It is not the radical nature of the extremists' beliefs, nor their fundamental personal commitment to their perceived ideal that is of concern to us. Nor should these beliefs and commitment be confused with a tendency for some young people to become more committed to open religious observance than their parents, in their search for their own identity. In a free society people are entitled to hold their own ideas, and wholehearted commitment to an ideal is often commendable. It is when the ideas and ideals are linked to the seizure of temporal power that freedom for all becomes endangered.

5.25.10. It is one thing to say, as the adherents of many faiths would, that faith should guide societal, as well as individual, transactions. It is quite another to urge the destruction of secular society, the only possible basis for a multi-faith city, in order to impose the social structure regarded by some adherents of one of those faiths as the optimum. The imposition of ideas and practices on others, and the treatment as worthless of all who oppose, is at one with racism and fascism, and should be rejected as such.

Little Support

5.25.11. Certainly, there appears to us to be little support for such fascist organisations amongst the population of Bradford, whether based on appeals to national or racial pride, or to religious and cultural loyalties. But although we are confident that, at the present time, extremism is not a major threat to the peace of the city, the most effective way of ensuring that this is, and remains, the case is for Bradford citizens to know each other better. Ignorance is the fertile source of extremism, and there is a lot of ignorance around.

5.25.12.   There are potential alliances, across the racial divides, which need to be formed by the overwhelmingly large number of people from all the different cultural groups who hold to decent values about living together in society. But this widespread sensible attitude needs clearer articulation, both to combat the bizarre appeal of irrational and unauthentic creeds to frustrated young people, and to put into realistic perspective the very limited extent of the White establishment plots, or the Muslim fundamentalism, which are so often suspected in our mutual ignorance of each other.

5.25.13.   We suggest, too, that it would be a useful step for very public condemnation of this kind of extremism to be made by **all** political, religious and community leaders as clearly and authoritatively as possible. Such a condemnation will have little effect on the zealots, but it would help to reassure all parts of the Bradford population that the threat of violent political or religious action is confined to a very small number of unrepresentative and ill-informed people.

5.26   Generation Gap?

Lack of Control?

5.26.1.   We have heard disconcerting evidence, from several sources, of parents from various cultural backgrounds feeling helpless to control their sons. To many, the current pressures to eliminate corporal punishment mean the removal of any effective deterrent to bad behaviour at school or at home, and they are uncertain of the extent to which they can punish their children.

Different Values?

5.26.2.   A number of commentators in the media explained the violent behaviour in the disorders of June 1995 by referring to a clash between the different values of older and younger generations in the Asian communities. For many years, if not generations, within the White population there has been talk of a generation gap which is characterised by a lack of mutual understanding, based on inadequate communication, between generations. The assertion is being made that this is now being replicated within the Asian communities, following the White example.

5.26.3.   Once again, we have to emphasise this recurrent theme – people are individuals, and it is foolish to stereotype beyond rather obvious levels of generalisation. But we think that this idea of a generation gap has to be handled with some care, quite apart from the dangers of generalisation. We readily acknowledge that a generation growing up in Bradford is likely to have many different ideas about how to cope with life here than did the generation which first came from the Indian sub-continent. Changing perceptions in the Asian communities are not new – in subsection 5.8. we outlined a changing Asian political agenda which, in part, antedated the lives of many of the violent protesters. Unless perceptions do change through time, young people will remain locked into very limited options.

5.26.4.   We have seen amongst the violent protesters' generation much evidence of a loyalty to, and respect for, the traditional **values** of their culture and those who hold them, but also a developing range of adaptations to the changes in society around them similar to those which occur amongst White young people. It seems inevitable, and a normal human reaction. We have heard far stronger evidence of the time warp of the older generation, in conserving some practices no longer followed in their places of origin, than we have of a rebellion by young people.

5.26.5.   Any generation gap needs very careful definition if exaggeration is to be avoided. We think the following quotations are relevant here:

"there is a growing divide within the Asian Community between young people and their elders." [From a note by some inner city Headteachers].

"Younger generations of Asians feel strongly that they have a stake in this country and therefore want to assert their rights in a way that their parents did not feel obliged to do so. It is this difference between the younger and older sections of the community which is often confused as 'the cultural fight' between two traditions – that is not the case." [from the Foundation 2000 Report *The Voices **Must** Be Heard*].

"It is a generation that wants a Muslim identity but does not want to carry all the baggage of its older generation; it is a generation that finds itself deprived with little hope of employment; it is a generation that finds it difficult to come to terms with the duplicity and hypocrisy of British foreign policy with Muslims (Bosnia and Iraq); it is a generation that sees its religion and culture ridiculed; it is a generation that prides itself in straight talking, and not taking any nonsense from anybody, including their elders. It is a generation who don't want to follow the old ways, they see themselves as British subjects, who know their rights. Despite all this, a majority of the young generation would abide by the law and live as peaceful and progressive citizens. There are, however, some hot-heads and it only takes an incident like the Manningham one [ie the Garfield Avenue and 'protest' arrests] *to set off disturbances. There is no reason why this may not happen again..."* [from a letter written by a professional man of Kashmiri background].

5.26.6.   We reject, therefore, the notion that the majority of young men in the Muslim communities have rejected the values of their parents, whilst recognising that normal processes of social change are taking place as new generations adapt to very different perceptions of the reality around them. In three respects, however, the generation gap in many Asian families appears to us to be different from that in other parts of British society, but of course the extent varies from family to family.

Three Exceptions

5.26.7.   The first generalised exception to the assertion that the generational changes in many Asian families are the same as those in White society is one of scale. All parents frequently do not know what their children are involved in, and children can easily deceive their parents, and others, as they 'play the system'. It is not that the Asian children are different from other children, but that they may have greater scope for evasion where their parents are less familiar with English, or with official practices.

5.26.8.   We heard of a young teenager who took a slightly older friend along with him, as his 'uncle', in police cautioning proceedings; of letters from school to parents either not reaching their destinations, or their significance being mistranslated to illiterate parents; of youths climbing out of their house to join in the disorders on the Saturday night after being kept in; and of parents only becoming aware of official concerns about their children when formal proceedings necessarily involved them directly, after many less formal stages had bypassed them. Although these were unconfirmed anecdotes, we respect their sources, and the generalisation they were used to illustrate.

5.26.9.   The second generalised distinction we would make is that in White society the role of community leaders is less pervasive than in traditional Asian society. Councillors here are widely known by White people not to have individual power to make decisions on behalf of the council, and the processes of public decision making are better understood. We detect a disillusionment with, and rejection of, the continuation of an intermediary role by 'leaders' amongst many young British Asians, often because the experiences of some leaders are not based in the British social, educational or political issues which confront young people today.

5.26.10.   We would agree with the following extract from an article in *The Independent* of 13 June 1995, immediately after the disorders:

"There is still a deep respect felt by the young for their parents ... But this respect is no longer extended to the older community leaders ... there is a vacuum which the older leadership, caught up in Kashmiri politics, caste and so on can barely come to grips with."

5.26.11.   The third generalised distinction is the range of pressures with which young people have to come to terms, whilst maintaining loyalty to their family faith and culture within the very extensive family networks in which they are known. We choose an external but informed view to illustrate this with reference to young Muslims. A worker with Touchstone, a Bradford church organisation which promotes inter faith dialogue, wrote to us:

"Many Muslim young people have to steer a course between at least eight different sets of expectations from:

1   home, where Bradford parents may follow a very traditional rural Pakistani form of Islam – or may be quite liberal, depending on the family.

2   the mosque school, where teaching of Arabic is largely by rote, without much explanation of the text of the Qur'an. Children finish these daily lessons at the age of 14, and as yet there is little provision for older teenagers.

3   mainstream youth organisations like Young Muslims UK, which encourage young people to study the Qur'an and to work out their faith as Muslims in Britain in the 1990s.

4   extremist Muslim groups which are hostile to secular British culture and to other faiths.

5   majority British culture, which is largely indifferent to religion, and tends to ridicule those who take it seriously.

6   the mass media, which often implies that all Muslims are extremist, violent, evil figures.

7   people of other faiths who want to convert Muslims, often with little knowledge of Islam.

8   *people with a wider interfaith perspective which values all faiths, encouraging explanation and*
sharing of ideals.

Young Muslims have to respond more often to the first seven attitudes than the eighth."

Redefinition of Traditional Values

5.26.12.   A well respected and experienced observer of community relations in Bradford, himself not
a Muslim, wrote to us:

"There is no real evidence to suggest that the young Muslims have lost respect for their
parents and that the social and moral fabric of the South Asian family is disintegrating. Their
respect for the immediate family has little changed but the extended social networks based on
caste, clans and regional loyalties have little relevance for them in the British context. They are
expecting many of the things which their local counterparts enjoy. They are redefining their
cultural and religious values in relation to the western standards and values. They are
aspiring to achieve more freedom in the choice of education, careers, friends, marriage, and
political activities. It is in these contexts that they see the broad ethnic social networks,
including their parents, as obstructive barriers."

5.26.13.   There is, then, in our view, little doubt that many of the younger generation believe that
their parents and grandparents have a partial view of British society, but they still try to
operate as dutiful sons and daughters within the context of the family. These attitudes are
not characterised by a desire to break away from family links and certainly do not indicate
lack of respect. It does mean that many young people consider the views held by their
parents, grandparents, and other elders to be antiquated and out of touch, in our view with
some justification.

5.26.14.   Conversely many of the older generation view their children as conforming to traditional
values, whilst making little or no attempt, or being unable, to scrutinise their children's, and
particularly their sons', behaviour outside the immediate family circle.

5.27   Public Provision of Activities

Marginalised Youth

5.27.1.   In this and the following four subsections (5.27–5.31) we deal with matters which relate to
young men, and to others. We showed the relevant unemployment statistics in Section 3.
As 45% of the youth in the local Asian community are unemployed, and 70% of the Asian
population (which is 55% of the total population) in Manningham is below 30 years of age,
there is a large number of local young people there with very little to do, and with very little
money. What is available and affordable to fill their time is therefore an important influence
on how they spend their time, and how they develop their citizenship.

5.27.2.   It has frequently been suggested to us that the development of anti-social street culture has
been aided by the lack of alternative social activities for young men in the Manningham
area, which is both appropriate for and attractive to them; that even the facilities which are
provided are not always available when young people need them, and/or have pricing
policies which tend to restrict access; that, in particular, there is a lack of secular meeting

places in which young people of different backgrounds can develop less alienated attitudes and behaviour; and that young peoples' views on their own needs are ignored.

5.27.3.   In the survey of young people's opinions in *The Riot Area Reviewed* of 5 September 1995 – inevitably a rapid indicator rather than an in-depth survey – the greatest concern expressed by young men was for new youth facilities.

" if the local survey is taken in context with other more detailed inner city youth surveys conducted in Bradford between 1992 and 1995, there is no doubt that there is a very real underlying lack of hope or expectation and boredom amongst young people. A significant percentage of young people perceive that...:

- *neither their circumstances or their opinions are thought to be important to other groups in society;*

- *they have failed in the education system or the system has failed them. A number truant from school regularly, though not necessarily continuously;*

- *both training and employment are a source of unpaid or cheap labour. Many young people do not undertake/remain in training even if they leave school at 16 years of age;*

- *their parents are beset by financial worries;*

- *there is real concern about possible reductions in benefits and health provision;*

- *leisure facilities are un-affordable;*

- *that the division between the rich and poor is growing and that life in England is for the fat cats..."*

5.27.4.   We endorse the accuracy of this description of the views of many young people in this area. Lack of something useful to do is a likely conseqence of no work, and no hope of work. We have therefore looked at recreational facilities, even though they are only a palliative, not a cure for unemployment. As one community leader put it:

"The problems of the area are long known: bad housing; lack of proper schools, staffing and equipment; poor job and training opportunities. These are the corner-stones of any community's well being. Least, but nonetheless important, are recreational facilities."

5.27.5.   We should stress that we are not here dealing with absurd notions of table tennis for the unemployed. We are concerned about how to deal with the boredom which inevitably flows from unemployment for young people. We are also clear that unemployment for young people includes many who have obviously much to contribute at a time of pressing but unmet needs in Bradford.

An Effective Response

5.27.6.   The need for more adequate youth facilities to occupy in a constructive way the large number of young men who have no work, and are unlikely to be able to stay in the house, even if they so wished, is a proposition which is beguilingly attractive, yet we suggest that great care is needed in working out an **effective** response. One non-Muslim Asian group wrote:

"It is imperative that in order to channel the energy of these youths constructively, the local area should have proper amenities and facilities. Realistically, perhaps, Manningham is in a

better position than its counterparts. There are for example the Manningham Sports Centre, the Pakistani Community Centre, the Manningham Swimming Baths as well as Football/Recreation Playing Fields. It is therefore, not the lack of amenities alone that triggered this unfortunate event [the disorders]."

5.27.7.   The *Riot Area Reviewed* contains a very useful and comprehensive account of the city council's considerable relevant activities, and other public and charitable activities, in the Manningham/Toller area. The council was recommended by that Report, not for the first time, to review what was available, and to rationalise the use of these existing resources. We strongly support such a course, and refer frequently in later sections of this Report to the need to tackle prioritisation more directly. Our first suggestion, therefore, is that the council should examine carefully the potential of existing provision, and make changes in the managerial arrangements to achieve the maximum potential from existing levels of expenditure.

5.27.8.   The reason for our caution should be obvious. The situation in Manningham/Toller is similar to that in other parts of the city, and an uncritical, enthusiastic response to the claim for more youth activities would have unattainable resource implications in the current political climate, even if it were accepted as an absolute priority.

5.27.9.   It seems to us highly unlikely that sufficient capital facilities could be provided to meet the existing demand from unemployed youths for alternative activities to life on the street, as noted in *The Riot Area Reviewed*, and the greater unemployment pressures caused by a constantly increasing number of young men, and the likely increase in the proportion of young women entering the labour market, make such an approach even more inappropriate. Even if the capital were made available we have no confidence that subsequent revenue support could be made available.

5.27.10.   We have also heard of too many examples of under-used, or inappropriately used, facilities already provided by, or with the help of, public funds, to believe that the provision of significant investment in new premises would necessarily be a cost-effective remedy. We were often told of the youth facilities which closed down in the school holidays, just when they were most needed. We were often told of the common practice whereby existing community centres are, to generate needed income, hired out for private occasions, such as weddings, just at the times when they are most needed for general community use.

5.27.11.   A particular instance that was drawn to our attention was that of repeated vandalism in relation to the bowling greens in a park not in Manningham, to such an extent that bowling had been abandoned on some greens, and might have to be abandoned altogether. The description we were given of the misbehaviour of local Asian youths ranged from stone throwing, verbal abuse and the deliberate disruption of matches, through spoiling the turf, to threats of personal violence, and arson of the pavilion. A permanent attendant could not be obtained, and the very mobile park ranger system was said to be ineffective for such a situation.

5.27.12.   We do not wish to exaggerate the problem. The person describing the situation in the park volunteered that the ones causing the trouble were *"a minority – but a large minority"*. Given the current, and the likely future population of the surrounding area, we dare to raise the questions "Are there now too many bowling greens there, and not enough provision appropriate for the needs of local people with other interests? What efforts have been made to involve older Asians in the problem of misbehaviour, or in bowling and other uses of the park?" We did not sense, from this information, that there was any conscious matching of the facilities of the park to the realities of the present day by the authorities or the users.

5.27.13.   In relation to parks and play spaces, mothers were reluctant for their very young children to use facilities which older children abused; parents of older children were apprehensive of the presence of drug pushers where older children congregated; the parks were 'no go' areas for many people who were frightened of gangs. The less the parks and other open facilities are used by the general public, the worse the potential for abuse, and the worse their reputation becomes. We wonder how the parks can be restored to full usage which, in turn, will promote safety. We suggest that this is an important subject for investigation, making use of local enthusiasms.

5.27.14.   Another complaint which, if true, gives us concern, is one made by the smaller ethnic groups, that the management of community facilities supported by public funds often fell into the control of one dominant ethnic group, and thus the facilities became unavailable for use by others. This is a serious allegation which should be examined closely.

5.27.15.   The needs of Asian girls are dealt with more specifically in the next Part of this Section.

Initiatives

5.27.16.   Individual initiatives in making more effective use of existing recreational premises are already taking place. One is a result of a joint approach in Manningham by police, local youth workers, and centre management, which involves local youths and has reduced the vandalism which had been prevalent at the Scotchman Road Sports Centre.

5.27.17.   During September to December 1994, 16 incidents were recorded by the police, involving damage to the building, pitch invasion and other violent disruptions of activities, and the dangerous throwing of fireworks. During a summer play scheme in 1995, which involved young people in very limited use of the facilities, no such incidents were recorded, and a follow-up 5 pm – 8 pm Monday Night Club, in which local young people undertook control of activities, resulted in only one recorded incident – of minor vandalism. The scarce resource, perhaps unrealised through lack of sufficient local leadership, is that of voluntary adult support, and we applaud the voluntary contributions which are made in many parts of the city.

5.27.18.   We have been impressed by the quality of detached youth work, its influence for good, and its flexibility. We think that detached youth workers, and a greater use of volunteers, is a more suitable way of motivating bored young people, in conjunction with those who manage relevant capital facilities. We understand that this is the approach now being considered.

5.28 Volunteers

Filling a Gap

5.28.1.   We now bring together two of the constant themes in this Report – the need for sensitively appropriate public services to meet politically prioritised needs and, because of the systemic mismatch between political and financial responsibilities in the British system of local governance, the lack of reliable or adequate public funding to pay for the costs of employment in those services sufficient to meet locally perceived needs. We make no judgements about the rightness of this situation, since that is not our task. Nor do we weaken the plea for tough prioritisation of such funding as is realistically available, which we make in Section 7 in particular.

5.28.2.   Unfortunately, given present financial restrictions, we do see an inevitable gap between what is clearly needed, and what can be provided by public authorities, in the extremely challenging situation in which Bradford finds itself. In these circumstances, if there is to be any bridging arrangement, the contribution of skilled, enthusiastic volunteers and temporary supporters to the established services from an informed citizenry has obvious potential.

Meeting Inner City Needs

5.28.3.   In Lord Scarman's report on the Brixton Riots, he wrote:

"6.28 ... Both the nature of the training provision to be made for the young unemployed and the wider economic issues are already the subject of vigorous national debate: it is unnecessary for me to comment on them.

6.29. I do, however, offer one thought for consideration in that debate. The structural causes of unemployment..... are deeper and more complex than the mere existence of the current recession. If this analysis is right, we shall have to face its implications. In order to secure social stability, there will be a long term need to provide useful, gainful employment and suitable educational, recreational and leisure opportunities for young people, especially in the inner city. For instance, it has been suggested to me that young people could be encouraged to participate in projects to clean up and regenerate the inner city. There is attraction in projects which could use the idle labour available in the inner cities to tackle the physical decay which is there so evident. It should not, I suggest, be too difficult to devise satisfactory schemes for such sorts of activities in place of current unemployment and social security programmes."

5.28.4.   The priority needs of the city which we identify in this Report are great, and obvious, and widely acknowledged, and so long as they are unmet their consequences are expensive to the community as a whole. Since one of the priority needs is for human resources to be switched from bored idleness to meaningful work, what is the political wisdom which prevents the costs of training, supervision and a worthwhile wage being found to make an appropriate match? We appreciate that this is not just a Bradford matter.

5.28.5.   We were particularly impressed by the volunteer 'Sunday School' which we visited one bitterly cold winter's morning in premises where the central heating had failed. The syllabus comprised English, mathematics, computer studies and other important subjects.

At the time of our visit there was an established morning session for boys, and an afternoon session was being planned for girls.

5.28.6.   The school was first set up in September 1995, and grew from 15 to 90 pupils in six weeks, and had an average attendance of 70 boys. Boys from a range of LEA and other schools freely told us how the teaching in basic subjects had improved their performance at their normal school. The Muslim teachers and support staff, as well as the pupils, were all volunteers. Some of the staff were well qualified, but unemployed, and were gaining useful experience of work as a basis for job applications.

5.28.7.   It was, in fact, a well organised effort by people from many parts of Bradford, determined to provide communal self-help, primarily to meet educational difficulties experienced by boys (and, since our visit, girls) from their religious community, though there was no deliberate exclusion of others intended. This example clearly demonstrates the point of creating socially needed jobs with the added value of real work experience.

5.28.8.   Throughout our Inquiry we have identified adventurous, and well established, voluntary or modestly supported initiatives, e.g. in the form of educational support, voluntary youth workers, neighbourhood watches, and local leadership. To this we should add the extra commitments of time and effort by many professional people beyond their contractual obligations. Much social support is provided by family and community networks. Surely this list of the existing less formal responses to communal needs could be extended, if more people were prepared to face up to the awful realities of life for many people in Bradford in the nineties and beyond. Or do we just wait for 'the Government' to change the financial regimes?

5.28.9.   The alternative to reliance on increasingly inadequate public services at a time of reducing revenue support seems to be civic chaos. We recommend determined exploration of the skills and enthusiasms of potential volunteers, particularly of the unemployed, and the terms on which they could be employed, as a means of helping to meet obvious needs, and as a means of providing constructive activity.

5.29   Segregated Sport?

5.29.1.   Experience of team Sports across the perceived divides was raised by some of those whom we interviewed in terms of its social importance, and also as a background for job applicants valued by many employers. We welcome the efforts that are being made to reduce the discrimination which so strongly exists in organised sport, both amateur and professional. Until the hesitations of young people from minority groups are understood, and racially offensive behaviour is firmly quashed, the potential opportunities for young people, and for Bradford's sporting reputation, will be unnecessarily reduced.

5.29.2.   The separate development of team sports leagues for Asians, particularly cricket, of which we have heard, is a symptom of divisions in the city which raises in an acute form the question "Do young Bradfordians of different ethnic backgrounds want to be entirely separate in their leisure activities, or not?" If they do, then there is little hope of harmonious relationships across what will be increasingly polarised groupings, as those young people become the mature citizens of the not-too-distant future. If they do not, what are those with the power to encourage joint participation doing about it? And how can we find out what young people want on this question which affects them so particularly?

5.29.3.   We heard that team games are now less available in and between schools; that non-White teams have to use pitches which are regarded as inadequate by established sporting leagues; that pitches are in short supply for the many young men who are keen on team games; and that Kabbaddi, a very popular Asian team game, receives surprisingly little formal recognition, given Bradford's ethnic mix of population. It seems to us to be important to establish whether these complaints are justified.

5.29.4.   We understand that Kabbaddi is traditionally regarded by many Asian young people in much the same way as games on spare land are generally regarded by all youngsters. A suggestion that the game had commercial possibilities was firmly rejected as inappropriate by one group to whom the suggestion was made, we were told. It is an interesting example of unrealised possibilities.

5.29.5.   We commend the beginning of interest shown in having a more representative crowd of supporters at the City football club, and the efforts of those who are making it more likely. Commercially, this makes as much good sense as socially. Sport seems to us to offer a very valuable return in helping Bradfordians to get to know each other, and we suggest it as another subject for dynamic exploration.

5.30   Art, Music, Poetry etc., ... and History

5.30.1.   We refer in para 7.5.13 to the absence of almost any evidence of the ethnically diverse nature of Bradford in its city centre activities. We have not investigated the specific issue raised by some people with us about the culturally limited range of shows and concerts put on at the Alhambra, or at St. George's Hall. However, we recognise both the attractiveness of the idea, and the financial risks involved. We were also told of the great financial cost of hiring these venues for occasions organised by cultural groups for their own purposes, but in these days of lack of public resources this is a more understandable situation. If it is correct, as was alleged to us, that art or music from the backgrounds of Asian Bradfordians was rarely performed at these central venues, it is regrettable, and appears to us to be another missed opportunity for the city to enjoy the riches of its peoples. On the other hand, it may be impossible to attract an audience, especially if there is only an occasional performance, and no prior marketing.

5.30.2.   We suggest that the alleged omission from Bradford's central activities should be examined. If proved to be true, it should be corrected, perhaps experimentally over a period and as part of a careful examination of Asian investment in the city centre. Bradford should reflect the ethnic diversity of the city in the activities in the city centre. It should trade positively on its composition. How many people from outside Bradford know of its Mela? Why is Bradford, for many outsiders, only synonymous with Asian cultures in a negative way?

5.30.3.   Though we have seen some diversity of exhibition at Cartwright Hall during our Inquiry, there appears to be little widespread positive dissemination of the Art, Music and other cultural expressions of the ethnic minority communities in Bradford, other than in the annual Festival and Mela, so that many people's experience of Bradford's cultural richness is located entirely in the separateness of their religious training and family experience. As a result their understanding is very limited. One White art teacher told us of his discovery of Asian art, and its value as a positive, artistic teaching medium. There is a growing contribution to English writing by British Asian writers which Bradford could develop.

5.30.4.   One valuable suggestion we were given was the desirability of knowing more about, and sharing, the different histories of the various communities in Bradford, their similarities, overlaps, and differences. How many Bradfordians have been taught about the history of Islamic Spain, which is geographically the closest place to Britain which has ever had a strong Islamic culture? To what extent is the shared history of the British Raj in India known beyond the level of slogans? It seems to us vital that Bradfordians are enabled and encouraged to understand both shared and separate, historical and present day, artistic and intellectual insights. Given the pressure of the standardised national curriculum, we doubt if this is a task to be left to the schools; we suggest it is a proper challenge to young people and to adults.

5.31   The Views of Young People

5.31.1.   Older people will surely recognise that there is nothing new in a claim by young people that their distinctive views are not valued. It is a normal part of growing up, and older people have enough difficulties maintaining their own agenda without having to take on new perceptions of wrongs to be righted! Nevertheless, the world and its prospects, with which today's young people have to cope, is very different, in its immediate impact on their lives, than it was for their parents and grandparents. The need to listen should operate at several levels, from family to the city council.

5.31.2.   As with the older people with whom we discussed life in Bradford, we were impressed by the decency and common sense of the children and young people who made their views known to us. Only in easily recognisable circumstances did the potential demagogues emerge. Yet, in a group of **youth** workers, we were told:

"We don't listen to young people's needs to influence the planning of our service. There are no young people at our meetings."

We cannot recall any instance of the views of young people being mentioned in any of our discussions of Educational policy. Is this just an unfortunate gap in our information?

5.31.3.   An Asian councillor wrote to us:

"In all cultures and communities, the youth play a definitive role as challenger to the system. This should not surprise any of us. This challenge can manifest itself as a radical lifestyle eg clothing, music, haircut etc on one hand and on the other hand it can be politically challenging. Only when the youth feel that the democratic political processes are not working or are too complicated or too time consuming, they can adopt a tactic of direct action [i.e. violent protest]. *A society where the youth are tame and docile will be a society without any progress.*
"

5.31.4.   The potential contribution of young people to the political life of the city is very important, though this will not be successfully achieved by the artificial promotion of a few who have the most to say. This is a particular challenge to the political parties, of course. The present level of alienation which has been represented to us should give them concern. But we hope for a wider base to political discussion within Bradford than just that of the organised parties. Young Asian men, aged say 15–25, are particularly suspicious of 'their' politicians, seeing them as factionalised and pursuing selfish agendas. We had no similar views from White youths; indeed we heard very few views at all from White youths, but we draw no conclusions from that.

5.31.5.   We have often heard, mainly from young men who have achieved an accommodation of their cultural background with life in Bradford, that the lessons from their experiences are rarely listened to. Partly the reason seems to be the isolated conservatism held by some of the traditional community leaders who cannot see the problems which face young people whose future is wholly in Bradford. Partly the reason seems to be the isolated conservatism of White officials and citizens who are similarly blind. Such young people have a valuable role to play – as bridges, as influencers of public policies, and as future leaders and representatives.

5.31.6.   We deal in Section 7 with the development of a prioritised, issue based local political agenda for Bradford. Such a process will help to produce young leaders of different backgrounds if it is properly and rigorously conducted.

Part 4   Young Women: Under-represented and Unheard

5.32   Our Focus and Sources

5.32.1.   *The Riot Area Reviewed* – of 5 September 1995 – stated that

> *"The needs of Asian male youth have been highlighted... The needs of 5200 Asian young women and girls... who also live in the area must also be considered."*

5.32.2.   In other Sections of our Report we have referred to women and girls, but in this section we discuss some of the issues raised with us by men and women from all backgrounds who had views on the position of women and girls and particularly, but not only, on Asian women and girls. Some of our informants were employed in public sector or voluntary services which brought them professionally or practically into contact with Asian women and girls, some were leaders in the minority communities, some were politicians, and others were citizens with views.

5.32.3.   Women of all groups were in a minority among those who gave evidence to the Commission, reflecting neither their numerical strength in the city, nor their formal rights as citizens, but rather their general under-representation in public life. This is caused by many factors, including their responsibilities for child care and other domestic obligations as well as traditional perceptions, which still restrict women's participation in civic affairs.

5.32.4.   Undoubtedly their own perceptions led, in many cases, to a reticence about contributing to public discussion on the disorders, or on Bradford's future. The Foundation 2000 report *The Voices **Must** Be Heard* recommended that

"Outreach work be developed to target women in the community who for cultural or other reasons do not or cannot access any decision making arena."

We fully endorse this recommendation and would want to see it apply to all women in any communities who are disadvantaged in this way.

5.32.5.   Despite this under-representation we did meet with many individual women from most backgrounds, including some holding public or professional positions, and we were able to meet with groups of women and girls in a range of situations. The questions and concerns they raised and views they expressed were in many cases the same as those raised by men. There was one marked difference between women and men in their approach to the issues and concerns. Men frequently excluded women and girls altogether from their contributions, or spoke as their representatives and, as with representatives in other situations, we were frequently unsure of the validity of their status in fact. Women did neither.

5.33   Women and the Disorders

5.33.1.   Women did not actively take part in the disorders and it was therefore commonly assumed that they were in no way relevant to any discussion about the disorders. This did not, however, prevent them being held responsible for some of the background reasons for the June events. For example, it was claimed that women could not cope with their sons because of 'the culture'. It was the rumour of alleged mistreatment by the police of a young woman, which spread rapidly and came to be widely believed, that initially fuelled male indignation.

5.33.2.   Some of the women to whom we spoke felt that the male dominated norms of their community encouraged some of the protesters to think that they were promoting the honour of the Islamic community. Others had then joined in, simply to show off, without any clear objective.

5.33.3.   All the women we met spoke of their shock at, and abhorrence of, the disorders, but not all were surprised by them. Whilst, some of them told us, some children were very successful there were also many bored, angry teenagers *"brought up with a ghetto mentality"*. They had no work, no money, no education – so jobs and better education were needed. Everyone, in their opinion, women, MPs, Mosque leaders, police, and those involved in the disorders, should sit down and talk about the situation, but above all they should listen to the young people.

5.33.4.   A well attended women's meeting in Manningham organised by a local councillor shortly after the disorders, had produced similar views. The women, the councillor told us, said the disorders had been a *"male event"*, and either they did not know what had happened, or they did not trust the men's reports. They did think that police treatment of Asian and White should be equal, which in their view it was not. They criticized the media for their portrayal of the events, and thought that it had been provocative to show them on TV. As we stated in para 4.26.12, a petition was organised which was eventually signed by 172 mainly Kashmiri women in Manningham, which stated:

"As women we feel sad about what happened at the weekend.

We want everybody to listen to each other.

We want peace."

5.33.5.   We were told of the women who had organised a march carrying a banner through the area on the Saturday night of the disorders (see para 4.21.1.) to demonstrate the need for peace, and although one woman reported that this had been shaming for the men who had a very traditional view of the place of women, others claimed this was not the case.

5.33.6.   Women living outside Manningham who spoke to us had a range of views on the events. Some dismissed them as of no interest, others feared there would be an increased hostility towards them from Whites as a result, and others told us of the concerns of their families in Pakistan for their safety.

5.34   Stereotyping

Misconceptions

5.34.1.   The pervasive stereotypes of Asian, and especially Muslim, women in Bradford, as well as elsewhere in Britain, do a great disservice to them, on an individual level, whether as members of families, or of diverse ethnic groupings, or as citizens. Such stereotypes lead to misconceptions and mis-readings of the lives they lead, the struggles they face, and the contributions they make, as well as disguising the many common experiences, situations and problems they share with other women. It is equally unrealistic and unacceptable for leaders, or other men from minority communities, to sterotype White women as lacking in morality in regard to themselves and to their daughters solely because of their more open lifestyle.

Shared Problems

5.34.2.   It is high time all such stereotypes were rejected by all those in decision-making positions, whether politicians or officials, employers or voluntary organisations. In particular, it is necessary for the police and those in the educational and social services to avoid using them.

5.34.3.   Many of the differences among women, of both the ethnic majority and the ethnic minority populations, derive from their economic positions, which influence their chances in all manner of ways. We have seen this in the availability to them of education, of jobs, and of good quality housing. We suspect the same applies to health care and other important services. In Bradford, as shown in para 3.4.13, a large number of women from ethnic minorities are living in 'areas of stress', and it is safe to assume that most, but not all, of them suffer, along with men, from the forms of deprivation which define such an area. The majority of other women do not live in these areas but, of those who do, many experience these same levels of deprivation. The differences on these measures are not **between** the minorities and majority, but **within each of them.**

5.35   Families

5.35.1.   Many kinds of family exist in Bradford and there is a wide variation in household composition. Compared with other districts in West Yorkshire Bradford is similar in the proportions of households with from 1 to 5 residents, but has a higher proportion of those with 6 and 7+ residents. In Bradford, households with 6 or more members number just below 8,000 or 4.6% of all households in the district, compared to an average of 2.8% for the county as a whole. The number of lone parent households in Bradford District is also just below 8,000 or 4.6%, and in the county as a whole it is 4.1%; Bradford West averages 16%, whilst in Manningham it is 4.3%. Overcrowding is found in 14% of Manningham households, compared to less than 4% in the district, and rises to 35% where there are dependent children. These measures are used as indicators of poverty, but they are also indicators of family structure.

5.35.2.   In the case of minorities from the Indian sub-continent the extended family, whether living in the same household or not, remains after 30+ years in Bradford a common form of family arrangement. This means that family obligations and support apply across generations, and cover a wider range of kin, than in the nuclear families which developed in British society over the period of industrialisation and which narrowed both family obligations and support networks. Though different in some respects, both types of family share values by which individual members are expected to care and provide for each other.

5.36   Male Domestic Control

5.36.1.   The degree of control over women exercised by their male kin varies significantly from one community to another, and from one family to another. It always relates to the father/unmarried daughter relationship and to that between husbands and wives. It may vary with age and socio-economic position, and may also involve a much wider range of male kin, for instance, brothers, uncles and adult sons. It is always imbued with moral values, frequently of a religious nature, and is often portrayed and understood simply as protection for women against those outside the family. But whilst the status and honour of the family are involved, so is the protection of the men's position within and outside the family.

5.36.2.   Control in personal relations within a family works not only directly through men, but women, as mothers, grandmothers, older sisters and mothers-in-law are also essential to it. It operates with the support of many institutions in the public sphere, though this is slowly beginning to change. The isolation of women varies – the experience of middle class women was always less isolated than their working class counterparts – but for those encapsulated within poor and restricted family settings there can be significant consequences, health workers told us, particularly forms of depression for which the only treatment available appears to be drugs, prescribed or otherwise.

5.37 Marriage

Arranged Marriages

5.37.1.   There were few direct comments on marriage from Pakistanis/Kashmiris who gave evidence to us. Arranged marriage was, however, implicit in much of what was said by people of all ages as part of the need to maintain traditional values and patterns of behaviour, and was most strongly supported among those men representing religious bodies. One young Kashmiri professional man did say that in his view arranged marriage *"is being pushed to the front, it is not the be all and end all"*, that is, though it is little understood, it is held to be the cause of innumerable problems by many commentators.

5.37.2.   Marriage in any community is rarely a matter for the couple alone. It usually involves the families of both parties, to a greater or lesser degree. It is regulated by the state in Western societies and in addition religious authorities make rules for their members. It confers rights and obligations on the partners, and on those related to them. Marriage is a matter of concern to families and to the public, linking past and future generations. It is a highly emotive subject, generating strong opinions and feelings within and between groups, and the subject of arranged marriages and some of the consequences assumed to flow from them was frequently raised with us by those unfamiliar with the practice.

5.37.3.   For those who are outside those communities which **explicitly** adopt the custom of older members arranging for marriages between suitable partners, there is a tendency to draw a stark dichotomy beween arranged and free choice marriage. This is unnecessarily divisive, because it fails to recognise that there is a continuum, with varying degrees of control and choice available in all communities. As well as the common parental wishes for their children's happiness and well-being, wherever family property exists to be inherited, wherever religious belief is crucial, wherever family honour is important, then whom one's children marry is a matter of grave concern to the family and to the wider kin group.

5.37.4.   Though some of these factors have lessened in importance in the White communities in Britain during this century, they have not disappeared. Most marriages are still between those from the same socio-economic group, the same religious background, the same nationality and the same ethnic and racial group. Those who do not conform to this pattern may in some circumstances suffer from sanctions, ranging from disapproval to total exclusion from their families of origin.

5.37.5.   We also heard from a White woman who was married to an Indian that Muslim women told her she was *"not married because he's an Indian"*. She commented *"they don't like White women marrying Asians."* The lack of open acknowledgement or discussion of mixed marriages in all ethnic groups is an illustration of the ambiguity and hostility extended towards those who do not conform.

Trans-continental Marriages

5.37.6.   In Bradford the term 'trans-continental' marriage means a marriage between a Bradford man or woman and a spouse from the Indian sub-continent, usually Pakistan or Kashmir. Such marriages are assumed to be arranged by older relatives both here and overseas. Though hard data about such marriages (except for the statistics referred to in para 3.4.7) on, for instance, their rates of success or otherwise, the personal and social characteristics of the spouses – age of marriage, language and educational attainments, etc. – are virtually non-existent, opinions are frequently expressed.

5.37.7.   For example, one woman expressed a commonly held view that, whilst she was not against arranged marriages as such, they should be more frequently between partners both of whom were British by background. Concern was expressed to us about the young men and women who marry and bring over non-English speaking spouses, and was related to the limiting effects on children one of whose parents, and particularly if it is the mother, does not speak English. This concern is then linked to the consequent inability of children from homes where English is not spoken to relate to their education in English schools, a concern which often ignores the competence in English of the Bradford born or reared spouse. We discuss the importance of the acquisition of English in subsection 6.5.

5.37.8.   Even when transcontinental marriages take place with full consent, it is argued that the mismatch between spouses of different levels of education, financial aspiration, and an ability to speak the same language, causes problems. A health worker told us:

"The life experiences of the partners are very different, and the difference is increasing in intensity."

5.37.9.   The subject of arranged marriage is one for informed choice between individual and family members, and we do not suggest otherwise. The traditional reasons for such marriages, in terms of property ownership, are lessening and the size of the communities and kin networks settled in this country is now such that earlier difficulties of arranging a suitable marriage here have decreased. If what is seen as an increasing social divergence between the two geographical communities is a reality, then it is likely that the number of such marriages will decline.

5.37.10.   However, those outside the particular Asian communities involved must remember that, for many people, links with the extended family members living outside Britain are precious, and obligations across generations are reciprocal, in much the same way as they are or were for other migrant generations, and for expatriates of all kinds. It is therefore essential that discussion is carried out in such a way that it does not threaten or demean the proper concerns of parents for their children and families as expressed through traditional customs.

5.38   Domestic Abuse and Violence

Allegations

5.38.1.   Only very recently has domestic violence begun to be taken seriously as a criminal act in Britain by the legal system and the police. Effective means to protect themselves and their children from such violence remain woefully inadequate for women without the economic means or other forms of support that independence requires.

5.38.2.   We heard many allegations about the oppression of Asian women. These included domestic violence, and the pressures being put on married and unmarried women to remain at home living lonely and unfulfilled lives, on young women to leave school or college and marry against their will, of young women seduced by men from the same community and then driven into prostitution, and of women in marriages arranged by their families being deserted and left to bring up their children alone. Such allegations appeared in many instances to be based on hearsay, but there can be little doubt that such cases exist. This leads to the indiscriminate condemnation of arranged marriages, and especially of those involving a spouse from the Indian sub-continent.

5.38.3.   Concern was expressed to us for young British women who go to their parents/ grandparents, homes in Pakistan/Kashmir to be married, and return to Bradford to await the arrival of their husbands after the formalities for his gaining entrance to this country have been completed. For outsiders, this concern related to young women being forced into marriage against their will, or to marriage with a man who had grown up in a totally different context, or to bringing in a man who, once he has achieved British citizenship, would live off income support, and in some cases later leave his wife and add to 'the single mother problem'.

5.38.4.   This concern was expanded in various ways: mention was made more than once of the drugging and forcible abduction of unwilling or unknowing girls and young women, before the journey from Britain to the family home in the sub-continent, of the abuse and violence to which the young women were subjected to obtain their consent, and of a general cult of silence which prevailed about such matters. Such perceptions exist widely, and specific instances were quoted. A view that a woman was sometimes used to obtain the right of entry to Britain and British citizenship for a male family member in Pakistan/Kashmir who would otherwise not be eligible was also expressed. This has for many years been a feature of debates and legislation to control primary immigration, that is of stopping men of working age, particularly but not exclusively from the Indian sub-continent, entering and residing legally in Britain.

5.38.5.   After campaigns by a number of organisations, including some concerned with the rights of British women to bring in spouses born and married abroad on the same terms granted to British men, the rules were changed following the 1985 decision by the European Court of Human Rights on equal treatment. This change applies to all women, and its use for reasons other than that intended is possible for any British citizen. In the case of British women with members of their extended family living in Pakistan or Kashmir, among whom there is an individual thought suitable as a marriage partner by them or their parents, it can not be assumed that this is a problem. Very many Asian young women accept the desirability of arranged marriages. Where problems arise later in the marriage, they may be due to any of the factors which lead to marriage breakdown. Again, we urge caution against making too much from limited evidence.

5.38.6.   One reason for the closure of an Asian women's refuge in Bradford, we were told by a man working in the area, was that *"it wasn't safe"* and he would not encourage women to come forward unless more resources were available. Additionally, we were told, the sense of shame and failure involved in a woman leaving her home both strengthened the determination of her male relatives to find and return her, and often deterred women from seeking external help in coping with abuse and violence.

Family Matters and the Authorities

Uncertainties and Misunderstandings

5.38.7.   In the past few years there has been further legislation relating to children, and changes in practice with regard to how domestic violence and abuse are handled. The responsibilities of agencies have changed, as have the rights and obligations of parents to their children, and of spouses towards each other. In practice there is not always a clear dividing line between what is a private matter within a family and what is open to public regulation. Case law is only slowly developing to guide appropriate action.

5.38.8.   This is an important subject for all communities, and the authorities, whether police officers, lawyers, social workers, or educationalists, are not yet fully cognisant of what is expected of them. In addition there are various voluntary agencies and charities, and pressure groups, particularly those concerned with the rights of women, of children, or of fathers, working out their roles in relation to the legislation. It is not therefore surprising that we met with diverse views on the subject. In the case of the Pakistani and Kashmiri communities the views which dominated were those of older males and professionals who themselves expected, and were expected by the authorities, to represent all members of their communities.

5.38.9.   The relation between these communities and the authorities with regard to family matters is highly sensitive not least because it involves issues of religious rules and the extent of the power of men to control women. There is a widespread belief within these communities that the authorities within Bradford have no understanding of, or sympathy with, families when a female member, either a wife or daughter, 'flees the home'.

5.38.10.   Indeed the belief is that all the relevant agencies, but particularly the police, conspire in order to ensure that the woman or girl is kept away from her family. This is one of the most traumatic events which can happen, we were told, and is seen as a point of irredeemable shame, to a family, who will go to almost any lengths in order to avoid public knowledge of such an event. It is plain, from what we have been told, that every possible pressure will often be placed by community leaders on complainants, witnesses and others involved, not to co-operate. We make no comparison with similar events or allegations of domestic violence and rape, child abuse and the like, in other communities.

5.38.11.   The reputation of social services amongst many Asian families is such that parents are frightened to have any problems identified at school or at hospital, for fear of having their children removed. The public disgrace involved in any official involvement in a family matter can also be supplemented by a genuine concern that strict codes governing behaviour towards girls would not be observed by the authorities and, in the case of boys, by fear of them being criminalised whilst in care. We were told by a meeting of headteachers that some of the families felt they were being targeted, and they did not want their daughters living under another's roof. The headteachers also said that staff shortages in social services meant that they did not often see the same social worker twice, and that building up close and continuing liaison between school and families was necessary to avoid misunderstandings about the domestic background.

5.38.12. Where so much of public regulation rightly depends upon a correct reading of intentions it is not easy for practitioners to draw inferences from a situation in an unfamiliar cultural setting. It seems to us that what is required is a clearer distinction between behaviour which is improper and unlawful, and behaviour which flows from different values and customs leading to unfamiliar situations.

5.38.13. There have been some horrific incidents of violence to women, up to and including murder, within Bradford, and the duty of the police is clear in these cases. All citizens are entitled to the protection of the law, and where a woman makes allegations, or where a woman or child appears to need protection, the duty of the authorities is clear.

5.38.14. Other instances may be less clear. There is official concern that women, and particularly young women, will be sent to Pakistan where family wishes regarding marriage can be enforced. Where the girl is under age, or where women of any age are subjected to criminal force, then the authorities obviously have a duty to take all the measures required to ensure that the woman concerned is safe, and the individuals responsible brought to justice. Nevertheless in some circumstances no criminal behaviour may be involved; the problem may be that of teenage rebellion being handled in an unusually strong way, or family hurt and upset resulting from a young woman leaving home or refusing an arranged marriage.

Mediation

5.38.15. The frequently held view in the minority ethnic communities is that, if such matters have to be dealt with, they are better dealt with tactfully by respected members of the community, in a firm, but understanding way. We do not doubt that there are situations in which such an approach can be helpful, as is the case within the White communities. Some of the younger men, who thought any police involvement unhelpful, put the emphasis on the mediating role of the wider family rather than on community leaders from whom they felt alienated. To what extent informal mediation is an appropriate option, and to what extent assurances should be given about cultural concerns not being diluted by White assumptions about 'rights', are matters to be considered in officially sponsored discussions with the ethnic minority communities. Ignorance of the law on the one hand and of different customs on the other, so prevalent in Bradford, are handicaps such discussions will have to surmount.

5.38.16. It is our view that some form of mediation, recognised by both the authorities and the communities concerned, is needed. This should attempt to reconcile rather than separate families, and allow controlled access to occur whilst at the same time ensuring that the women and girls concerned have real control over their own decisions. There is a clear need for the authorities to have people who understand, in detail, the issues concerned, and carry the confidence of the community more widely than is the case at present.

5.38.17. Once again, we have a challenge to the way in which public services equip themselves to provide an appropriate implementation of standard objectives by way of staffing, training, planning, and implementation. Not only the ethnic, but also the **gender** composition of the representatives of the authorities involved is of the greatest importance, so that understandings fully reflect the communities they serve.

The Need For Open Discussion

5.38.18.   Public debate in Britain on the subject of domestic abuse and violence, and the attempts to provide refuges by women's organisations, began only in the early 1970s. For many, in all ethnic groups, the subject remains an uncomfortable one, as do other domestic matters, such as rape, child abuse and incest. No one knows the frequency of such criminal behaviour overall, nor the relative incidence of it in different classes or ethnic communities. These are matters which, in practice, cause great antagonisms, particularly between the police and Social Workers, on the one hand, and the families concerned and their community representatives, on the other.

5.38.19.   It is quite impossible for us to measure and compare the frequency of these forms of domestic violence and marriage breakdown among minorities, as against those in other communities. The entrapment of unwilling girls and young women undoubtedly does occur in Bradford, and in some cases criminal methods are used. This is not only completely unacceptable, but calls for action by the families, the communities and the authorities.

5.38.20.   The question is, what can or should be done, and by whom, to provide the same degree of support and protection, in an appropriate manner, as is intended to be available to all citizens? We do not criticise those who struggle with the problems of providing the relevant services, nor with those who are very properly seeking to protect important family values. We do say that the present situation is unsatisfactory, and urgently needs open consideration.

5.38.21.   It seems to us that these family matters are subjects which can no longer be suppressed on the grounds that they are too sensitive. There is much confusion and anecdote, stereotype and extrapolation, and a lack of open and constructive dialogue.

5.38.22.   Those involved professionally or personally, or as representatives or concerned members of the communities, need an organised forum for discussion to take place, informed by relevant data, and based on a clearer understanding of professional practice, legal obligations, and the concerns expressed to us. These concerns can only be discussed satisfactorily when the views of the women themselves play a substantial part, when women are listened to within their families, and by the authorities and professionals who have relevant responsibilities. It is one more example of the concerns which we express about the appropriateness of public services in the next section of our Report.

5.39   Work and Employment

5.39.1.   Women from all backgrounds expressed concern about the changed employment situation and the consequences of unemployment, low wages and poor conditions, on the lives of families. Many were fearful for the young people growing up without work, or of leaving school with no prospects of jobs. The growing proportion of women in the labour market was noted by many, and projections from the Chief Executive's Research Section, made in 1995 on assumptions agreed by Research Officers of Bradford Council's Economic Development Unit and Bradford Training and Enterprise Council, indicate that proportionally, the greatest increases are occurring in female groups.

5.39.2.   Comparing the 1991 female labour force with that for 2011, an increase of 9 per cent is projected. For each of the Census categories the increase is given as: White 2%, Black 48%, Indian 33%, Pakistani 147%, Bangladeshi 150%, Other 141%. The categories differ greatly in terms of population size, and start from different levels of recorded economic activity, which vary with age in all groups. For instance, the rate for White women in 1991 varied from 84% for those aged 40–49 to 2% for those aged 60+; for Pakistani women the highest rate was 52% for women of 20–24 and 3% for those of 60+ and for Bangladeshi women the highest rate, 54%, was also in the 20–24 age group and the lowest, 2% for the 60+ group. The rates of economic activity for both Pakistani and Bangldeshi women in Bradford over the age of 24 are lower than the national rate of 22% for these groups.

Under-recorded Work

5.39.3.   Statistics on labour market participation are only a very rough guide to the level of women's involvement in economic activity. This is so for all women, but stereotypes about Asian women not being allowed to work, and so not being perceived as working, distort their economic contribution still further. The official figures on women's economic activity shown above are highly likely, on the basis of research evidence from studies in Britain and in most parts of the world, to be systematically underestimated.

5.39.4.   There are many reasons for this which we do not go into here, but it should be noted that in Bradford the homeworking undertaken by women from all backgrounds, and the labour of women (and children) in micro-businesses is rarely, if ever, counted in the statistics, and part-time work and self-employment are poorly recorded. With the increase in male unemployment, women's economic contributions may be the only source of earned income to a family.

Changing Work Opportunities

5.39.5.   With the changes which are taking place in the type of work available in Bradford, the skills and working patterns traditionally associated with women's labour market work may be in greater demand, both in low paid jobs with poor conditions and in relatively well paid jobs offering better conditions.

5.39.6.   One upper school Headteacher wrote to us:

"Research indicates that many employers prefer to employ women because they are more flexible, better motivated and often better qualified.

Women are often already more used to the flexible portfolio of jobs concept which experts say will encompass everyone in the future. Working women are already often familiar with part-time work, career breaks, flexible arrangements etc....

Among the Asian community, some families are aware of many of these trends. More Asian women work and more families expect their daughters to work when they leave school. Only a few years ago many families refused to allow their daughters at [this school] *to go on work experience placements. Nobody objected this year; and the range of placements and the geographical spread of them increases each successive year."*

5.39.7.   Other teachers who spoke to us were less sanguine about the access to placements *"for those with Asian names",* which indicated continued discrimination by employers and agencies.

5.40   Public Provision of Activities

5.40.1.   Frequently we were told of efforts being made to provide for the social, educational and leisure needs of women and girls by both public and voluntary agencies, but it was recognised by most of those involved that they were only scratching the surface. Several reasons were advanced for the present situation, in which most of the effort and resources are used for boys and young men.

5.40.2.   Some of the existing provision in the Manningham area was listed in the *The Riot Area Reviewed* Report, and we were told of several initiatives in the area and elsewhere in the city. For instance, one centre in Bradford Moor, supported by city council funding, provided both mixed and single sex facilities. 80% of those taking classes were women, and a youth club for girls was held once a week. We were told that few women were willing to serve on the management committee, but some had been co-opted, there was a woman volunteer who had responsibilities for services for women, and a women's sub-committee had been set up at the beginning of 1995, 13 years after the centre opened. The members of this centre whom we met included both men and women, and a variety of views concerning the development of young people and women were expressed.

5.40.3.   A number of the local youth and community centres make some provision for women and girls. These centres are, however, male dominated and the time and facilities devoted to women and girls are in all cases very much less than those available to men and boys. In some cases this can not be construed as a deliberate policy: it is a consequence of the kinds of activities deemed appropriate, such as 'male' sports, an absence of awareness of women's and girls' rights to share in public provision, or a lack of effective demand by the women and girls themselves which may be due to pressures to remain at home or to lack of interest in what is on offer.

5.40.4.   The Noor e Nisa Centre and the Millan Centre, both of which have provided training facilities for women, funded by public bodies, address a range of developmental needs. Originally started as a grassroots organisation, the Millan Centre has been described in one report as bursting at the seams with training activities in inadequate buildings. On our visits there we were impressed by the efforts being made by the women on behalf of their communities. They were concerned not simply with women's needs, but with all those deprived of opportunities in the area. Experiencing the uncertainties of short term funding and the effects of the lack of strategic planning, they nevertheless had a more rounded grasp of the situation and how much needed to be done, far outweighing other views we heard. What such a centre demonstrates is the resourcefulness of women themselves in tackling the problems they live with on a daily basis, and how more effective they could be with more support.

5.40.5.   Other small groups and projects providing single sex activities exist, and the Bradford Asian Girls' Educational Association, which is Grant Aided, distributes small pump-priming grants. The initiatives taken by Bradford College in adult and continuing education, and by the women's centres in Manningham, over several years have met in part some of the needs of women from deprived communities. None of these, however useful the work they do, is able to provide the basis for on-going development work which is needed in the inner city. Moreover, a co-ordinated approach to identifying needs, and then prioritising them in relation to an agreed strategy, is missing.

5.40.6.   The needs of women can not be taken out of the context of wider developments, in particular, those of building a viable local economy and all aspects of the environment, including housing and open space, security on the streets and in play areas, appropriate refuse collection schemes, and an effective use of existing buildings; and access to more adequate health care and education services. The women we met, old and young, speaking English fluently or hardly at all, from minorities, from the majority population, or in ethnically mixed marriages, who lived in Manningham or the inner city more generally, were fully aware of the issues which needed tackling. Their contribution is vital, particularly in helping children to gain from available education, if appropriate strategies are to be devised and implemented.

5.41   Social Change

5.41.1.   Informally all groups of people have ways in which accommodations to social changes are made, so that behaviour is allowed which does not fit the norm, whether because of material necessities, changes in the demands placed on groups by external pressures, challenges from within the group to unequal treatment or unacceptable restraints,. These accommodations may be by turning a blind eye, or by not flaunting or denying such behaviour publicly, especially in the presence of those who have moral, political or economic power to wield. For minority, as for all, groups these conflicting pressures exist, and though the situation may be portrayed by the majority as generational conflicts, this is by no means an adequate representation.

5.41.2.   The experiences of men and women in mediating conflicting demands are essentially different. For instance, the adherence to 'traditional' modes of dress and behaviour expected of women from many Indian subcontinental families is not equally applied to men. As one commentator has written:

"There is a whole gamut of definition of immodest clothing for women, where I know of none for men living in the West".

5.41.3.   We spoke with several Muslim young women who had, sometimes after a long and painful struggle, achieved the right to live independently. This they did through a synthesis of their religious beliefs with the freedom to be educated and to work in occupations outside their homes. Some of their parents had unquestioningly maintained the attitudes and views of a woman's place with which they had grown up, and had been baffled and enraged at what they regarded as their daughters' adoption of Western-style values, mixing with others freely, going out to work, refusing an arranged marriage, or limiting their family to two children. The parents were fearful of the opinion of others in their community who would see the new ways in which their daughters behaved as a slur on the family's honour, and as a criticism of men who could not, or would not, control them properly.

5.41.4.   The parents had often been supported by the young women's brothers, who saw their own status threatened by these changes. The young women had thought out their positions carefully, and had pioneered courses which they now saw other daughters following more easily within their families. They forecast that these changes were slow, but inexorable. The number of arranged trans-continental marriages breaking up, they told us, was increasing, particularly where it was the woman who was confident in the ways of this country because she had grown up here. Many families were learning that a male spouse from the family's original home did not necessarily reinforce the old ways, and the failure of an older daughter's arranged marriage underlined this experience when it came to the turn of younger daughters to be married.

5.41.5.   There are no statistics on which the representativeness, or the accuracy, of these views can be judged. What was evident, however, was the deep thought which these women had given to how they could fuse their loyalties to their family and religious background with a way of life to which they felt properly entitled. The impact of these social changes, whether in relation to the job market, the pattern of local purchasing, the size and location of families, or the contribution to the political and cultural life of the city, must not be underestimated.

5.41.6.   We should note that it is not just the **young** women born and educated here who are developing a different lifestyle. We learnt that some older women who had had no opportunity to learn English were now anxious to do so, and we met one who was attending classes for the first time after 30 years in Bradford. The stereotyping of older women as unchanged and unchanging is common, but seriously mistaken.

5.41.7.   The women who migrated to join their husbands in Bradford some 30 years ago had to adapt to a very different way of life. Those with husbands on shift work, often on permanent nights in the textile mills, or on rotating shifts on public transport, took on responsibilities for their families with less support than they would have had in their home villages, and had to meet the demands of an educational system for their children, and other unfamiliar demands, with little or no help from the authorities. It should not be forgotten how successfully many of them adapted their lives in this way, nor the extent to which they were involved in contributing economically to their families, doing paid work inside and outside the home.

5.42   The Contribution of Women

5.42.1.   Within the minority communities it is women in negotiation with men who will work out viable strategies for the future. Increasingly women in Britain, including Bradford, and in the Indian sub-continent, are making their voices heard and both young and older men are learning from them. Those outside the minority communities, in particular women, have a role in promoting in their own groups an understanding of customs different from theirs and a change in the climate of the organisations in which they work. Open and informed discussion, and changes in practices, will take place when improved opportunities for education and employment are available.

Section 6
The Public Services

6.1 Special Programmes?

6.1.1. We turn first to the two Public Services whose interrelationships with the "ethnic minority" communities caused most concern to our informants – Education, and Policing. Yet we came across so many similar symptoms in these and other public services that we believe the general criticisms of these two services brought to our attention probably apply also to other services, reinforcing our view that the common cause is the lack of mutual understanding within Bradford which we described in Section 5. Public services, which in theory are democratically accountable, ought to be able to take the lead in overcoming obstructive social problems and tensions.

6.1.2. In this Section 6 we explore in Part 1 the concerns of people about Education, and in Part 2 the concerns about Policing, which were repeatedly drawn to our attention in both cases. In Part 3 we explore more generally the responsibilities of the public services in relation to the special needs of a multi-ethnic population.

6.1.3. Despite the strength of expression which we have heard from some people, in criticism of those responsible for these services, we have to insist that there are very few in senior positions within the public services who could be properly described as wilfully racist. The difficulty seems to be more an unwillingness to direct operations and organisation so that racism is eliminated as unprofessional conduct, and so that the undoubted challenge of providing appropriate service delivery to take account of different needs is met. There are undoubtedly some, however, at all levels of organisation who are incapable of relating to people who do not share the same history or the same cultural assumptions, and sometimes they are proud of it. They, in turn, are matched by those people from the ethnic minorities who are unwilling to explore and understand the majority culture, in all its variations. In between are people trying to understand and bridge the cultural divisions involved. Once more we see our task as being to strengthen these bridge builders, in relation specifically to the public services.

6.1.4. Lord Scarman, in his 1981 Report on the Brixton Riots, wrote:

> *"6.31. ...... there is a lack of a sufficiently well co-ordinated and directed programme for combating the problem of racial disadvantage. Unless a clear lead is given by Government, in this area as in others, there can be no hope of an effective response. ...."*

Although we share this view, we can do no more than note it, insofar as *"Government"* means the Central Government in Whitehall. However, we apply the same message to Bradfordian self-government in Section 7 of this Report, where we deal with political responsibilities.

6.1.5. Lord Scarman continued:

> *"6.32. This leads me to the question how far is it right to go in order to meet ethnic minority*

needs. It is clear from the evidence of ethnic minority deprivation I have received that, if the balance of racial disadvantage is to be redressed, as it must be, positive action is required. .....
Given the special problems of the ethnic minorities, exposed in evidence, justice requires that special programmes should be adopted in areas of acute deprivation. In this respect, the ethnic minorities can be compared with any other group with special needs, such as the elderly, or one-parent families. I recognise the existence of a legitimate and understandable fear on the part of both public and private institutions that programmes which recognise and cater for the special needs of minority groups will stimulate a backlash from the majority. I suspect that this fear, rather than "institutional racism", is the primary factor inhibiting the necessary development of such programmes. I believe that if the justification for any such special programmes were fully explained, the backlash threat might prove over-rated. Nevertheless, it must not be allowed to prevent necessary action. ...."

6.1.6.   We find ourselves in agreement with much of this; however, it would be unwise to neglect the part played by institutional racism and its consequences.

Part 1. Education

6.2   The Basic Duty

6.2.1.   The basic legal duty of the Local Education Authority (LEA), i.e. the city council, is still that contained in the Education Act of 1944:

"to contribute towards the spiritual, moral, mental, and physical development of the community by securing that efficient education throughout those stages [of the progress of a pupil through the system] *shall be available to meet the needs of the population of their area."*

6.2.2.   We emphasise that the duty is to make education *"available to meet the needs of the population"*, which clearly means that the LEA's duty is to recognise the special circumstances of pupils, as well as those circumstances which are common across diverse cultural backgrounds, and to ensure that the best practice is developed, understood, and practised effectively. In our view, it is not so much *"positive action"*, as the appropriate carrying out of a common obligation, that requires stressing in this situation.

6.3   The Challenge

6.3.1.   Lord Scarman also wrote:

"2.18. ....The problems which have to be solved, if deprivation and alienation are to be overcome, have been identified – namely, teaching a command of the English language, a broad education in the humanities designed to help the various ethnic groups (including the "host community") to understand each other's background and culture, and the basic training in the skills necessary to obtain work in the technological economy of the modern world; ...."

6.3.2.   In its recent publication *The Way Forward*, the Bradford organisation Quest for Education and Development, familiarly known as QED, sets out the challenge in Bradford very clearly:

"Economic deprivation amongst minority ethnic people is a fact of life. Poor economic

*circumstances too easily become the breeding ground for crime and anti social behaviour and a vicious circle can be created which spirals ever downward. Bradford District's economic decline has borne especially heavily on minority ethnic people where they are **twice as likely to be unemployed** as similar minorities in the UK as a whole. Asian school leavers gain only two thirds the qualifications of the average for Asians in the UK as a whole."*

6.3.3. We have been impressed by the strength of the representations made to us about the quality of Education, and the disappointment at the results, especially in relation to children from Pakistani and Bangladeshi backgrounds. However, the unfavourable comparison by QED about qualifications has to be put right against the background of the children in Bradford, for which national comparisons may not be entirely appropriate.

6.4   Bradford's Schools

6.4.1. Bradford's LEA schools are organised, after some Nursery provision, as First Schools for children aged 5–9, Middle Schools for children aged 9–13, and Upper Schools for those aged 13–18. There are no single sex First or Middle Schools, but there is an LEA Upper School for Girls only, and one for Boys only. Applications by parents for a school place should be made 18 months in advance to the Headteacher of the school to which they wish to send their child. The city council also gives some financial support to 23 'supplementary schools' in the Manningham area which are organised by religious and community bodies of various ethnic minority groups, to encourage the teaching of minority languages, and cultural and religious values.

6.4.2. In addition to the LEA schools, and the Church of England Aided Schools, there are grant maintained schools, private schools, and a City Technology College. The Roman Catholic schools are Primary, for those aged 5–11, and Secondary, for those aged 11–18. Given the focus of our investigations, and the limited time available, we have concentrated on the work of the inner city LEA schools.

6.4.3. In a Survey of Bradford Schools conducted by the city council's Education Directorate, published in November 1995, the current statistical breakdown of the 'pre-1974 Bradford City' area's school population showed that 60% were White, and 37% were Asian. Just over 30% were Pakistani, with Indian and Bangladeshi pupils making up the largest other groups in the standard OPCS classification structure. It predicted that for this geographical area half of the school leavers would be from minority ethnic origins within 4 years.

6.4.4. A more detailed survey of the Manningham area, *Manningham – in Context*, was published by the Education Directorate in March 1996. Of the pupils in the group of 15 schools in Manningham expected to be inspected by Ofsted, 94.9% were Asian, and 92% had an Asian mother tongue.

"A significant fact ..... is that the great majority of pupils of Asian ethnic origin, despite nearly all having been born in the UK, have Asian home languages. As a result very few speak any English and need language support on entry to school."

The issue of language was raised with us by many and it takes a prominent place in most discussions of education in Bradford. For this reason we look at it first.

6.5   English Language Competence

Political and Professional Significance

6.5.1.   The acquisition of fluency in written and spoken English is an obvious necessity for taking a full part, not only in the formal education system, but in most aspects of life in Britain. It is therefore imperative that ways are found to enable everyone to acquire these skills. For those of compulsory school age, the direct responsibility for seeking appropriate policies, and implementing appropriate practices, to achieve this lies with the educational administrators, school managers and the teaching profession. But they can not do this alone. Political decisions on the provision of resources at local and national level are crucial, and so too is the development of teacher education adequate to the task.

6.5.2.   The acquisition of language is not a simple technical matter of linguistic fluency, but a complex social process on which community and personal beliefs, values and practices impinge. The many studies carried out, and the experience of innumerable teachers in providing effective learning environments for the acquisition of English for speakers of other languages, constitute, we were told, a sufficient basis on which to make rapid inroads into what is seen as such a great problem. Given the lack of city-wide strategic professional leadership to individual schools of which we heard from almost all the individual teachers and Headteachers who spoke to us, perhaps the social, and therefore political, issues around language acquisition, rather than the technical issues, are the more intractable.

6.5.3.   Examples of these political and social issues are legion and we can refer to only a few. The value attached to one's mother tongue, and to the values of those on whom we depend as young children, cannot be over-emphasised as a basis for security. The learning of English or of any other language starts with this recognition.

6.5.4.   How well we learn is dependent on what opportunities we are offered, and on our socio-economic circumstances and their associated health and housing conditions. For instance, we were told of an investigation carried out by a GP and Health Visitors, which indicated high levels of anaemia in pre-school children in part of the area covered by the *Manningham – in Context* report. Until the relatively few resources required to remedy this deficiency are forthcoming the children and teachers in that area are being unnecessarily disadvantaged. Such steps call for greater co-operation between different services. Many teachers raised issues to do with poverty, overcrowding, and poor health which, combined with the poor conditions in schools, set problems for them and for the children which neither could solve.

6.5.5.   It is not therefore simply a matter of too few resources for education, but a much greater issue which faces the city council and other institutions and agencies in Bradford, if better standards of education are to be achieved.

6.5.6.   There is a political position, often held by people who are themselves mono-lingual English speakers, that there should be no special provision for children born in this country to learn its common language when in school. Their argument, as it was put to us, was that it is the responsibility of parents to ensure that their children are equipped to benefit fully from the education that is made available by the school, and that scarce resources are therefore being unnecessarily diverted from the education of the majority of children.

6.5.7. We agree that educational resources are very scarce, and that their use must always be fully justified, but future prosperity and better relations in Bradford depend heavily on the competences of its school leavers including, especially, competence in English language. It is unrealistic to imagine that this important objective could be achieved in the foreseeable future if there were to be no support for children needing help in coping with the English school system. In any event, their situation is no different from that of any other school child with particular needs. It is foolish to think that children are standard raw materials, to be shaped mechanically in an educational factory into educated widgets! We are convinced that the provision of **effective** language support for **all** children who need it is indispensable for the future well-being of Bradford. 'Effective' necessarily means that the support must be related to individual needs.

6.5.8. One Kashmiri parent put it to us that:

"Children starting at school still can't speak English. People like me should have been pointing it out. Our children are not White, and don't feel British. The identity of our children is the crux. Language is important for that."

6.5.9. A Sikh leader told us that many Sikh parents insisted that their children should first have a good command of English, and then attend the Temple school.

6.5.10. An Upper School Headteacher wrote to us at some length, and we quote this as an example of the way in which many of those at the chalk-face have given a great deal of thought to the political and bureaucratic context in which they and the school pupils have to work:

"It is clear to anyone working in Manningham schools that rigorous English acquisition has been soft-pedalled. For example, over 80% of [the pupils in this school] *have been in the Bradford school system since they were five (or in many cases three) but teachers here estimate that up to 50% of* [pupils] *would benefit from English language support. Such* [pupils] *are not peculiarly "dim" – they just have not been given an awareness that* **competence in standard English is crucially important** *for future life chances. The corollary of this is represented by those pupils who have arrived late into England with little or no English, but whose families are well aware that good English is a basic pre-requisite for opening up opportunities in England – these youngsters often seem to learn English in a trice and, in some happy cases, end up at university etc.*

So, we have a sadly ironic situation whereby in a laudable attempt not to appear too Eurocentric, Bradford's educational policy planners may well have increased inequality of opportunity by not emphasising the centrality of effective English acquisition, which I firmly believe is the key to helping Asian families prosper in England.

We need to realise that equality of opportunity for Bradford's Asian citizens is **enhanced,** *not diminished, by emphasising effective acquisition of standard forms of English. There have been years of confusion and mixed messages from the Education service on this topic."*

6.5.11. One former First School Headteacher, who had struggled with the problem for years, was convinced that, for many children, the home background made it impossible for the school to cope with teaching English language successfully until there was some special provision made, such as a special reception process for children entering school with inadequate English. She thought an undue fear of accusations of racial discrimination had prevented the free professional discussion of the challenge, and such a possible solution, and hence of leadership by the LEA – a sentiment we heard more than once, both from teachers and from some Asian parents.

6.5.12.   We cannot stress too strongly the need for more open discussion of this pressing local educational issue, among those involved professionally, or as parents, or as political decision makers. That there is an unwillingness to discuss such educational, or other civic matters, because of fear of demagogic consequences is to be regretted. There can at best be only limited progress in dealing with Bradford's problems if such an atmosphere prevails.

6.5.13.   We must, though, insert this caveat: the lack of ability to read, write, and speak standard English is not a problem of ethnic minorities alone. As one man whose work takes him to all parts of Bradford, put it:

"On council estates the kids can't speak decent English. Education doesn't prepare kids to stand on their own two feet, still less introduce them to the rewards of reading."

This was an important point which no one else made to us very strongly, though from other sources we know it is the subject of much comment among those who have introduced changes to the Schools system over the past decade, and has been of concern professionally for a much longer period. The title to Section 3, Shared Problems: Perceived Divisions, is again relevant.

Section 11 Funding

6.5.14.   The uncertain future of 'Section 11 funding' makes this an opportune time to review the situation thoroughly. At the time of writing we understand that the Government is shortly to announce what the future of this temporary funding is to be. Since its introduction some 30 years ago, the Home Office has given this exceptional financial aid to local authorities to meet the special needs of members of ethnic minority communities whose language or customs differ from those of the locality. Most of this aid is given for expenditure on education, and in particular for teaching English.

6.5.15.   One experienced officer from a department other than Education, but whose work gave him frequent contact with schools, put the challenge this way:

"What happens at the First School is most important. Often the children cannot access the curriculum. They can't sit down, can't use scissors, can't identify colours. Education, like all public services, tends to have to be a mass production line. If the entrants don't fit the norm ....."

He did not finish the sentence, but spoke of the need for a much more individualised entry process which would remove both the need for continued special support throughout a child's school career, and the poor results which are such a feature of the present system.

6.5.16.   There has been much disagreement on how the Section 11 money should be used, with claims that it did not benefit those for whom it was intended, but that it had been used instead to supplement the general needs of schools in the face of imposed budget cuts. Since April 1992 the use of these funds has been more strictly monitored by the Home Office and, when it was announced that such funding was to end, Bradford bid successfully for its extension, on the grounds of the city's special needs. The equivalent of some 500 educational posts are currently supported in this way: teachers, classroom assistants and liaison officers. According to *The Riot Area Reviewed*, the report produced at the request of the Leader of the Council immediately after the disorders:

"The Manningham/Toller area is the principal recipient of Bradford's Section 11 funding to schools."

6.5.17.   The temporary nature of this funding amidst continuing acute financial pressures is a matter of great concern, and this has inevitably inhibited open and systematic educational discussion of how best to deal with the continuing need for language support in schools. The lack of competence in English is suspected to be overstated by some, and understated by others, depending on their particular interests, and whilst this is the case no workable strategy can be developed.

The Need For Leadership

6.5.18.   It is clear to us that puzzlement at the lack of priority given to tackling this problem is very strongly, as well as very widely, held. We certainly found it to be a major concern in schools among teachers and heads. We expected that these by no means new challenges would have been a major theme for the educationalists who advise or direct the council's operations, and we are aware of their relevant work.

6.5.19.   During 'the Honeyford controversy' and its aftermath (see para 5.8.18) too much emphasis on English as a pre-requisite to economic and social integration was accepted as devaluing other languages and cultural backgrounds, and as racist. Many who spoke to us thought that there was now a more balanced view, but some people suggested that community leaders, who held their privileged position because of their own facility in speaking English, did not encourage parents and others to take advantage of the available facilities, or to explore other ways of developing language competences. We do not know if this is a factor, and no community leader we heard subscribed to this view.

6.5.20.   We would like to have found a clearer, politically accepted and prioritised strategy for dealing with the problem, drawing upon the best practice which is surely by now discernible. Clear leadership is urgently needed. It is vital that explicit political discussion and prioritisation of this challenge should be undertaken urgently.

6.6   League Tables

The Results

6.6.1.   There was a general concern expressed to us about the league table results of Bradford's inner city schools, and a considerable gap as to the causes and remedies between those most familiar with the schools and those who depended on rumour and hearsay for the opinions they expressed.

6.6.2.   The kind of comment about Bradford's results found in the national media is illustrated by the following quotations:

"in three of the city's comprehensives less than 7% of teenagers obtained five or more grade A–C GCSEs. ..... such figures compare badly with the national average (43.3%)"

"An average of 26.7% of pupils passing five or more GCSEs at grades C or above left it [i.e. Bradford] *languishing tenth from bottom in last year's exam league table of LEA's. Four inner city schools returned single-figure percentages, while relatively high-achieving schools in the richer suburbs and outlying towns and villages made the average appear more respectable ....."*.

6.6.3.   There has also been local comment, such as:

"Pupils in Manningham are likely to come from deprived and over-crowded backgrounds and, with a few exceptions, will have Asian home languages. Reception-level tests show that Manningham pupils on average have fewer relevant skills than other pupils from deprived backgrounds. However, their progress through school is comparable, given their starting circumstances. At both upper [single sex] *schools the GCSE performance at 5+ A–C grades is well below their peers' both locally and nationally but the ... Girls' results compare well locally on other measures."* (from *"Manningham in Context"*).

6.6.4.   We were told that, in one Upper School with largely Kashmiri and Bangladeshi pupils, an overwhelming proportion of new entrants achieved very low levels in maths and science, and half did badly in English. The headteacher was confident that these poor results were **not** due to low abilities. Some pupils subsequently were able to achieve remarkable advances.

The Need for Leadership

6.6.5.   It would be most unfortunate if this rather dismal commentary were to give too widespread a picture of inadequacy. There is good education being provided, several exciting initiatives being taken, and there are many pupils who achieve outstandingly. In identifying and exposing problems, we do not wish to give a false impression that nothing is being done well, or that nothing is being achieved. But problems clearly exist which need to be addressed. The seeds of Bradford's future well into the next century are being sown and nurtured now, for good or ill. We were very impressed by much of what we heard about, and saw of, the dedicated work of teachers, governors, parents and pupils in identifying and tackling the challenges they face.

6.6.6.   The city has a council which is one of the largest Local Education Authorities in the country, a University, a College of Higher Education, and many committed, experienced teachers and other workers in Education. Yet there appears to be no cohesive, organised forum for identifying and voicing professional advice on the priorities for the solution of the educational problems which are so peculiarly pressing in Bradford, nor for identifying the lessons to be learned from the various initiatives that have been locally pioneered. This challenge is not so much one of power or, in the first place, of resources, but for a strategic consistency based on sound advice and clear choices.

6.7 Parental Responsibilities, Concerns and Battles

Making Education Available

6.7.1. The responsibility of the LEA is to make appropriate education **available,** and we therefore also recognise an equivalent need for parents to respond constructively to ensure that what is available is both adequate and well used. It is clear to us that this equivalence necessitates a joint approach by schools and parents, as well as the involvement of the pupils. Without dialogue and mutual respect between teachers and parents, it would be foolish to assume that children can meet the problems created by adults.

6.7.2. We apologise for stating the obvious to those who spend much effort in enabling such an approach, but the need for good practice to be recognised and spread is urgently needed. Unfortunately parental involvement in the work of the schools remains inadequate, whether as Governors, or just as individual parents, though we were favourably impressed by the growing capacity of the leaders of the Bangladeshi community, in particular, to contribute to current educational discussions in a constructive, professionally persuasive, way.

6.7.3. Bradford has now had more than 30 years experience of educating pupils from diverse backgrounds in the Indian sub-continent and more than 20 years educating the second and third generations born and brought up here. Various policies have been adopted during this time, some encouraged by national direction and funding, and some in conflict with them. The parents of the different generations have faced a number of challenges and have been subjected to not inconsiderable stereotyping, indifference, misunderstanding and blame for the educational performance of their children. It is the responsibility of educationalists to take a fresh look at what too many of them presently see as parental failings.

6.7.4. There can be no doubt that schools do have difficulty in involving parents, and that many schools do try to solve the problem, and some examples of effective practice were drawn to our attention. We were, however, disappointed to hear of schools 'discovering' for themselves successful practices which had been followed for some time elsewhere – in the case of one school, a practice which we knew had been followed in a very nearby school for some years. Once again, we have to urge a more strategic leadership to meet the challenge.

Parental Interest

6.7.5. One Kashmiri, who is himself well educated, told us:

> *"The original immigrants were not usually well educated. There is no history of family familiarity with the British educational system. Therefore there is a gap, and no heavy involvement of parents in the work of the schools."*

6.7.6. In parts of Bradford, including the Manningham area, it is the case that many parents from almost all ethnic backgrounds are unable to relate confidently to the educational processes affecting their children and, not surprisingly, those whom we met were mostly from economically impoverished households. But the concern of many for their children's education was manifest in many of the meetings we attended. Amongst many parents there was genuine surprise and anger if their children had not done well from what seemed a long period of compulsory education. Such realisation is too late.

6.7.7.   In the early 1990s the largely unquestioned assumption amongst Asian parents that Bradford schools were satisfying good educational standards for their children was dispelled by a realisation of the relatively poor position of Bradford in the national league tables, and it was replaced by a general sense that Bradford's schools were failing their children.

6.7.8.   Some Bangladeshi parents sought judicial review of the council's allocation policies and practices, claiming that 31% of Asian applicants in Manningham were not admitted to any of the three schools of their choice, compared with only 5.3% of non-Asians. They also pointed to 'good' schools whose catchment areas excluded Manningham. The parents lost their case, but the council was forced to become more aware of the growing importance of educational standards as a concern of these parents.

6.7.9.   It would be unfortunate if the issues raised by their continuing campaign about educational achievement were to be defensively rejected by the LEA. We cannot judge whether all the criticisms being made are correct. We certainly think that the right questions are being asked, and that they are not relevant only to Bangladeshi concerns. Those asking the questions deserve support from parents of all backgrounds who are concerned about the standards of achievement in Bradford's schools. The issue is properly a political matter of great importance. Unfortunately, many worried parents do not see the political processes as being open to their concern.

Absences in Pakistan

6.7.10.   We frequently heard from people of different backgrounds about the adverse effects of long visits by pupils to family homes in the Indian sub-continent. Although long absences are disruptive, many teachers were confident that the disruption could be reduced significantly if parents woud co-operate with the school in selecting the least damaging timing. In one largely Asian upper school we were told that there could be 5% of the pupils away on a long visit to Pakistan at any one time. There has been some inconclusive research on the educational effects; much seems to depend on the age of the absentee, and on the attitude of the school, e.g. in giving work to the pupil and using the experience gained. Very young children can be set back in their acquisition of English, and the 13+ pupils miss out on GCSE preparation. As one Headteacher told us:

"You can live with it in Year 9, but not in Year 11."

6.7.11.   Again, there is need to open out the discussion. Some Asian parents told us that they did select a time for visits which would be least disruptive, and several teachers shared the educational potential of such visits with us. But there was a widespread feeling that many parents did not realise the importance of appropriate timing, and the adverse effects on education of inappropriate timing. Such visits are obviously important in maintaining family identities, and are likely to be a feature of life for many Bradford children for the foreseeable future.

6.7.12.   One practical suggestion put to us was that in schools with a large Asian population the timing of the long summer school holiday should be varied, so as to miss the extreme heat at that time of the year in the Indian sub-continent. We mention this suggestion for two reasons. First, it was put forward seriously by a representative body, and therefore needs to be examined on its merits. Secondly, it is a nice example of the usually dominant cultural assumptions and practices being challenged, instead of the reverse!

6.8 Ethnically Integrated or Segregated Schools?

6.8.1. This is a challenge which Bradford needs to take on board more openly, despite the restricted scope of intervention by the city council. There are two separate, but related aspects. The first is that, given the residential concentrations of the White population in the suburbs and on former council estates, and that of some ethnic minorities in the inner city, how and from where schools draw their pupil populations will affect their overall profile. The second is that, given the importance of a 'good' education, parents will try to obtain entry for their children into what they consider, or are told, are the better performing schools. This may lead to intense competition, resulting in frustration and anger for many of those who are disappointed.

The 'Preference' System

6.8.2. If an LEA school cannot accommodate all those whose parents have applied for places, a 'preference' system is operated by the Education Directorate. The formal rules give first priority to the sisters and brothers of existing pupils, then a geographical catchment area is drawn to include enough pupils to fill the remaining places. A catchment area has regard to the proximity of the child's home to the school, the availability of other schools, areas from where children have traditionally attended the school, access to transport, and awareness of natural obstacles, e.g. major roads. Special provision is made on medical or special needs grounds. There is a two stage appeal process for parents who are disappointed at the unavailability of a school place of their choice. Grant maintained and private schools have their own catchment/selection criteria. Such rules are always likely to be open to criticism and misunderstanding.

Parental Attitudes

6.8.3. Why, say many of the Asian parents in Manningham, do other schools produce better examination results than those available to them? Many think that the reason for the better results is the presence of a significant number of White children in the other schools, which guarantees better teaching and other resources. Many White parents think the presence of Asian children reduces the quality of their children's education because of the English language issue discussed in subsection 6.5. The result is a general pursuit of 'good' schools by concerned parents on the basis of the schools' records. The result is also increased segregation along ethnic lines in which narrowness of cultural understanding is constantly reinforced.

6.8.4. An Upper School Headteacher told us:

"Polarisation in schools is taking place. The Hindus have stopped coming, and the Sikhs.

There is a perception that this is a Mirpuri school. There is also a movement away by the upwardly mobile Pakistani classes."

6.8.5.   He was quite clear that this did not mean his school was an 'Islamic' school. The parents and pupils clearly wanted good GCSE results and an ethos which included their children within the normal educational system, whilst affirming the value, and the values, of their own culture. He was aware, too, that providing this, whilst avoiding a *"White backlash"* was extremely difficult.

6.8.6.   In 1983 the Muslim Parents Association pressed for five LEA schools to become voluntary-aided Muslim schools, on the pattern of Anglican and Roman Catholic Church schools. The LEA sought to counter this request by responding to specific Muslim needs. The LEA promoted awareness of Muslim dress codes for girls, and single sex swimming and PE, flexibility over extended visits to relatives' homes in South Asia, and the introduction of Halal meat in school meals.

6.8.7.   Many of the parents were concerned about the drawbacks of separate education, and supported the LEA's approach. We find that this is still the wish of most Asian parents who have discussed this matter with us, but it is a fact that some LEA schools do exist where almost all the pupils are Muslim. Concern was expressed to us by parents that this did not help their children to become part of the life of Bradford.

6.8.8.   Given the strongly held preference expressed by representatives on behalf of many Muslim parents for a girls-only School, the LEA has provided a School to meet that need. It is therefore, we were told, legally necessary to provide an equivalent boys' school, and one exists for that reason. Both these schools, despite overcrowding and poor buildings, are now achieving improving academic results.

6.8.9.   Parents with the financial means to educate their children in private schools in Bradford are in a minority. However, in some of these schools there is a more ethnically integrated student population and the performance of children from ethnic minorities is, we were told, indistinguishable from those from other backgrounds.

6.8.10.   Parental choice of school is, in fact, absent for many of the Manningham parents who believe that their children would achieve higher standards at other schools than those actually available to them, and the extent of restriction on choice appears to be peculiar to Manningham. Unfortunately, we have not been able to obtain published detailed statistical information from the LEA about the comparative success of parents throughout Bradford in obtaining places for their children in the Upper schools of their choice. This is a subject of great concern, and nowhere more so than in the Manningham area, where it was the first focus of the Bangladeshi campaign to improve educational standards for the under-performing inner city children. It is another example of 'sensitivity' preventing open discussion and, hence, the establishment of open decisions.

The Views of Teachers

6.8.11.   We have not conducted research to enable us to indicate a professional consensus, but one inner City upper school headteacher reflected the views we heard from the teachers who spoke to us about this subject. He told us that in his view integrated schools were best, but that they would have to be explicit about the teaching of moral values and the provision made for religious education, not just in the formal arrangements, but also in the basic attitudes which a school promoted.

Confusion of ethnic and educational factors

6.8.12.   On our visit to the boys' upper school, which has had a poor reputation, our impression was of a well-ordered school with a good atmosphere, and a determination to help pupils cope with the harsh realities of their future constructively. This challenge had to be met in cramped premises, with poor facilities. Attendance records at this school had improved, and there was clear determination by the Headteacher that the trends should continue to improve. A considerable change for the better had been achieved with the help of the LEA in supporting a massive change of staff, to obtain teachers who were able to be constructive in meeting the special challenge which the school now presented.

6.8.13.   It was a matter of regret to the staff to whom we spoke that, with the exception of the Chairman of the Education committee, Councillors only visited the school to accompany complaining parents. Once more, we heard of the difficulty of getting parent governors, with the inevitable result that the governors were not typical of the community being served by the school.

An Evaded Issue

6.8.14.   There is no simple solution to this social and educational problem of ethnically segregated schools, but it must be addressed by those responsible for educating Bradford's children. At present it is evaded. Greater openness about the relevant information is one step which should be taken, but more crucially the criteria being used to determine catchment areas should be kept under constant review as part of the open political process, and justified within an **overall** educational strategy. In the absence of conscious social engineering, the only solution which will not create other problems is for the schools to produce better results. It is not the presence of Asians in a school which, of itself, causes bad results, though the timing and effectiveness of language support is relevant; many outperform their White contemporaries. Nor is it simply a lack of funding, though the Newsome Report reminded us decades ago that the proper education of the economically deprived is always expensive, and the case for more educational funding does appear persuasive. But the Muslim Girls' School in Bradford is, we were told, grossly underfunded, yet its pupils are achieving excellent results.

6.8.15.   The basic question of the civic pros and cons of ethnically integrated or segregated schools should be openly on the agenda not only of the Education Committee, but of all the groups and institutions which are concerned about Bradford's future. Only then can a strategy be confidently developed to accommodate the educational and civic needs of a multi-ethnic city. We note that this is not a matter which affects Bradford alone, but also other parts of Britain, and indeed of the world, where people of different traditions and backgrounds live within the same society.

6.9   Religious Education

Inside Schools

6.9.1.   The place of moral and religious teaching in schools is a matter on which there is a range of divergent views, and it seems to us that respect for diverse beliefs is an essential basis on which to proceed. We would include in this, of course, those who have an agnostic position. In Bradford schools our main focus inevitably has been on Islam and on Christianity.

6.9.2.   An agreed syllabus for religious education in multi-faith Bradford was first negotiated in 1983, and a new, locally agreed, syllabus, *Faith in our Future,* has been prepared for use in Bradford schools from September 1996. One might have thought that agreement on a syllabus between all the main religions in Bradford would have been impossible, given historic tensions and misunderstandings. In fact, it is an outstanding example of what has been achieved by Bradfordians, using relevant skills, to solve a very challenging problem satisfactorily. The Bradford Inter-Faith Centre which has pioneered this work was founded in 1986, is nationally recognised, and makes a continuing contribution to the life of the city. We have detected very little disharmony that is religiously based, apart from the activities of a few extremists.

6.9.3.   It is not our role to assess the technical or theological excellence of the syllabus, though we think that we would have heard significant criticism if any existed. We commend it as an example of what can be done. It is essential, if the LEA schools are to retain the confident support of parents from different traditions, that those traditions are valued, and used constructively as part of the process of education. At least in this important area of possible social division we found no cause for concern, with people from several different backgrounds cooperating with understanding of, and respect for, each others' belief systems in order to serve the best interests of all those who live in the city.

In relation to Schools

6.9.4.   Religious education outside school is the province of religious institutions and their followers, and here we comment only on those issues which have been raised with us which are relevant to school education.

Eid

6.9.5.   Forecasting the precise date of the religious festival of Eid is a matter which schools, seeking to accommodate appropriately those who wish to observe the Festival, see as a problem because of differences of practice adopted by different mosques. There is now recognition of the holiday by the school authorities, but the solution of relying on the expert forecast of astronomy, which we understand has been adopted elsewhere in Britain, has not been universally acceptable to Bradford's mosques. Until such time as it is, the uncertainty will continue to cause friction and disruption, and put parents and children under cross-pressures. Further discussions are obviously necessary.

Attendance at Mosque Schools

6.9.6.   This was raised with us, and has appeared as a problem in some education reports, in terms of the length of the day of the school children involved. One view was that there was clearly an effect on mainstream education, because young Muslim children were spending in further study two or three hours a day more than non-Muslim children. This again appears to us to be a matter which all those directly concerned must discuss.

6.9.7.   The view was put to us by a number of people from a variety of backgrounds that many Muslim parents view the religious education given at 'supplementary schools' run by the Mosques as the most important part of their child's education. There is a religious obligation on all Muslim parents to ensure that their children read and understand the Qur'an. These schools are therefore central to Muslim parents' religious duty to their children. The Qur'an is, of course, written in Arabic and the believer must study it in that language. Genuine understanding takes years of intensive study.

6.9.8.   The traditional way of understanding the scriptures in Pakistan, we understand, would be to study Urdu texts and then refer back to the original Arabic. Since very few Mosques recognise their capability to provide English tuition or translation many children have to learn both the Urdu and Arabic versions. As they are in most cases already speaking both English and Punjabi there are issues to be discussed by all those who are placing what may be very strong pressures on them. As far as we know there has never been any attempt to understand or address these issues within the mainstream curriculum, nor by the Council for Mosques.

6.9.9.   It seems to us that the still extensive influence of the Imams could be applied with advantageous directness to the task of translating the basis of the Qur'anic faith to the circumstances of those growing up in contemporary Bradford. In the case of many children here, the Imams already run the risk of that influence being marginalised, even for their basic purpose of religious and moral instruction, because English is rarely the medium of instruction. We believe the mosques could, and should, do much more to assist young people seeking a Muslim identity to grow up as Muslims in Bradford, by providing more effective teaching, organising educational support, and providing organised social facilities. Their role in affirming to successive generations, and to others, the value and values of the belief system they represent, quite apart from the formal religious significance of their basis, is extremely important.

6.9.10.   Insofar as the teaching of languages other than English is concerned, the development of real language skills in those other languages could provide a means of strengthening both cultural confidence and a greater facility in the use of English also. The mosques, and their educational activities, often represent a major financial investment by local Muslims, many of whom are poor, and their potential should be maximised. Insofar as the supplementary schools run by the mosques receive money from the Local Education Authority for such purposes, more clearly accountable mechanisms for its use, linked to a clear Local Education Authority strategy, should be introduced.

6.10   School Experiences

6.10.1.   Two teachers, who had had experience of teaching in multicultural and predominantly Asian areas in other cities before coming fairly recently to two different Bradford inner city schools, separately spoke of their shock at the tensions in these schools between some of the

White staff and the Asian pupils, and the lack of investment over many years in appropriate staff training. We were relieved to hear them both say that things were now improving.

6.10.2.   They also spoke of the low self-esteem of many of the pupils, and their lack of facilities to help them relate to British life. One teacher who spoke to us had introduced lunchtime discussions on contemporary topics which caused the pupils concern, but which the pupils had had no other opportunity to confront and learn about. These had proved to be well attended and produced a wide range of views and requests for information. This was despite warnings from other teachers that no-one, or only those with 'extremist' views who would disrupt the meetings, would attend.

6.10.3.   If, as seems likely, there is a growing gap between generational perceptions, and between young people from different ethnic groups, such opportunities for discussion are vital.

6.11   The Explanations

6.11.1.   We wish to make it abundantly clear that our Report, in raising issues of concern to many people about Education, is not an attack on Bradford's teachers and educationalists in general. That there are some poor teachers, as there are poor members of every profession, is not in doubt, but the concern we wish to reflect is that the educational system is not producing the results that Bradford people expect, and that the future of the city needs, despite some very commendable work.

6.11.2.   The reasons given to us for the poor average of Bradford's educational results include:

a)   from the schools: lack of clear **intellectual** leadership by the LEA in seeking solutions to the professional challenges facing individual teachers in the current situation;

b)   from the schools and the LEA: the diversions of effort caused for teachers and educationalists by nationally imposed changes to educational management and administration, and especially by those changes which ignore the very significant impact of Bradford's ethnic minorities on appropriate educational provision;

c)   from the LEA: inadequate finances, poor buildings and equipment, and reduced powers to intervene;

d)   in relation to some of the pupils: ill-discipline, a poor grasp of English, and poor self esteem; lack of role models; parental ignorance of the British educational system;

e)   from parents: unchallenged low expectations by some teachers.

6.11.3.   All these reasons for poor performance would benefit from collective political and professional consideration within Bradford. We understand the pressures, but the fact is that the present system does not work as it should. Some of the main challenges are known; some of the successful responses are known; yet there appears to be insufficient political, intellectual, and professional leadership to overcome the institutional incapacity at a national and local level to deliver what is required. What we have missed is a sense of collective endeavour which is synergistically powerful.

6.12   Staffing

6.12.1.   We were provided with an Education staffing profile for 1995/6. Of course an overall profile can only have a limited value, but the overall division that we were given was between 'White Staff' and 'Black Staff', which is not particularly relevant in addressing some of Bradford's problems, particularly when so much emphasis needs to be given to the issue of language.

	Officer	Craft and Manual	Teacher
Central Staff			
White	81%	93%	74%
Black	19%	7%	26%
School Based			
White	91%	91%	97%
Black	9%	9%	3%

6.12.2.   We were told in January 1996 that only three Headteachers were from the ethnic minority groups, two of First Schools, and one of a Middle School. There were none from these groups then in the Inspectorate, and none in the ranks of senior Education officers. The central officer statistics, however, do reflect the efforts of the city council to recruit so as to reflect the needs of the local population in the advice and implementation which its officers provide.

6.12.3.   The centrally based teacher statistics reflect the inclusion of the temporarily funded "Section 11" staff (see paras 6.5.14 – 17), even though the latter are mainly school-based. The statistics, however, support our concern, and that of several teachers who commented adversely on the selection processes for teachers at multi-ethnic schools, that the multi-ethnic nature of the population is, for whatever reasons, insufficiently integral to the Education Service as a whole. That only 3% of **school appointed** teachers should be from the ethnic minorities is a gross under representation which must inhibit appropriate responses to current challenges. One of the purposes of the formal education process must be to enable young people to have access to a wide range of opportunities for employment and Further and Higher Education. One of the advantages of having teachers from all ethnic backgrounds in schools is that they are more likely to provide children with immediately available role models and advisers.

6.13   Self Help

6.13.1.   We were made aware of initiatives by the LEA, by schools, and by teachers individually, to support pupils who would otherwise be denied a good education. The 'Asian Tuition Association' is a voluntary organisation, based in Manningham, which offers support, guidance and tuition, and we are aware of other initiatives. Homework support, liaison with parents, and supplementary teaching are all being promoted, but not in any co-ordinated way which could lead to switching of resources from less successful to more successful methods.

6.14   Need for a clearer strategy

6.14.1.   The council has recognised many of the current challenges, and developed some supportive responses, e.g. the Governors' Support Service supports a 'black school governors' forum'. The council has also sought to protect the Education budget for schools, despite the cuts in expenditure it has been forced to make. It is clear that there are not the funds available within the present budget to support the extension of successful initiatives to meet the challenges in the schools, without openly choosing priorities. This lack of funding seems unlikely to change in the foreseeable future; certainly we did not hear from anyone who thought it would. In these circumstances the need for ruthless prioritisation is clear.

6.14.2.   Given the amount of individual expertise and experience which is available in Bradford schools it ought to be possible to arrive at the optimum way of using the available resources, even though they are obviously limited. The present situation, in which individual teachers, schools, parents and others have to discover for themselves better methods which have often been long used in other Bradford schools, and the consequent misdirection of resources, is not satisfactory. Unfortunately, the abandonment of front line workers to find their own way through the uncharted waters of contemporary Bradford without ever drawing their experience together is a common feature of Bradford's public services. The result is a lack of coherence in a service's understanding of the problems, and a lack of clear direction in the allocation of priorities and resources.

6.14.3.   We were surprised to hear one very experienced first school teacher wondering aloud whether it might be better to have more rote learning of basic language, reading and maths, at the expense of play and painting. Surely the Bradford teaching profession is capable of exploring the relevant evidence on questions such as this, and adapting practice accordingly? Why has this not happened? What forums has the LEA established to enable it to happen? Why has such a matter become the subject only of rather superficial political debate at a remote national level?

6.14.4.   We appreciate that the powers of the LEA to control schools are now very limited, that it has taken a great deal of political courage to protect its underfunded budget, and that there is no permanence to the special Section 11 government funding, for the retention of which it has been necessary to fight so hard. We understand something of the huge organisational upheavals which have been imposed on LEAs and schools alike in the past decade. We sympathise with the many Headteachers and teachers who work so hard to make sense of children's school careers whilst observing nationally dictated systems which are often inappropriate for the actual situation in their schools. We are not suggesting greater control, nor more expenditure, nor new administrative systems, but intellectual leadership backed by political will in making some uncomfortable decisions – about how the skills and other resources which are presently being used can be used more effectively.

6.14.5.   Given the social problems which stem from the poverty of widespread unemployment, we are in no doubt that Bradford will continue to suffer tensions amongst its young people unless its strong efforts to increase employment are complemented by success in overcoming the inadequate educational attainments of so many of its school leavers. The School system and its achievements are of critical importance for the future of the city.

Many of the city's present tensions will worsen if the generation presently in school is not better equipped than those in the recent past. The growing number of young people in Bradford ought to give Bradford many advantages. It will only do so if appropriate education can be achieved.

Part 2 Policing

6.15 Introduction

6.15.1. In view of our description of the unfavourable perception of the police in the Asian communities in Manningham at the time of the disorders, it is probably not surprising that we should have heard many complaints about the police from such sources.

6.15.2. But although our remit arises from the disorders, and we have already set out our account of those disorders and our related comments in Section 4 above, we heard so many complaints from a wide cross section of the public about policing, its relationship to the disorders and to the general background to the disorders perceived to be applicable also in other parts of Bradford, that we have to deal with a wider subject than just the policing of the disorders, or of Manningham.

6.15.3. The reasons we have to emphasise particularly these wider concerns about policing, despite our understanding of the obvious difficulties which the police face in dealing with a population which has various cultural assumptions about the work of the police, are twofold: first, an inadequate relationship between the police and the people of Manningham created, in our view, a clear predisposition to violence; secondly, the police, who are charged to uphold the law and to maintain public order, are properly a prominent and intrusive public service, about which there are high public expectations and concerns.

6.15.4. It should be made clear that this part of our Report is not hostile to the policing function. The need for the enforcement of 'law and order' is widely recognised amongst all sections of Bradford's multi-ethnic population; indeed, a major part of the expressed concern about policing was that there was not enough of it, though the specifics varied! We understand that ill-informed, generalised, criticism of the police immediately after the disorders caused a lowering of morale amongst Bradford police officers, most of whom are conscientious citizens of this, or similar urban areas, and are committed to achieving a high professional standard of policing, despite many frustrations and provocations.

6.15.5. Lord Scarman wrote in 1981:

"5.47. The value of the current debate about policing lies in the fact that it has revealed, or, more accurately, re-stated – for they have always been part of the British policing tradition – three fundamental points:

(i) the importance of policing by consent;

(ii) the need for this approach to policing in all aspects of police work. It is not something which can be put in a separate box labelled 'community relations';

(iii) that keeping law and order is the concern of the whole community, something in which all sections of the community have a responsibility as well as an interest."

The wisdom of these words, in particular, has become increasingly clear to us throughout our Inquiry.

6.16   The Police Force

6.16.1.   The West Yorkshire Police Force is responsible for policing Bradford. Their Headquarters are in Wakefield and their area also covers Calderdale, Kirklees, Leeds, and Wakefield. This total area covers 784.5 square miles, and has a population of 2.1 million people. Bradford's population constitutes 23% of the total population of this area.

6.16.2.   Although too much should not be read into one year's statistics it appears that recorded crimes in Bradford increased in 1995, whereas in the rest of the West Yorkshire police area they decreased.

Divisional Organisation

6.16.3.   The Metropolitan District of Bradford is divided into five separate police Divisions, each headed by a Superintendent accountable to HQ in Wakefield. The Superintendent of the Central Division is often regarded as the Chief Constable's principal representative for City-wide purposes but, at the time of our enquiries, he had no operational precedence over the other Divisional Superintendents. The exact nature of the relationship between the Bradford-based Superintendents was not clear to us. One issue of concern within Bradford is the perception that divisional loyalties and structures obscure the definition of, and responses to, Bradford-wide problems. The concern has been expressed by a surprisingly wide range of people, and not simply from nostalgia for the days of the former City Police Force.

6.16.4.   It is an organisational issue we do not feel able to pursue, beyond emphasising that the problems we are highlighting in this report are Bradford-wide, and can only be tackled successfully on that basis. Whether or not the relationship between the Bradford Superintendents can be properly described as 'first amongst equals', the present local arrangement can do little to match city-wide needs to police accountabilities, and therefore Bradford must currently look to a more distant and higher level of rank than Superintendent for solutions to Bradford's city-wide policing problems.

6.16.5.   Two of the five Bradford divisional areas, Central and Toller Lane, were directly involved in the disorders which began on 10 June 1995, but only the area covered by Toller Division was involved in the originating events and in the disorders of the 9 June. We have therefore concentrated most of our attention on the Toller Division in considering policing matters. The small part of Manningham to the eastern side of Manningham Lane is in Central Division; the rest of Manningham is in Toller Division.

6.16.6.   The Toller Division, we were informed, serves a population of approximately 90,000, of which 64.5% are White, 32.5% are Asian, and 3% are from other ethnic groups. The majority of this Asian population reside in Manningham and Girlington.

6.16.7   The Toller Division's organisation was unusual in having a divisional Vice Squad to deal particularly with the entrenched problem of prostitution within its area, an arrangement which gave rise to a number of local residents and professional workers in the area noting for us their concern at what they saw as the unfortunate influence of the Divisional boundary on policing the prostitution. As a result of the campaign to which we referred in subsection 5.22 the area frequented by the prostitutes has now changed, and is the subject of co-operation between Toller and Central Divisions.

6.16.8. The Division was also unusual, we were told, in that a number of uniformed officers had been removed from 'reactive' policing, to work with detectives in a unit to deal with rising problems of serious crime, and particularly drug dealing. This change in policing resulted in the Division reducing its crime rate by 4.1% more than the Force average, and increasing its detection rate by 1.2% more than the Force average, in 1994/5.

6.16.9. Particularly impressive was the reduction in burglaries of houses by 22%, compared with a Force average of 5%. These are considerable achievements, and demonstrate the different advantages which flow from different policing strategies. Insofar as such 'pro-active' policing reduces the amount of time available for other policing activities, the reduction in 'visible' policing regretted by the public can only be made good by sacrificing these gains, or by radically different ways of providing communal policing, in the absence of increased financing.

6.16.10. No organisation is static, and we are conscious of the constant process of change since the disorders, in the Toller Division in particular, resulting from local and Force initiatives. Many of the concerns which we heard from the public have been recognised and addressed in changes in the deployment of the Division's resources, but it seems unlikely that all the concerns can be met, given the limited resources available to the Force. Yet many of the concerns are very proper, and if the police cannot meet them, then other means will have to be sought.

6.17 · Policing by Consent

The Weekend of Disorder

6.17.1. It would be easy to dismiss the evidence of the events immediately prior to the disorders as no more than a series of unfortunate mistakes by individual police officers in misreading the situation in which they found themselves. We have asserted boldly in Section 4 that a much deeper problem was involved, and consider that looking for individuals to blame for the specific situation would be no more than diversionary scapegoating. Our commentary on the whole of the weekend was not so much critical of the police operational decisions, but of the misunderstandings and attitudes which caused the police to act as they did, particularly on the Friday evening.

6.17.2. To us, the evidence pointed inescapably to an institutional incapacity to understand, and to relate to, other cultural groupings than the traditional White culture, and in particular to the local Kashmiri community. This is not a matter of blame for those directly involved, but a consequence of history, except that the situation has been around now for a very long time. It was not new in 1981, when Lord Scarman made his recommendations. Nor is it confined to the police.

6.17.3. Our overall conclusion had to be that the present basis of policing in an area such as

Manningham was fundamentally flawed, and that the officers whose conduct may now be seen to have been mistaken were having to cope with the consequences of that fundamental flaw. In Manningham, and in many other parts of Bradford from which our witnesses came, policing does not carry the confidence, and therefore the consent, of a large proportion of the local community of various backgrounds.

6.17.4.   An Assistant Chief Constable was quoted in the House of Commons on 21 June 1995 by the M.P. for Bradford West, from an article in the Telegraph and Argus:

"There are lots of things that are a matter of frustration for the community there [i.e. Manningham] *including education, employment, and inter-racial tensions. The police are trying to find their way through that. It would be easy to say that the racist police caused the disturbances but there were tensions there anyway that we have to deal with. Loose comments in the press aiming barbs at the police become received wisdom.*

He feared the police could be stereotyped as racist because of one incident, which would be wrong. 'The search for a cause and effect relationship of what happened is too simplistic. There was obviously more to it. It's too simple to point to the arrest of two people and blame the disorder on that. The disaffection of youth generates the sort of scenes we've also seen on the streets of Northumberland and Oxford. We all have to try to find an answer, and the police are only partly responsible. We are one of the few agencies in these areas working hard to maintain control and we get caught in the crossfire when the fuse blows'."

6.17.5.   We agree with what the Assistant Chief Constable is reported as having said. Dividing the world into predetermined large groups of 'baddies' and 'goodies' is unrealistically unhelpful, but we have found it to be regrettably common in Bradford in discussion of several of the important themes we have pursued. The situation is complex; we do acknowledge the existence of *"a set of social conditions which create a predisposition to violent protest"*, to quote Lord Scarman again; we do recognise the scarcity of understanding which is needed to provide an appropriate basis for service provision; but we do not regard a general condemnation of the police as racist to be accurate or helpful.

Previous Experience

6.17.6.   Nevertheless, antagonisms between local young men and the police, based upon a longer memory within the community of inappropriate, unfair, or racist treatment by individual police officers was, in our view, undoubtedly a most powerful motive for the indignation of the Kashmiri community. However wild some of the rumours, the crowds of people of all ages were ready to believe them, to be indignant and angry about them, and to provide at least apparent approbation of the anti-police actions of the violent protesters sufficient, initially, to remove one normal obstacle to the unacceptable behaviour of the violent protesters.

6.17.7.   There is still considerable concern by older and younger members of the Manningham Muslim male community that their strongly held criticisms about police behaviour may be side-stepped as a result of the existence of the other tensions to which the Assistant Chief Constable referred, and which we have also identified in this Report. The Manningham/Toller Report *The Riot Area Reviewed*, commissioned by the Leader of the Council immediately after the disorders, stated:

"Young people from the Manningham/Toller area, including some who were involved, have met with the police, the REC [Racial Equality Council], and attended open meetings held in the community. The young people maintain that policing was the major factor that led to the riots. There have been allegations by local young people that they have been targeted and subject to harassment by the police. It has led to a growing resentment of the police. This was followed by the particular incident which sparked off the weekend riot.

When formulating strategies to improve the social and economic welfare of young people in the Manningham/Toller area, building bridges between the police and the young people as a basis for good community relations is essential.....

...... A survey investigating young people's perspectives of racial prejudice identified that 72.5% believe that they suffer from prejudice from the police amongst other forms of institutional racism"

Reflecting Local Society

6.17.8.   Once again, it is interesting to read what Lord Scarman wrote, in his 1981 Brixton Report:

"5.6. There is widespread agreement that the composition of our police forces must reflect the make-up of the society they serve. In one important respect, at least it does not do so: in the police, as in other important areas of society, the ethnic minorities are very significantly under-represented. The real problem is not that too many members of the ethnic minorities fail to meet the standards for appointment, but that too few apply. .... The reasons most commonly given for lack of interest in a police career were a basic lack of interest in the job, a fear of being alienated from family and friends, and a fear of being ostracised because of colour prejudice within the service ......"

We have found that this inadequate reflection of society, this lack of interest, and these fears, existed in Bradford, in 1995.

"5.13. I therefore recommend that the Home Office, with Chief Officers of Police, and in consultation with Police Authorities and representatives of the ethnic minority communities, conduct an urgent study of ways of improving ethnic minority recruitment into the regular police and of involving the ethnic minorities more in police-related activities such as the Special Constabulary. The object of policy must be that the composition of the police fully reflects that of the society the police serve. Nothing less will suffice. ...."

This *"object of policy"* is still an essential, urgent, priority, in our view.

"5.15. It is unlikely, however, that racial prejudice can be wholly eliminated from the police so long as it is endemic in society as a whole. The destruction of racial prejudice requires a determined and concerted effort throughout society, including an unwavering lead from those in positions of authority in public life and in our major institutions. The police, of course, must make a parallel effort. We cannot rest on the cynical proposition, which I have heard, that, since the police will necessarily reflect social attitudes, racially prejudiced people are bound to be found in their ranks. ...."

6.17.9.   For so long as 'race' is an unintelligently divisive subject in society, we do expect to find racially prejudiced people, in all walks of life, and in all cultures. The current challenge in

Bradford is to minimise the occasions of racial prejudice in this important part of the criminal justice system, to minimise the occasions of misunderstanding which allow racial prejudice to be falsely imputed to the police, and to optimise the effectiveness of the police. All these are matters requiring the participative co-operation of many people beside the police. In short, we must have 'policing by consent'.

Wider Public Concerns

6.17.10.   The conclusion we have reached about the institutional incapacity to provide an appropriate public policing service in the Manningham area is underlined by many of the concerns expressed to us other than in direct relation to the events of the weekend. We have deliberately used the abstract noun 'policing' in relation to these concerns, rather than 'the police', because there is also considerable support for the police force, a realisation of the difficult task police officers are called upon to perform, and a wish for them to do more.

6.17.11.   Even where the criticism of police officers is strongest, amongst young people and particularly amongst young people from the ethnic minorities, the initial general accusation of the police being 'heavy' or 'racist' is often tempered by a subsequent acknowledgement that they are not all so. Some of the 'community leaders' who have been involved in discussions with the police, when there have been difficult situations to confront in the past, were surprised at the strength of feeling which was so obvious at the time of the disorders, and their obvious anti-police content, recalling the sensible management of previous tensions which had been achieved.

6.17.12.   The particular concerns about which we heard in relation to the police can be grouped under four headings. We put them in quotation marks to emphasise that they are allegations, not necessarily our conclusions:

1.   "In relation to the disorders, the following questions were asked, or were implied:

Were the police heavy handed?

Why should there have been any negotiations?

Why did the police not follow the advice of the "community representatives" on the Friday and Saturday?

Why did the police not deal more rigorously with the trouble-makers during the disorders?

Why were more trouble-makers not charged?

Why were charges later abandoned?

Why was the city centre not better defended?"

We have covered the facts raised by these questions about the disorders in Section 4 above, and we do not deal with them further here.

6.17.13.   2.   "The design of Lawcroft House, the Toller Divisional Police Station, is a threatening example of the gulf deliberately placed by the police between themselves and the local citizens";

3.   "The police are not concerned about people";

4.   "The police are not sufficiently active to deal effectively with the level of crime".

We now deal with these outstanding headings.

6.18   Lawcroft House

6.18.1.   Lawcroft House is the Divisional Police Headquarters of the Toller Division. It was built and opened in 1994. The yard on the Heaton Road end is protected by a high solid stone wall which, at its lowest, is approximately the same height as the ground floor ceiling of the police station itself, rising with the slope of the ground to the approximate height of the first floor ceiling. It is broken by an emergency exit gateway, but presents a most intimidating aspect to the passer-by. We have heard incessant criticism of the design of this police station because of this wall, and it certainly reinforces the pre-existing adverse views of police practices and attitudes held by local people.

6.18.2.   It is nicknamed 'kila' – 'the Fort' by local people. One local White man's equally imaginative description was *"It looks like the Bastille"* ! The only exception to this local criticism which we heard was from a group of Asian women who live in Manningham, and who were unanimous in their favourable opinion of the building!

6.18.3.   In the House of Commons on 21 June 1995 the local M.P. gave voice to this criticism. He said:

"Lastly, we need to ask about the brief given to the architect for the building of the expensive new police station in the Toller division. If the brief was to build a fortress or a castle to give out the wrong signals – to suggest that there is an army that is sent out from behind high walls to quell local trouble – the architect succeeded. The police station, by its design, gives out entirely the wrong signals to the local community."

In fact, the wall merely contains garages and a car park, and frequent public tours are now encouraged by the police to discourage any sinister connotations.

6.18.4.   Three factors are said to have influenced the architectural design of this perimeter wall (which was not the subject of adverse comment on the lines we have indicated during the public processes of obtaining planning permission). The first factor, we were told, was the existence on the proposed site of the Lister's Mill former dam, the stones from the wall of which were re-used to form the new wall. The second was the proximity of a stone-built Victorian School building and the massive stone-built (and listed) Lister's Mill buildings, the latter being directly opposite the proposed police station. The third was the slope of the land.

6.18.5.   We can understand the influence of these three proper factors, but we, too, dislike the domineering and fortress-like result. We understand why an adverse public reaction to a public service building with a wall such as this should exist so strongly. However, given the lack of equal protection afforded to other parts of the site in the new construction, we do not consider that there was a secret conspiracy to provide a fortress-like structure. Of much greater significance is the existence of suspicion which gives rise to such widely, and strongly, held reactions. If a beefburger chain were ever to take the building over, we doubt if the wall would get a second glance!

6.19   Concern about People

Racist Police Officers

6.19.1.   We first must refer to our findings in relation to the disorders, which we have already rehearsed, and which are also at the heart of this allegation. We have written above that we do not regard police officers, in general, as 'racist'. That there are some police officers who are 'racist', and who cannot see the need for even elementary courtesy and consideration in dealing with the city's multi-ethnic population, is also very clear, and their repeated bad behaviour has a far greater impact, like all bad news, than does the routine good policing. As one elderly Asian man, who has served Bradford with great commitment over many years, put it:

"How can I have respect for the policeman who calls me a 'Paki bastard', and Whites 'Sir' ?"

We are satisfied that such officers do not reflect the policies of the Chief Constable and the Police Authority.

Regrettable Experiences

6.19.2.   In this subsection of our Report we now refer to some of those who told us of their experiences of the police. One very responsible Kashmiri young man told us:

"Our elders teach us to respect the law. But there is very little policing on the street. They [the police] are not visible. There is no connection between the community and police officers. Nor are there good visible role models who relate to the community. The only experience most people have of the police is when there is a problem."

6.19.3.   Because the police are White dominated, and inadequately related to the people in areas of Asian settlement, they often reflect an ignorance of other cultures in unconsciously offensive attitudes, which are nonetheless regrettable. In other cases the rudeness is not capable of rational explanation, though there may be a doubt whether the behaviour is exclusive to dealing with people of a different ethnic background: White people can suffer from police rudeness, too. In the following examples, chosen to give a range from the examples quoted to us, the persons concerned had all been deeply affronted, whatever the explanation for the police behaviour.

6.19.4.   We heard of a young Asian man, born and educated in Bradford, a graduate, being told in an uncontroversial conversation with a police officer:

*"In **British** law .... In **this** country ......"*

In addressing a general readership, we ourselves have found it difficult to avoid such expressions. They are not inherently wrong, but they need to be used with care in personal discussions.

6.19.5.   More seriously, we have heard from several police officers, of differing cultural backgrounds, about a racist 'canteen culture', which may often be no more than a consequence of ignorance, but nonetheless is unconstructive, divisive, and hurtful. We do not shrink from saying that it is unprofessional.

6.19.6.   An older resident from Garfield Avenue told us:

"In 1965 the police were so good. Now the police have youngsters who don't know how to deal with coloured people. Half of them don't like us. Some, a few, are very good. You can feel they don't like you."

6.19.7.   One non-Pakistani Asian community representative made clear his community's acceptance of the rule of UK law, and the need to punish those who broke it.

"The community therefore have to trust the police to be as professional in their activities as they were confident in doctors. We do difficult jobs and have to take responsibility. I am willing to put my trust in independent police, and so do most people. This demands in return exemplary behaviour by police at all times. I am sorry to say this does not happen. It is the view of our Society that there are very many bad policemen."

6.19.8.   He went on to state that this was not necessarily because the police were racist, although some clearly were. Generally, he thought the police were very bad at answering the telephone – they showed no sympathy, no sense of an emergency, and seemed to have a general lack of interest in the situation and concern for the person making the call. If the contact was at a police station:

" 'B...r off and claim from your insurance, if you are not hurt', is the attitude."

6.19.9.   On the street, the police often *"made a meal"* out of a situation, instead of being tactful. The experience of his community was that

"We used to regard the police as friends. Now, they worry – what am I going to be done for?"

6.19.10.   A police officer told us:

"Too many police regard 'immigrants' as ignorant. I cringe at how some of my colleagues treat them as nincompoops. The result is suspicion, unfairness, and mistrust. It is amazing how little most police officers know, even about how to address people."

6.19.11.   We were told by one non-Muslim Asian cultural group of an insensitive police response to an incident in which they had asked for protection when attacked by a gang of youths at a communal festival, but were treated as *"nuisances"*, indistinguishable by the police from the gang of another Asian cultural background who, they said, were the aggressors.

6.19.12.   Recently, a young Kashmiri man, well known to all three members of the Commission, accidentally reversed into the stationary car behind him whilst parking his car in Bradford. The other car was unattended, and the young man was conscious he had caused minor damage to its number plate. He wrote its registration number on the back of his hand, and came to our meeting. When he came out the other car had gone. He then went to the local police station to enquire how to trace the owner of the other car. The police officer at the public reception desk, to whom he spoke, at first refused to assist and, when the young man persisted, the police officer threatened a charge of failing to report the accident! Only with great persistence did the young man achieve the advice he was so properly seeking.

Another Side

6.19.13.   We should counter this rather bleak catalogue by repeating something told to us by a resident near the Infirmary, who saw policemen held in reserve on the Saturday afternoon of the disorders informally playing cricket with local youths as the policemen waited to respond to any trouble. Even in the tense situation of that weekend, common sense and decency kept breaking through. We have also met police officers who are working hard to eradicate professionally inappropriate behaviour by police officers.

6.19.14.   In West Bowling there have been outbreaks of violent public disorders by young men, though nothing on the scale of the 'Manningham Riots'. The record given to us by local people referred to such incidents in July 1989, November 1992, July 1994, November 1995, and December 1995. There may be lessons to learn in terms of the different levels of community organisation and, from what we were told, the more knowledgeable police responses, which existed in this different geographical community.

6.19.15.   There is a strong feeling that police attitudes to members of minority groups have been very different in different areas of the city. Police attitudes prior to the disorders were seen as much more 'hard line', and dismissive, in the Toller Division, which includes Manningham, than would have happened in Central Division, or in Odsal Division which includes West Bowling. One of the organisers of the West Bowling Youth Initiative was, for instance, quoted in the Yorkshire Post of 5 September 1995 in the following terms:-

"The police [in Toller] *were seen as the root cause of the trouble, but in this area we have a direct, face to face relationship with a local inspector, and this enables any potential problems to be nipped in the bud...."*

6.20   'Insufficient Activity'

Equality Before the Law

6.20.1.   Few are likely to argue with the principle that 'Equality before the Law' is a basic necessity for a harmonious society. There were many people who complained that the police, in practice, do not observe this principle. The attack came from opposing sides – from those Whites who thought that the police were *"soft"*, and *"turned a blind eye"*, when incidents involving Asian youths were drawn to their attention, and also from members of several ethnic minority groups who thought that the police treated them as second-class citizens, as stupid, and assumed them to be criminal.

6.20.2.   One former policeman, long retired, claimed that many police officers who spoke to him were *"fed up"* at instructions to be *"sensitive"* where *"race"* might be a factor. As a result, youths were becoming arrogant, and had little fear of the law. He gave us several examples from his own observations in the inner city .

6.20.3.   It is tempting to say that since the police are criticised from opposing directions they must be getting it just about right. We resist the temptation, not only because these views were so strongly held, but also because they were based on relevant personal experiences of apparently reliable people, and because we could see how both sets of accusations could exist simultaneously. We could also see some explanations, based on propriety (e.g. lack of evidence), or sound operational priorities (e.g. arising from lack of sufficient manpower), as to why the police sometimes have to behave as they do, to the disappointment of members of the public.

Timeliness of Response

6.20.4.   A group of inner city headteachers told us:

"police response times are inadequate and support from the community constable is not consistent due to a number of factors, in particular 'shift patterns'.

Relations with the police are low because of the operational priorities of the service.

... there is a high level of youth crime in the area."

6.20.5.   Again and again the difficulty of getting a timely response from the police has been raised with us, in terms of delay in getting through on the telephone to someone who could deal intelligently with the subject matter, and in terms of an adequate response by way of immediate action. Judging by what we were told, if a situation was not life threatening it was a common experience that an immediate response was not possible, even where a serious crime like housebreaking or drug dealing was being witnessed by the caller.

6.20.6.   Where there is delay in responding to an appeal for help from an Asian or African Caribbean source, the cause is often put down by the caller to racist indifference. When we heard of a delay of one and a half hours in responding to a telephoned message from an African Caribbean business man that an armed gang robbery was taking place at his premises, we could understand why.

6.20.7.   Some of the complaints of delay were about experiences which happened some time ago, and the police may have since improved their responsiveness, e.g., by the formation of 'help desks' at Divisional HQs. But some complaints were recent, and we understand from the police that these problems arise not just because of lack of officers.

6.20.8.   The police equipment for receiving telephone calls, chosen on the advice of external experts, has been found unsuited to the needs of Bradford's police work in practice, acting as a barrier to communication rather than as a bridge, but the cost of replacement is daunting, the police told us. We can only register the deep dissatisfaction of so many citizens who have thought that they were being responsible in reporting something they thought important, and who could not understand what appeared to be the lack of seriousness with which the police responded. Dealing with this particular root of the problem will have to wait until the priorities of an already overstretched, Government limited, police budget permit. In the meantime, there are other roots to the problem which can be dealt with.

Public Disorder

6.20.9.   The following quotations are taken from the T&GWU paper previously referred to in paras 5.14.7 and 5.21.8.

".......... On most occasions the police do not take any action whatsoever ....

Once an assault has been reported the question of prosecution arises. In the majority of cases the police are informed either when the assault occurs or, if not then, when the report is made (cases of spitting are no longer reported as the police refuse to make any record of the incident.........)

We do know that the police may charge an offender with Common Assault, however, we still have to experience this in Bradford. The alternative is for the victim to take out a private prosecution, however, without the benefits of professional police detection and identification procedures, there is very little opportunity for success. It is no wonder that Bus Workers feel aggrieved at the lack of support provided by the Police Force.

The nature of many assaults, a blow struck from a passenger as they alight, means that it is difficult for the police to trace and apprehend an assailant. This low level of apprehension may also contribute to the feeling by Bus Workers, that not enough is being done to protect them....

However, if an assailant is caught, the police may charge the alleged offender, in most cases, with Assault, however, most incidents are considered by the police as Common Assault, and the Driver would be informed of the options available through a private action, and that the police do not take action on such occasions.

This is a complete contradiction to the views of the Crown Prosecution Service, who have assured us, that they would take action in circumstances where a person providing a Public Service has been attacked, while carrying out their normal duties....

Bradford's Bus Workers have suffered more assaults than any other city outside London, and although 50% of the work force are of Asian Culture, there is very little evidence, that the increasing number of incidents are a result of racial tension.

It would be wrong to say that on some occasions the attacks are not racially motivated, however, this is only a very small percentage of the overall total."

6.20.10.   Much of the concern expressed by members of the public was about the marked deterioration in the quality of urban life as a consequence of the quantity of unchecked minor crimes, ranging from foul or insulting language, or obstruction of the footway, through vandalism or petty theft, to minor motoring offences. Their view was that because these minor crimes were not dealt with adequately, even when reported, more serious crimes were attempted, and respect for the enforcement of the law decreased. In the Manningham area specifically, there was a view that a sense of arrogant invincibility to discipline by the law held by a relatively small but significant number of youths was now far worse than before the disorders.

Drugs

6.20.11.   A resident in one area of the inner city told us:

"I have seen drug buying and selling, but the police were not doing anything although they know who is doing it. If anyone helped the police and the drug dealers know – he has had it and the police cannot protect them. The police must keep information confidential or all the family gets into trouble."

We made reference to the extent of drug dealing in Bradford in subsection 5.23, and the above quotation fairly represents the views we were frequently given.

Open Discussion

6.20.12.   We strongly suggest that the police at all times should be more open with the public about the constraints within which they operate, so that public criticisms, which are important both individually and as comments on general policy, become better informed by an understanding of public financial policies, legal requirements, and priorities. This would also enable more focussed criticism of improper or ineffective performance. We have rarely found that the police have explained their situation successfully to local people. We have found much criticism of the police to be ill informed and generalised, with the danger that criticism which has some substance becomes easier to ignore.

6.20.13.   We were told by one politician who has been closely involved with police matters, though not speaking officially, that *"minor crime is not a police matter"*, and that *"police intervention in a Public Order situation is usually counterproductive"*. Neither of these assertions is as daft as it at first seems, and they both need public discussion.

6.20.14.   Is the involvement of scarce, highly trained professionals justified by minor crime? If it is not, then what is the alternative? It is the de facto adoption of the answer 'No' to the first of these questions, without the development of an adequate answer to the second, which has justifiably caused people to say that the police have ceded control of the streets for most of the time, and when they do intervene it is as strangers to the people of the area. Hence, the counterproductivity which was seen at the time of the disorders.

6.20.15.   We are aware of the urgings of the Audit Commission that the police need to move away from the known public preference for 'visible policing', in order to achieve greater impact on the more serious crimes, and the benefit of doing so is apparent in the Toller Division's serious crime statistics. Here, we are at the heart of the policy dilemma: the public, rightly in our view, attach importance to visible policing as an essential part of policing by consent; but visible policing does not make the impact which the public also rightly desire on the detection of the many serious crimes committed by the few serious criminals in any given area.

6.20.16.   We have also been made aware of some of the difficulties of providing policing by consent in the Bradford of today. Many of these difficulties, such as funding and related manpower and equipment restrictions, lack of public cooperation in providing evidence, or the distancing, which professionalism requires, of officers from possible sources of inappropriate pressures, are not peculiar to Bradford.

6.20.17.   What is peculiar to Bradford is the significance of its population's particular ethnic mix, with a pace of social change which emphasises for the foreseeable future the practical importance of dealing with people of different background cultures appropriately in order to provide a proper level of service to the city .

6.20.18.   It is plain to us that much more is needed than the Police Forums, to bridge the gaps which exist between police and local people. We make the same comment about what is perceived, when it is perceived at all, as an impotent Police Authority, about the useful but limited contacts between senior police officers and community representatives, and about what Lord Scarman called *"separate box[es] labelled 'community relations'"*, which have been the current formal methods of bridging. As an exasperated leading member of the Pakistani communities put it to us:

"We have had Forums all our lives. We want better relations with the police, and they should be fair and honest and polite."

6.20.19.   One Muslim organisation was particularly scathing of the Police Forums. Their view of them was that a few people went there regularly to criticise the police, and the police went there to defend themselves. There was a bureaucratically correct procedure, but a lack of constructive discussion and follow up. In the meeting we had with this organisation it seemed to be a general view that, as one member put it:

> *"the problem lies at constable level. We discuss with the higher ups but they don't, or can't, put their house in order."*

6.21   Need for Policing by Consent

6.21.1.   We have set out the above complaints, and given them prominence, because we cannot emphasise sufficiently the extent of the public concern about policing which we heard. We recognise that the police do not deliberately set out to disappoint the public. We know that there are often reasons and pressures why the police have to act as they do. Nevertheless, we warn that public confidence in the present policing arrangements is not strong. Active steps must urgently be taken to make good the large deficit in meeting reasonable public expectations, which the near monopoly of policing by an extremely expensive professional force dictates at a time when public funds are restricted.

6.21.2.   Leaving aside the undoubted existence of individual racist police officers and an organisational ethos which is only slowly adjusting to an intelligent appreciation of minority cultures (as is the case with other public services and the White community generally), our criticisms of policing lead us to press for a much more radical examination of the options that are available to bridge the widening gap between the professional Police Service and the needs perceived by the citizens of Bradford. If the gap is not bridged, the basis of *"policing by consent"* will be destroyed. The alternative options, of opportunist self help and/or a breakdown in public order, are both unacceptable.

6.21.3.   We are confident that these challenges are increasingly realised by the most senior police officers, and that operational arrangements are constantly being improved by Divisional Commanders. We have noted with approval a number of local initiatives taken by various police officers. As with the challenge in Education, we see a need for more open and focussed political discussion, and clearer political accountability for actually achieving measurable results in the practical, city-wide, strategies which are needed to realise *"policing by consent"* in Bradford.

6.22   Police Responses

Building Bridges

6.22.1.   One Bradford ethnic minority group wrote to us in relation to the disorders:

> *"The Asian community has built up a very good working relationship with the police authorities and we believed that sort of approach* [the handling of the original events in Garfield Avenue on 9 June 1995] *by them was a thing of the past."*

6.22.2.   The following quotation is taken from a 1994 *"Background"* section of a police paper describing a local police initiative:

"In January 1993 Bradford Central Division increased its operational area to encompass the much larger residential area [of X]

This has brought about a large variety of policing problems, including a high proportion of juvenile crime and incidents of stoning of police and other emergency vehicles.

This has highlighted the need for police to integrate more and to develop their understanding of the problems associated with living in an inner city area. In turn, residents need to look to the future. In Central Division's area this means local Asian communities and in particular the youth within that community. They will be the investment for the future.

It is therefore essential that the two parties form a co-operative role and not a confrontational one..... Otherwise there will be a deterioration in the quality of life and the loss of Law and Order is inevitable....

Whilst there is no large problem currently, trends tend to suggest that there is a potential for future unrest amongst the Asian Youth. This is indicated by drug dealing, shootings, armed robberies, and damaged police vehicles, all involving Asian youths aged from their late teens to early twenties. Of course, there is no suggestion that this is merely confined to the Asian population."

6.22.3.   In the Toller Division efforts have continued to be made to involve the police more deeply in the life of the local community, and some initiatives have been particularly aimed at Asian youth. We were particularly impressed by an Action Plan prepared by the Toller Lane Division in January 1996

"to improve the communication links between the police and the young people of the Toller Lane area of Bradford"

and we find its basic analysis is often parallel to our own:

"The key effects seen as emanating from the present situation were identified in brief as:

- *Lack of Trust/Confidence – both Asian youngsters towards the police and the police towards Asian youngsters.*

- *Outbreaks of Disorder – serious and minor*

- *High Crime Rate*

- *Poor Quality of Life*

- *Low Representation of Officers from the Ethnic Minorities.*

To combat and resolve these it would be necessary, in the first stage, to create an atmosphere which will lead to a better understanding and avoid misconceptions.

The causes of the aforementioned were identified as:

- *Lack of understanding – both ways*

- *No existing arena to begin communication*

- *High density of population*

- *Drugs*
- *Vice Issues*
- *High Unemployment*
- *Poor quality housing*
- *Perceptions (correct and incorrect)*

Many of these are matters over which the police have little or no direct influence. It was decided that three areas would be selected where the most effect and influence could be envisaged, with the intention of making some change...."

6.22.4.   This analysis follows many years of attemps to build a better relationship between the local police and the local community. The need for such a relationship is also openly accepted by at least some people in the local community. We have already quoted several relevant remarks. At a public meeting held in Manningham early in 1996 there was the following exchange between three Asian members of the public:

Mr. A: *"In my opinion community policing is not as it should be. The community police should know all of the residents but do not appear to. It would help if the police were trained in the community more than they are at the moment."*

Mr. B: *"We are not here to defend the police and as the police are by nature cynical because of their job it is perhaps unfortunate that in riot situations they will not always act correctly. You should be aware that some police officers have been sent to Pakistan to assist in their learning about how to deal with communities but what we do not want is for them to bring back to this country the method of crowd control adopted by the police in Pakistan."*

Mr. C: *"There is no one here from the police and we should recognise that the British police are far more lenient than many other police forces in the world. How much do we involve the community constables? How often do we take action to ensure that street lights are repaired, and other things done to assist the community?"*

Mr. A: *"More police are needed who know the community and so if this problem occurs in the future it is much less likely to end in a riot."*

Community policing

6.22.5.   Toller Division reduced its Community Constables from 20 down to 8 over the two years to November 1995, in order to provide more pro-active and carefully focussed policing. The beneficial results can be seen in the statistics quoted at para 6.16.8. The Community Constable for the Oak Lane area remained, however, and, immediately following the disorders, another constable was appointed to the Division's Community Involvement Unit as 'Projects Officer', specifically to work with young people in the Oak Lane/ Manningham area. This Unit includes a Crime Prevention Officer, a Youth Services Officer, and a School Liaison Officer.

6.22.6.   The West Yorkshire Force already invests in formal training in community and race relations, with an extra day's opportunity for probationary constables in Bradford to experience Asian cultures. As is the case in Bradford's public services generally, however, the approach seems to be more an attempt to explain peculiar variations from the norm, to almost exclusively White trainees, rather than the building up of an intelligent team approach to working with the various groups who constitute the Bradford public. Certainly, in one or two key instances, we were not favourably impressed by the practical results of the training; the superficial knowledge gained seemed dangerously thin.

Recruitment

6.22.7.   The police informed us:

> *"In June 1995, Toller Lane Division had an establishment of 171 officers .... 8 officers from minority ethnic backgrounds (this is 4.67% of the strength – the West Yorkshire percentage being 2.06%)."*

Reference back to para 6.16.6 shows that if the establishment were numerically representative (a crude comparison we use to make a simple but important point) the Toller Division's population would mean an Asian strength of 32% compared with the actual 4.67%. Given Lord Scarman's warning in 1981, this is unacceptable performance by the Police Authority – unless the advice of Lord Scarman has been rejected on an occasion, and for reasons, of which we are unaware.

> *"Three officers were of Pakistani origin (1 Detective Sergeant and 2 Constables); two were of black Caribbean origin (both Constables); two were Indian origin (both Constables) and 1 other ethnic origin (Constable)."*

> *"At present, Toller Lane has a 13 strong Special Constabulary. This is made up of 10 male officers of which 6 are Asian (including the section officer and his deputy), 4 are White and 3 are female (2 Asian and 1 White)."*

6.22.8.   The recruitment, promotion and support of police officers from the ethnic minorities in West Yorkshire appears to us to be crucial to the development of appropriate policing within an area like Manningham. It is not sufficient merely to adopt formal policies to this effect.

6.22.9.   There is no doubt that senior police officers do see the need to recruit more entrants to the police service from the Asian communities, but we were told that there is only limited interest from Asians. The entry standards for all applicants are rightly very demanding, and vacancies within the force are few. On present reasonable predictions it will be some considerable time before the local police service is likely to reflect the ethnic mix of the city's population, particularly in the senior ranks, and so to have an innate capacity to relate to all the population.

6.22.10.   The position of the Special Constabulary might, if adapted after research, be more hopeful, and we are aware that its role is already the subject of review. We were, however, disappointed to hear of the experience of one man whose application to join the Specials had taken months for the initial process of selection to begin. We were told by the police that they had been understaffed for the relevant personnel work. We sympathise with both sides of this experience.

6.22.11.   The complaints we received about the reception of both telephone and personal callers raises questions about the appropriateness of training for dealing in a helpful way with the public, and suggests the recruitment of civilians who could help to bridge some of the gaps in understanding.

6.22.12. There are mixed views within some of the Asian communities about the desirability of the police force as a career. In a small group of 8 year olds in a First School we asked about their ambitions. When one boy said he wanted to be a policeman he was immediately rebuked by another:

"No. That is not a nice job."

6.22.13. In the *Telegraph and Argus* of 21 June 1995 was the following report:

"RH has had his heart set on becoming a police officer since he was a child.... And he is applying to become a special before trying to get into the force. R is keen to build links between Asians and the police. Ideally, he would do that here, in Bradford. But, he says: "Theoretically, that's perfect, but it can't be done. It would put me in an awkward position, knowing so many people. I would lose my friends. It could be difficult for my family and myself if I arrested someone we know. I would be sworn at because I'm Asian". He believes the barrier is partly due to traditional beliefs in India and Pakistan where police officers can be held in low regard. R said young Asians fear they will not be promoted in the force, may be picked on by fellow officers, and will lose their friends."

6.22.14. Waiting until the regular or special police forces have recruited, and promoted, a proper reflection of the population cannot, on its own, be an adequate course for meeting the clear present needs of Bradford. Nor is this the only source of alienation. Genuine *"policing by consent"* requires an effective system of political and professional accountability to ensure that progress is achieved by monitoring a range of measures.

6.23 The Local Community's Responsibilities

Supplementing the Professional Police

6.23.1. In a democracy, and with a dominant principle of policing by consent, the expensive and professional police officers represent only a part (albeit the most effective part) of the community's policing arrangements. Another part, though at the other extreme of expertise, is an increasingly anxious law abiding majority of the population who wish to see the law observed, but who presently often find the professional police unresponsive and unavailable. In between are the Specials, and the undernourished Neighbourhood Watches.

6.23.2. The money for the extension of traditional responses is not there. How can the non-professional concerns be constructively harnessed? We urge investigation of the possibilities, to the extent of unorthodox experiments and pilot schemes. These alternatives may risk losing some of the advantages of orthodox professionalism. It is for politicians, acting after expert advice has been given, to weigh the balance of advantage to the public.

6.23.3. Such experiments have been forthcoming in other countries with similar problems, we understand. A Canadian arrangement called 'Citizens on Patrol' was particularly drawn to our attention, and it appears to meet at least the obvious requirement of avoiding lawless or provocative vigilantes. In close association with the police this organisation's functions are to patrol designated areas; to record and report suspicious activities and those involved; to remain within the bounds of the law and in full co-operation with the police, observing commitments to training and to confidentiality. Its members have no special powers and do not investigate. We do not go so far as to commend this model, but it represents an approach which should provoke emulation.

6.23.4. We were particularly impressed by the initiative of one inner city Upper School in establishing a previously unknown post of security officer. The testimony of senior staff was that the particular person appointed (who was an African Caribbean dealing frequently with Asian youngsters and their families) had, over a period of five years, made an enormous difference not just to the security of the school, but to the standards of behaviour by pupils in and out of the school. His visits to the homes of pupils were particularly effective. Parents were properly responsive to his reports of their children's misbehaviour. Equally, the children were responsive to the threat of direct parental involvement. We admired his expertise, his dedication, and the initiative of the school. We also noted the advantages of his flexibility of operation. Again, we note the approach as a model for emulation.

6.23.5. We were told that, in the past, one Upper School had paid bus monitors to keep discipline on school buses, but this had been discontinued for financial reasons. It seems a pertinent question to ask how, in making the current arrangements, a balance is struck between the costs of imposing a proper discipline and the costs of not doing so. The fragmented nature of public and quasi public services prevents the question being answered easily.

Public Recognition of the Problem

6.23.6. Although there is widespread general public recognition of inadequate policing, in the form of the complaints which we have received, there appears to be little public discussion about self-help. Again, we are proposing nothing that is new. We emphasise what must have been said many times before – that only when the effects of crime become sufficiently unacceptable to a community that its members are prepared to use the police and other Public Services as a support to their own efforts will a real impact on the problem be possible. The Home Office has published *"A Practical Guide to Crime Prevention For Local Partnerships"* which could be a useful starting point.

The Expression of Public Complaints and Concerns.

6.23.7. There were only 13 formal complaints against the police in the Toller Division, despite the general dissatisfaction we have recorded, during the year prior to the disorders, and none, we were told, had racial overtones. That may be a function of public ignorance of, lack of confidence in, or indifference to, the complaints process. Indeed, given the level of indignation against police treatment of local citizens in Manningham which is one of our findings, it certainly cannot be a reliable indicator.

6.23.8. The local police, the local community, and local politicians, have to ask themselves why a minimal level of formal complaints should precede public disorders which were based upon considerable anger at the attitude of the police towards local people.

6.23.9. The police have made efforts to explain their perceptions and their changing methods in the local Police Forum, but at no time, we were told by the police, has the subject of unsatisfactory relationships with the public been raised in those meetings (although we did find one expression of concern from the Oak Lane area to a **Neighbourhood** Forum in February 1994, that the local police were not building links with the area). As with the formal complaints process, we have to emphasise that the effectiveness of the Police Forum has to be questioned until both local citizens and the local police are satisfied that it represents local opinions effectively.

6.23.10.   It is perhaps indicative of the problems of effective consultation with the different sections of the local community that in December 1994, the Toller Divisional Commander had invited local religious leaders and two detached youth workers, to discuss the provision of premises for facilities for young people in the area. The several churches and the synagogue were represented, and the Imam of one of the mosques attended, but the secretaries of two other mosques did not even reply to the invitation, we were told. Even if the mosques do not consider that they have a relevant role, the large local Muslim communities cannot reasonably complain about police lack of cultural understanding when their distinctive institutions do not respond constructively to police initiatives.

Providing Evidence

6.23.11.   If the concept of policing by consent is to have real meaning it is not good enough to regard crime as exclusively a matter for the police, especially when a dishonest defence is a frequent reaction to a criminal charge. It is difficult for the police to get people to understand the need for witnesses to support a criminal charge with evidence, given the high standard of proof required by the Courts in criminal prosecutions. People who do report crimes to the police are often disappointed that, despite their positive identification of the criminal, no charge is made against that person. They fail to appreciate – indeed they resent – the response of the police that the informant's word alone will be inadequate to overcome a denial by the criminal, and the police are then accused of inadequate response.

6.23.12.   When, as happened recently in inner Bradford, a murder allegedly took place in the presence of many people, but the police had difficulty in getting witnesses, it is difficult to be sanguine about a peaceful city. As one White citizen put it:

"We can only meet each other on equal ground when both sides admit to their rogues."!

In the case of Asian areas the consequences of public failure to volunteer evidence must severely limit a largely White Police Force for the purpose of intelligence gathering.

6.23.13.   It has, we were told, proved difficult to establish 'Neighbourhood Watch' schemes in areas of heavy Asian settlement. In the Toller Police Division there is *"almost Nil"*, according to a police report. But, the report continued:

"One such scheme was recently launched, predominantly Asian in make-up. It came about after residents in a very close-knit community became intolerant of the level of crime and the fact that they saw youths from within the community being responsible, or at risk of becoming involved. Since its launch, links between this community in general, with the police, have grown, with improved communication and trust."

6.23.14.   Unfortunately, the general mistrust of the police makes some responsible Asian leaders reluctant to become more openly involved in helping the police. They feel they will both lose the trust of their community, and be marked out for reprisals by the criminals. If crime is not to flourish leaders will have to consider how they can encourage the people for whom they speak to co-operate more readily with the police.

6.23.15. We should also report that we heard of an Asian father who encouraged his children to stick to their duty to give evidence, despite threats of violence, whose children later suffered badly as a result, and who eventually had to abandon the family house. The outcome in this case was a plea bargain, and a Conditional Discharge, we were told, for the criminals!

Letting the Law take its Course.

6.23.16. One particular set of cultural assumptions which causes suspicion and misunderstanding between the police and the older members of the Asian communities is the proper role of the police in dealing with inter-personal disputes. The traditional way of dealing is for a senior and respected member of the family or local community to attempt to mediate between contending parties. This tradition is clearly rooted in the situation in rural India, Pakistan, or Bangladesh, where there was no ready recourse to the courts for formal methods of resolution.

6.23.17. This can mean that, even in quite serious criminal cases, a third party may talk to a complainant and witnesses, and succeed in persuading the complainant and/or witnesses to drop the complaint or refuse to give evidence, perhaps on payment of compensation to the complainant in recognition of guilt. To the participants, operating on inherited assumptions, it may be a normal, indeed an expected, process. The police, however, see this as corrupt and frustrating, and potentially as criminal interference with the due process of the law. It cannot be wondered at if the police become cautious about pursuing some complaints. The potential for misunderstanding and resentment in these situations is obvious.

6.23.18. There is also an inter-generational problem – when young people brought up in a predominantly 'Western' society are subjected to such an informal process they often resent what they see as unreasonable pressure, even though they may feel obliged to submit to it because of respect for the older generation.

6.23.19. In these circumstances we conclude that the police are unlikely to be able to provide the standard of policing that is normal. That, presumably, is to the detriment of the whole city, since the effects of crime are not merely very local. It is also necessary to point out that such communities cannot at the same time complain that the police are unresponsive to them when they want police help.

Parental Control

6.23.20. Causing trouble in public places begins at an early age. The descriptions we have been given of life for people using streets, buses, parks, etc., in many parts of Bradford, to go about their normal lives, demonstrate an intolerable presence of unruly behaviour by children, some very young, and by youths. Countermeasures are needed, of which the simplest would be greater control, of young boys in particular, by their parents. If this is not done then talk of curfews, and other extreme nationally devised solutions, will continue, and may one day be imposed. The problem is widespread, but our understanding is that many parents often do not know what their sons are doing, rather than that they are indifferent. They, at least, should consider what steps they could take.

Part 3   The Public Services

6.24   Introduction

6.24.1.   In this Part we very briefly relate the considerable amount of material we received about Education and Policing to the much smaller amount of material we received about other public services. We wish to make it clear that we are not confining the definition of 'public services' to those provided by the Bradford Metropolitan District Council.

6.25   A General Problem?

6.25.1.   We are firmly of the view that the failures in the Education and Police services to which we have referred are not just the result of some self-contained individual service ethos peculiar to those services alone. Their institutional incapacity to cope with the very great changes which have developed over the past thirty years in the ethnic mixture of Bradford's population is rooted in the general incapacity of the city to cope. It is extremely unlikely to be the case that this institutional incapacity exists only in the Education and Police services. We have received some evidence which confirms, and none which denies, its existence in other public services, though we were heartened by the TGWU paper referred to in para 5.14.7, in the case of the local bus industry – a former public service.

6.26   Leadership

6.26.1.   We are aware of some leadership, already given in the two services we have emphasised, and in other public services, which is working hard to move on realistically. We are disappointed, however, to find a lack of clear, driving political commitment to making progress in the public services, accompanied by measurable and monitored targets which reflect enthusiasm for the benefits to be gained. The strategic assumption for dealing with a substantial, and growing, proportion of the permanent population seems to be to ignore the significance of the differences except insofar as circumstances enforce recognition. Where recognition is unavoidable, special arrangements – often cosmetic – are then tacked on to the main body of activity in order to look decent (or formally to comply with the law).

6.27   A Secular Basis

6.27.1.   We are firmly of the view that the political objectives of the public services in relation to all the various religiously or ethnically defined 'communities' in Bradford, including the Whites, normally require a strong, undifferentiated, secular basis. Any special **policy** to meet distinctive religious or ethnic claims on public services should be the subject of conscious, careful and open justification.

6.27.2   However, we distinguish clearly between undifferentiated, secular, policy objectives and the need for differentiation in the practical implementation of policy. Attempts to justify so-called 'positive action' can themselves be divisive, yet so much that is called 'positive action' is no more than the application, in the particular circumstances of ethnic or other minorities, of a normal individual differentiation to meet the circumstances of the users of a public service in the implementation of general policies. Knowledge-based understanding of how to make a general policy work most effectively in relation to the people directly involved is preferable to the ineffectiveness caused by ignorance and reluctance.

6.27.3.   We are, therefore, decrying a wooden and unsympathetic uniformity to the delivery of public services which ignores legitimate differences. We have already illustrated this point with reference to the standard duty of the council to make Education

"available to meet the needs of the population ..." (Education Act 1944; see para 6.2.1.)

6.27.4.   Similarly, we have advocated a standard need for 'policing by consent', which in turn requires special implementation to meet local circumstances. If all public service users and recipients were to be standardised in order to receive identical services then the whole nation must prepare for a considerable shock! The conceptual framework which we suggest, to minimise unnecessary friction about meeting different needs, is simply that an equal emphasis on matching the agreed common standard of service appropriately to an individual's, or a locality's, needs should be made in each case.

6.27.5.   A Service provided in a particular locality should obviously take into account the needs and preferences of the particular people living there. A particular Service's general policies should be implemented in accordance with the distinguished needs of a particular group of people, e.g. the provision of large print books, or with the needs of a family, e.g. the size of accommodation, or with the needs of an individual, e.g. adaptations for a physically handicapped person living at home.

6.27.6.   In just the same way, a policy to provide school meals properly should take into account the religious, medical, and cultural background of the recipients. Providing Halal meat is in no different category than providing vegetarian food in a restaurant for those who cannot eat the meat normally provided. If the purpose of a service is to nourish schoolchildren, there is little point in providing meat that they cannot, for whatever reason, eat.

6.28   Communication

An Old Lesson

6.28.1.   Appropriate services cannot be delivered unless effective communication is seen as of first importance. The inappropriateness of Service Delivery is not a new subject. As with every part of our Report we are repeating lessons already learnt in particular circumstances, but not examined for more general application. In January 1994 the Bradford West Area Panel considered a report by its Co-ordinator and, as a result, a follow up study was commissioned into the dissatisfaction of Asian residents with the council's services in Girlington, which was much greater than amongst White residents. It needs to be remembered that the term 'ethnic minority' is a misnomer when applied to Asian in most of Girlington. The dissatisfaction was of a majority of the majority of residents. The follow up report, *Service Delivery and Service Quality in Girlington – A Perspective from the Pakistani Community* was published in September 1994.

6.28.2.   The report of the Area Co-ordinator on the research report took seriously the point we wish to emphasise for more general observance:

> *"...It was felt that it would be inappropriate to conduct another survey ..... as the survey method of research is too structured to allow the researcher to explore attitudes and beliefs in great detail. ..... It was thought that the type of information collected from residents taking part in these interviews would offer a much more meaningful insight into their feelings and attitudes towards the Council. ..."* (at 3.0).

It would be surprising that direct involvement of users should need to be suggested, were it not that we have found it fairly standard practice not to consult with service users other than by inappropriately formal ways.

6.28.3.   The same lesson was given in a publication by QED:

> *"QED achieves its mission by accurately defining the needs of ethnic people, targeting priority groups and implementing specific programmes of action..... In Enterprise development we are confronting the problems of the Asian business community, who make little use of mainstream agencies which provide advice and help. The problem is two sided. Mainstream agencies have an inadequate understanding of the needs and cultural background of Asian business people who, in turn, have low awareness of the services. "*

6.28.4.   The Girlington research indicated that:

> *"Not many people had complained to the Council although there were many occasions when householders wanted to complain but had no knowledge of the Council's complaints procedure."*

The research revealed that some were unsure whether their complaint would be acted upon; others did not want to *"rock the boat"*; the few who were working did not have the time.

6.28.5.   The Area Co-ordinator's report continued:

> *"This research .... has identified a lot of dissatisfaction with Council services amongst the Pakistani community in Girlington. Some of the problems faced by these residents may also be pertinent to ethnic minority communities in other parts of Bradford. This research has highlighted that a lot of improvements need to be made to the way in which Council services are delivered. These improvements will have implications for the way Council services are delivered not only in Girlington but throughout the Bradford District."* (at 4.0).

6.28.6.   The Co-ordinator's report had some pertinent recommendations to make on *"Communications"*: more English teaching facilities for adults; an Urdu/Punjabi speaker to provide a telephone 'Helpline'; a network of male and female 'Information Contacts' to pass on information to other residents, especially those who were illiterate; research about languages used and understood; etc. We were particularly pleased to note the understanding of the report about the strength of oral, rather than written, communication for many people, paralleling our own experience in communicating our desire to hear from all sections of the Bradford public. Translating official messages into officially recognised community languages is a significant, and expensive, gesture, but it is not communication in many cases.

6.28.7.   We understand that some progress has been made in implementing the recommendations, and a review of progress is planned.

"Some of the findings of this research has resource implications. However, a lot can be achieved by resource rationalisation and targetting of resources .... in response to the identified needs ...."

A Practical Example

6.28.8.   One important aspect of life in Manningham which was raised with us occasionally, though it has little bearing on the disorders, was that of the uncleanliness of the back streets. This was readily apparent to us as we became familiar with the area. One immediate source of the litter was burst bin bags.

6.28.9.   The Council has a basic duty under the Environmental Protection Act 1990 to arrange for the collection of household waste within its area free of charge. It is a duty going back to the establishment of the Victorian Public Health standards which we now take for granted and, of course, there are more detailed statutory provisions governing the discharge of this duty. It would not, however, be an appropriate fulfilment of that standard duty to ignore the consequences of the larger number of people who live in, or visit, many Asian households, or the greater vegetable, but lesser packaging content, we were told that the household refuse from many Asian homes contains, and to treat every house in the District as a standard unit with a standard volume entitlement. The common (and legally required) standard of service is to remove household refuse; the actual service needed will vary.

6.28.10.   According to the Girlington Survey reported to the Area Panel in September 1994, part of the problem about bin bags was the failure of the Refuse Collection Service to communicate clearly to local Asian householders the circumstances in which household refuse is collected. We understand that this deficiency has now been recognised, though we hope that it will not be left to men exclusively to decide on appropriate arrangements for the disposal of household refuse which is, within a household, the traditional responsibility of the women.

6.28.11.   The manner, rather than the matter, of discussion of this and similar subjects certainly needs diplomacy. The fundamental reasons for the general untidiness appear to be a lack of awareness of many local people of their civic responsibility to prevent the spoiling of public places, and in part an inability to organise a voluntary, collective, response to a common local problem. In relation to the first reason, which is believed by many people not from such areas to be the only reason, the lack of awareness needs to be addressed openly, instead of being stifled by fears of causing offence.

6.28.12.   But in relation to the second reason there was an encouragingly constructive response of local people recorded in the Girlington survey, and an encouraging extent to which young boys and girls were growing up conscious of the offensiveness of litter, graffiti, and pollution. In our visits to Manningham schools such reactions were often volunteered, and we realised the value of the now discontinued initiative which had funded a youth worker to concentrate on this topic. Once more we make the point that ignorant stereotyping of large groups of people deprives public policy making of a realistic basis.

6.28.13.   It seems to us that this interesting Girlington study is a valuable pointer to what the proper delivery of public services should mean in Bradford. Its implications are of major political significance, and that is the subject of the next Section of our Report. We have taken the subject of Communication seriously in considering how the contents of this Report should be communicated. The Report is lengthy, complex, and difficult to read, despite our efforts to make its main messages clear. We have therefore emphasised the need for the Congress to consider very carefully the practicalities of communicating effectively the messages of this Report to the public, in Section 8.

6.29   Time to Think Again

6.29.1.   The city council has, over two decades, sought to adapt to the needs of the newer cultural groups the services which it provides. It has devolved some decision-making to Area Panels. It has sought to increase the number and influence of advisory officers from these groups. All of this deserves praise for the general intention, and the achievements. What we fail to see, in the council's and other public services, is an adequate driving through of the logic that public services are there to fulfil general objectives, but they will only achieve their objectives if their managers are capable of understanding the people they serve.

6.29.2.   We are concerned not to be critical of the past, so much as to be constructive about the future. We suggest that it is time, indeed it is overdue, for a major reappraisal of the appropriateness of the services provided in a multi-ethnic city by all public service providers.

6.29.3.   Bradford has come through the stage of pretending that nothing much needed to change in response to substantial immigration. That ended in the 1970s and 1980s. We are coming through the stage of conscious 'sensitivity' towards ethnic minority cultures by almost entirely White controlled services and politics. We need now to move as rapidly as possible to public services in which members of all ethnic communities are realistically represented in the consideration of direction and operations, and in which the same standards of service are knowledgeably provided to meet different requirements in the specific situations of Bradford as it is and as it will be.

6.29.4.   In the public services which have been drawn to our attention the established ways of doing things exert too strong a drag on those within them who are striving hard to meet current and future needs in realistic ways. Brave objectives are not being set. It is time to think again.

Section 7

Local Politics and Self-Government

7.1 Terminology

7.1.1. We have chosen the title of this Section, and avoided the use of the term 'local government', to distance our paragraphs from sole linkage with the council of the Metropolitan District and its organisation, and we have throughout this Report used the word 'politics' in its basic sense of 'the affairs of the city and its citizens'. Even where we have referred to local government organisations like the council, or the Police Authority, readers should understand that Central Government is heavily influential in their apparently independent activities. It is a curious but unavoidable fact that Central Government is now the most powerful actor in local governance.

7.1.2. We have been concerned to avoid direct involvement in current 'Party politics', which is a particular, though highly organised and dominant, way of informally influencing the making of decisions by local political bodies, of which the local council is the most democratically significant. But we are not so naive as to think that our comments will have no Party political resonances. It is inevitable that they will. We simply ask that readers accept that we have not applied our minds to what those resonances might be, and so they have not influenced us in writing our Report.

7.2 An Unflattering Description

7.2.1. It will already be apparent from our Report that we are very concerned about two fundamental political problems:

1. Bradford citizens' mutual ignorance about each other (mainly Section 5 above); and

2. Bradford public services' institutional incapacity to relate properly to all the different needs of the people they are obliged to serve (mainly Section 6 above).

7.2.2. In this Section we add two more criticisms which have been repeatedly drawn to our attention:

3. 'The failure of the local political system to prioritise the most important problems to be tackled, from out of a very long list of highly desirable projects and politically sensitive present expenditures'; and

4. 'The failure of the local political system to reflect public concerns which are so strongly and widely held that they ought to be obvious candidates for purposeful political consideration.'

7.2.3. A leader of one of the smaller Asian cultural groups, repeating representations made to us by people from all backgrounds, pleaded that we would raise, in our Report, the fundamental issues underlying Bradford's current problems, so that the many concerned people who are unwilling to become involved in what they see as the silliness of the present knee-jerk formal Party political culture can become involved in sensible discussion.

'Our elected leaders don't have a vision. They are only in it for the prestige. Which political leader is thinking about 2011? Councillors are only thinking about the next elections".

7.2.4.   This unflattering description, we consider, contains enough substance to require us to examine it in more detail. We now examine the two outstanding criticisms, numbers 3 and 4, just mentioned.

Part 1. Deciding Priorities

7.3   Introduction

7.3.1.   Criticism number 3 was 'The failure of the political system to prioritise the most important problems to be tackled, from out of a very long list of highly desirable projects and politically sensitive present expenditures.'

7.3.2.   Lord Scarman, in his Report on the Brixton Riots in 1981, wrote:

"6.5. The failure of many attempts over the last three decades to tackle the problem of inner city decline successfully is striking. The proportion of national resources devoted to resolving the problem is clearly an important consideration: but it is noticeable that large sums have been spent to little apparent effect. The underlying national economic decline is no doubt one important reason ....

6.6. There may, however, be other factors. One of these, I suggest, is the lack of an effective co-ordinated approach to tackling inner city problems. ..... conflicting policies and priorities – as between central and local government or between different layers of local government – appear to have been a frequent source of confusion and reduced drive. ...... I conclude that much could be done to achieve a better co-ordinated and directed attack on inner city problems,..."

Once again, there is a striking similarity with the situation in inner Bradford.

7.3.3.   Because the city council has been extremely co-operative and open with our Inquiry, most of this subsection uses examples taken from council activities. The city council is active, often in ways which are taken for granted, throughout the city, and particularly in areas of stress. In making criticisms we intend to be helpful to those who are struggling with the day to day, as well as the longer term, problems of the city and its citizens. It would be inappropriate and unfair to draw critical conclusions about individuals from our Report. The council has to work within a larger system, and individuals have to work within the council's systems.

7.3.4.   The emphasis on the council is not unfair, however, even though we suspect our criticisms should range more widely, since the council is the only local means of expressing democratic choice on local practical matters. Our criticism should be set against the many achievements in ad hoc urban regeneration which stand to the credit of the council and, more recently, of its partners in the Congress. There have been many successful bids made for the central funds which have been on offer. Not having a clear strategy, which is the essence of the criticism in this Part 1, does not mean that nothing is being done.

7.4   A Public Begging Bowl Culture

7.4.1.   From Bradford city council's viewpoint, as the economy of the city has worsened, the freedom of the council to spend money has been increasingly restricted, and in recent years the contribution of future central grants and permissions to spend has become ever more uncertain. We make no direct comment on the desirability of this position, but we do not detect any sign that it will change in the foreseeable future; more importantly, nor do the expert public finance specialists to whom we have listened. It is for this reason, amongst others, that we strongly urge a greater effort to prioritise existing local expenditures strategically, so far as possible.

7.4.2.   Nor is this Report the place to discuss the political arguments about proper levels of public spending, yet what we can say, without fear of contradiction from almost all those who spoke to us, is that in the two public services on which we have concentrated, Police and Education, there is considerable evidence of significant underfunding in Bradford to meet current reasonable needs. Furthermore, there is considerable evidence that lack of expenditure on these services is causing, and will continue to cause, heavy expenditure to the community in other ways, as material on which we have reported shows.

7.4.3.   The sources of public finance available to the city council and other local public bodies, and the systems which govern those sources, are complex. We did begin to try to set out the various Government financial regimes and initiatives which have dominated Bradford's abilities to deal with its problems in recent years, of which several are quoted in para 3.3 of the *Resources Study* (see para 7.7.10). There are, however, few people who understand the system, and it has taken a lot of effort for us even to understand the relevant acronyms! In the end, we decided, with relief, that the effort needed was not justified.

7.4.4.   Suffice it to say that control of financial sources is largely with Central Government, as is control of the limit on total expenditure by the council. In a Report which studiously concentrates on what Bradford can do, we nevertheless have to acknowledge the existence of Bradford's Central Government-promoted dependency on centrally controlled public expenditure. There is little matching sense of direction between such a system of funding and the theoretically devolved responsibilities of a democratic local authority. The general systems for financing local authority activities are now so complex that it is difficult for a local authority to plan ahead in accordance with its own local strategy.

7.4.5.   One particular concern was expressed by several people active in the promotion of public investment in Bradford – that there appears to be an inadequate relationship between the capital expenditure made available under various schemes, and the revenue needed to make the capital investments work. In some instances the capital needed is small, but the revenue implications are more significant. In some of the situations we have considered, investment in people both to provide a service and to produce desperately needed local jobs, would pay better returns than building projects, but it seems it is difficult for the present systems to accommodate that.

7.4.6.   For example, we were impressed with the 'Jobsmatch' Initiative, when we visited the Grosvenor Centre in Manningham, one of many initiatives properly pursuing sensible objectives on a basis of only temporary European funds which may soon expire. This is an approach which places people with appropriate language skills and cultural understanding in a locally based office, to help local unemployed people to follow up their desire for training, or to match their skills to any jobs which are available. From where does Central Government think any replacement finance can come, for apparently worthwhile initiatives such as this, in the present economic plight of Bradford, given the relatively limited amount that prioritisation would produce and the scale of other important demands. This is as much a mystery to us as it is to most people in Bradford seeking to improve matters.

7.4.7.   The temptation to the local authority, in the circumstances we have described, is to try to spread available money as widely as possible so as not to incur unpopularity by cutting existing activities and then, with some justification, to blame Central Government that new challenges cannot be met because of the unfair and insensitive allocations to Bradford. The dominance of central financial control encourages short term planning and the pursuit of whatever are the latest nationally determined criteria for the allocation of resources and permissions to spend. Yet although the city council has only vestiges of the powers formerly exercised by local authorities, it does still have some influence, and indeed some control, over the distribution of public funds for local public services.

7.5   The Criticism – No Clear Strategy

7.5.1.   We have asked front line workers, in a number of disciplines and working for different public sector employers, if they knew of the strategy for the inner city to which their work was contributing, and we have never had a clearly satisfactory answer. Instead, they said, there was a plethora of beautiful statements about what would be unquestionably desirable – *"apple pie or pie in the sky"*, as one informed observer put it. Image making appeared to be more dominant than the stark exposure of the limited choices available.

7.5.2.   An experienced Asian worker in the Manningham area said:

> *"The Youth Service has never taken stock of facilities in this area, to redirect resources to areas of need. If there is no new money, it is obviously necessary to reprioritise."*

7.5.3.   At the other extreme of organised political activity we sought to discover a common agenda provided by the city to, or organised collectively by, its Members of Parliament as a collective force for Bradford in Whitehall and Westminster, given the constant references we heard to the dominance of the Central Government over the activities of the council. We were unsuccessful on both counts.

7.5.4.   The cause of this absence of a council strategy, it was widely said by people likely to know (including by some political activists from both major Political Parties), was that there was a preference for keeping the lid on discussion of unpleasant facts or controversial issues. The management of news which might invite knee-jerk sniping from the opposing party, or which might affect the public brand image of a party, dominated the arrangements for discussion.

7.5.5.   At a more practical level, it was said, although the council had always managed its expenditures to keep within Government prescribed limits (not an easy task) it had not yet tackled prioritisation by discontinuing some expenditures to pay for the continuation of others in accordance with an openly agreed strategy. The discredited old tradition of seeking to maintain a base budget, whilst adding on the cost of new needs, had been superseded merely by attempts to maintain the existing range of services in the face of the externally dictated cuts in total expenditure, in order to avoid controversial choices.

7.5.6.   Furthermore, we were told that there was a wilful separation of different council service hierarchies and their related party political and operational power bases, despite the increasing number of problems, opportunities and trends which defy the service boundaries determined by the political definition of problems, opportunities and trends of up to a century and a half ago. This, in turn, also led to another level of sectionalised struggle to hang on to existing allocations, with no-one able to fight for an overview. It is certainly not uncommon for the different council Departments to be listed as separate components of 'inter-agency' action.

7.5.7.   When the Commission wanted to know what problems, in the area where the disorders began, had been identified, and what measured progress was being achieved in meeting those problems, we had to discuss our interest with what seemed like 57 Varieties of organizations, each separately dedicated to meeting those problems. Bradford currently lacks a capacity to sort out the wood from the trees.

7.5.8.   Another repeated criticism, by those not involved in them, was of the dominance of local Party political battles about local issues on national Party lines, so that local concerns were trivialised or distorted. The result was a minimalist impact by the council on increasing local problems. As one Asian middle aged man rather bluntly put it:

"We want to know the politicians' vision for Bradford, and how to achieve it, not arselicking. They mustn't hide any more, now.... Politicians have got to justify themselves".

7.5.9.   We have set out all this criticism directly, because it would be foolish to ignore the widespread nature of its existence, the strength with which it is held, and the evidence which appears to support it. We have not considered it our role to conduct a management consultancy type of exercise, but we have come across several important examples which support the criticisms.

Education

7.5.10.   We have dealt with this subject specifically in Section 6, and reached a conclusion that a clearer strategy was needed. We can say that a formally articulated 'strategy' for Education appeared in February 1996, despite the obvious, and critically important, questions about, for example, proficiency in English being of concern since the 1960s. We understand this strategy has now been formally adopted by the council, as Local Education Authority, but we have searched the document in vain to find any prioritisation, matched realistically with likely resources. Inevitably, in these circumstances, there is no evidence of the focussing of intellectual leadership and political pressures required to achieve implementation of priority choices, whether those to which we have pointed, or any others.

The City Centre

7.5.11.   In June 1995 the Bradford Congress published a *"strategic"* document dealing with the needs and opportunities in the city centre – *"Vision into Action"*, a strategy which we readily accept can only be developed over a long time, and as opportunities offer. In terms of our own remit we have not had to pay much regard to the needs of the city 's commercial centre, but its prosperity is obviously of some relevance to almost any question about the future of the city as a whole.

7.5.12.   Most of the comments we have heard about the city centre from members of the public were extremely pessimistic. Whites found it decreasingly attractive; Asians had no real stake in its commerce. A particular indicator of limited activity in the city centre was that given to us by someone whose work and voluntary commitments were indivisibly linked to the city centre. He described to us how it was a different place by night than by day. The lack of 'ordinary' people around at night, we were told, highlighted the violence, drunkenness, homelessness and vulnerability of those who were there. It also highlighted the public order problems related to the night club scene in the early hours, and the frequent absence of services other than the police to deal with the problems which the people who were there have, or cause. How can there be an attractive city centre if this is the situation? How can the strategic importance of the city centre be asserted other than by a determined effort at a strategy in the interests of all, given that the centre itself has such limited direct electoral punch?

7.5.13.   One of the striking features of Bradford's city centre is the almost complete absence of activities which reflect the ethnically diverse nature of the city's population, but we have not been able to find any evidence of this strange fact being thoroughly investigated. In relation to entertainment we have made a similar reference at para 5.30.1. As the numerical and economic balance of the city's multi-ethnic population changes, it is inevitable that retailing in the centre will suffer so long as it appeals only to a diminishing local White clientele.

7.5.14.   But what is being done? Where are the practical proposals which follow up this rather obvious, and overdue, insight? If there is not a radical reappraisal of the role of the city centre in an ethnically diverse population's lives, there is every reason to be pessimistic. The forces which shaped its past prosperity have declined, yet we question whether the relatively new forces that might contribute to its future prosperity have been engaged. *"Vision into Action"* deals specifically with this subject matter only in relation to retailing.

"A growing ethnic minority population, and the potential to attract shoppers from outside the District, provide an opportunity to encourage the promotion and establishment of a quality Asian shopping area in the city centre with its own character and specialised retailing."

7.5.15.   Once again, we have a nice idea, but not a strategy. Once again, the Asians are tacked on.

Housing

7.5.16.   There is a clear Housing Strategy, adopted by the council in September 1995, which forms the basis of the joint approach to the city's acute housing needs by all housing agencies. Bradford's Housing Needs Index is the highest outside London, we were told. The strategy's proposals are related to a view of finance and other practical influences, but it is not clear how this housing strategy relates to the needs of the city as a whole, as the recent contest about whether the Single Regeneration Budget, Round 3, bid by Bradford should be for housing estates in Bradford North, or for the general needs Manningham/Girlington, has shown.

An Integrated Strategy

7.5.17. A method for achieving a synthesis between Bradford's several Economic, Social, and Physical Strategies is set out in the document *"An Integrated Regeneration Strategy for the Bradford District."* No one referred to it in our many discussions on this subject, other than those responsible for its production. It includes many of the key ideas and statistics which indicate the economic potential and the current problems of Bradford. It is again deficient in having almost nothing to say, in any hard edged, managerially meaningful way, about priorities.

7.5.18. The March 1996 replacement Draft of this document contains a new section on *"Implementing the Urban Regeneration Strategy"*, which does raise the profile of the inner city as a priority. This new section highlights that all the geographically defined stress areas should be addressed as a priority, and there is a general let out clause about *"other smaller areas"*, which suggests that stark choices have still to be made. Again, we cannot find a sufficient link between politically inoffensive verbiage and the challenging realities which should shape the action. The new subsection is a welcome step forward, however, and provides a basis for hard decisions when there is a willingness to take them.

'The Non-Statutory Sector'

7.5.19. Bradford spends more than most other local authorities on the 'Non-Statutory Sector', i.e. non-governmental bodies which provide services to the public. Sometimes it is referred to as 'the third sector', or 'the voluntary sector', though we think the latter misleading. The council is spending about £6.5 m per annum, but this grant aid is, we were told, allocated as a continuation of past decisions, not based on a constantly renewed evaluation of needs and achievements.

7.5.20. One council insider, who has closely observed the subject, reflected the views of several of those who spoke to us when he told us:

"The grants originally arose from a Government special grant, therefore they are now historic. Since there was no exit culture laid down in the past it will take unpalatable decisions to make changes, and there are a lot of time-expiry time-bombs ticking away, anyway. There is no clear strategy. The distribution is stuck in patterns which may not reflect current needs. Bradford has the data, but not the will to be more strategic. One consequence of this is the pursuit of 'gatekeeper' roles by local Councillors. Young people are increasingly sceptical, and no clear message can be given why grants are allocated as they are."

7.6 There is No Clear Strategy

7.6.1. We have searched avidly, from the first sessions of our Inquiry, for a strategy which is rigorously being followed to cope with the challenges of the multi-stressed areas of Bradford's inner city. Either we have been told that there is none or, more surprisingly, uncertainty was expressed even at the highest levels as to whether there was one or not. We have looked at several documents in which we hoped to find a pragmatic bridge between the important, but obvious, broad political concerns for the city (which are clearly expressed in, for example, the city council's "Service Plans 1996–97" [Draft Revision March

1996]) and the work of the various public Services, or of the many 'partners' in the city who seek to line up their strategies alongside each other, for the benefit of the city as a whole, in the work of the Congress.

7.6.2.   All that is desirable obviously cannot be achieved at once. What are the priorities? How do Bradford's attempts at a strategy get beyond the stage of *"apple pie or pie in the sky"*? Much has been done to express what is desired, but the much more demanding task of marrying the vision with the practical realities of available finances, skills, and powers to shape the priority direction of those resources has not been articulated in any clear, publicly accountable, way. There is already considerable machinery for inter-agency co-ordination, and a fund of knowledge, expertise and commitment on which to draw. Our constant observation was that all this potential was limited in practice by lack of a clear strategy which can be used to prioritise the direction of scarce funds and other resources, to knit together the many separate strategies of the various agencies and sub-agencies involved, and to monitor success with a view to further prioritisation.

7.7   The Consequences

No basis for decision-making

7.7.1.   In the absence of any authoritative overall strategy for Bradford's future as a viable city, to act as a base line for individual initiatives, most political discussion will inevitably degenerate into competition for local or sectarian advantages. In the absence of such an overriding strategy it is inevitable that people will seek to maximise their own bit of the action, leading to accusations of favouritism or political opportunism. The council has properly recognised that there is need for decentralisation of some decision making to communities defined by reference to Parliamentary constituencies and wards, but the process is unhealthy so long as there is no tension between the needs of these individual localities within the city and those of the whole city. Only a more transparent system can overcome the widespread suspicions that individual decisions owe more to influence, or even corruption, than to strategic reasoning.

7.7.2.   The Foundation 2000 Report of 1995 said:

"Local politics seem to have been ambushed by vested interests of a narrow few. Both parties need to ensure that accountability is essential in local politics ....".

As one mature and experienced Pakistani leader put it to us:

"Under the present arrangements it is those who shout the loudest who get what they want, and keep the others out."

A leader of one of the smaller ethnic minority groups said:

"The council always seems to be firefighting. We feel we have not had a fair deal. We will have to demonstrate, like the Muslims did."

7.7.3.   An election address we were shown, in an area outside the city as we have defined it, made particular, if superficial, play of the use of educational expenditure to meet the special language needs of inner city children, and made critical general references to the refurbishment of inner city schools at the expense of other areas' needs. The ad hoc bidding process adopted by the council for Government financial assistance also promotes tensions between different areas of the city who see themselves as rivals.

7.7.4.   The recent dispute about 'Westbourne Green', the subject of another revealing study by consultants, illustrates a problem typical of the inner city to which a solution had to be found ad hoc, and amidst great local tension.

7.7.5.   All parts of the Metropolitan District's area produced people who told us that their part was unfairly neglected because of the influence of other sections of the total community. There appears to be no way of coping with the charge of neglect of the inner city which we so frequently heard from a very wide range of people, even though the council, and other public bodies, contribute a great deal to the resourcing of life in the inner city. There appears to be no way of dealing with the charge of neglect of other parts of the city which we heard from other groups of critics. Several people spoke to us about the difficulties of rationalisation, making sneering references to *"postcode politics"*. There is no clear strategy to use as an explicit, reasoned guide to explain why a particular activity is, or is not, being carried out.

7.7.6.   So far, in the above instances, we have tried to reflect the concerns of people who were involved with, or were very interested in, local political processes or the implementation of the results. The less involved, who do not understand the processes, perceived close connections between the personal influence of individual Councillors and the successes of some initiatives over others of at least equal merit.

7.7.7.   We close this subsection by quoting from a letter we received from a Pakistani member of the public living in Manningham. He wrote to us about the accountability of the local authority for its community spending projects, and his helpful analysis and comments were:

> *"It is important to determine:*
> * *How much and how the local authority allocated public funds for various community projects. What were the criteria for allocating these funds?*
> * *Who and how many benefited from those funds?*
> * *What was the outcome of the monies allocated? Where is the evidence? Has there been any evaluation / audit of the projects? Are there any reports etc?*
>
> *I believe that before these questions are answered, allocation of any further funding will not necessarily improve the quality of life, remove the fears of further riots, or bring about economic and environmental development and regeneration of deprived and disadvantaged inner-city parts of Bradford...."*

No one has been able to give us a rational explanation for the broad basis of detailed decision making by the city council.

Local Confusion

7.7.8.   The criticism we heard was not just directed at the absence of a strategy at the broad, city-wide level, but also at the unfortunate consequences locally for those who try to deal in practice with current problems.

7.7.9.   This is illustrated by the fate of the *"Manningham/Girlington Community Resources Study"* of September 1993, in which many of the concerns which were repeatedly put to us by those whom we interviewed were also described. The Resources Study was an independent review commissioned jointly by the Bradford Task Force (a Government sponsored body which has now lapsed) and the council's Housing Directorate, and it clearly demonstrated the complexities and overlaps of social provision which then occured in the locality, and underlined the lack of guiding priorities.

> *"The study arose out of an inter-agency seminar on the area held in September 1992 which concluded that there was an impressive commitment to the area both by agencies and individual workers. However, the multiplicity of projects, lack of communication and lack of an overall strategic focus for action gave rise to a suspicion that both statutory agencies and community organisations might be 'underachieving' in the area in relation to the resources and efforts they put in."* (from the Introduction).

7.7.10.   The Resources Study calculated that Manningham/Girlington received:

> *"about one eighth of all of the city council's neighbourhood based grant funding."* (Finding 5).

> *"3.3 With other statutory funders, Manningham and Girlington have mixed fortunes. Task Force concentrate a lot of spending in the area but this rules out most available support from the City Action Team whose priorities are areas outside City Challenge and Task Force boundaries. Safer Cities has had only a minimal impact on the study area while the TEC has been very active but now plans to prioritise non-neighbourhood-based initiatives. The area is notably lacking in European funding as far as the local voluntary sector goes.*

> *3.4 The study identified twenty six different statutory funding sources (counting the various budget heads within CBMC* [City of Bradford Metropolitan District Council] *separately) funding the organisations studied, as well as a host of trusts and private sources, large and small. Such variety is potentially an asset but there was little evidence of co-ordination.*

7.7.11.   *"4.1 There is no shortage of strategic thinking about the study area, and about Manningham in particular. But again there were signs that agencies were developing their own strategic thinking in isolation – which is not, after all, a very strategic way to behave.....*

> *4.3 A second problem is the absence of context and leadership.* [The City Council], *which ought to be setting the pace in terms of community strategy, appears to have so many separate, and tenuously related, "strategies" running or being developed concurrently that one is reluctant to suggest anything more! The recent review of Community Education appears not to relate to the authority's Community Development Strategy (which itself has not moved forward perceptibly in almost a year) and the relation between either of these and other "strategic" initiatives including Area Panels/ Neighbourhood Forums; Anti-Poverty Strategy; and comprehensive Community Regeneration, for example, is by no means clear. We also found that people we interviewed who had strategic roles often seemed unclear about the roles of their counterparts in other Directorates or agencies.....*

> *4.6 Fifth, there is an external problem with policy, resources and political attention. After the late 1970s/early 1980s focus on the inner city, the policy spotlight is now increasingly on peripheral estates and smaller towns in declining industrial areas. It could be argued that the*

pendulum has swung too far; certainly it is now more difficult to attract resources into and to develop policies for areas like Manningham and Girlington than it once was."

7.7.12.   A further Report – *"The Riot Area Reviewed"* of 5th September 1995, stated:

"7.2 Large amounts of Central Government funds to Urban Programme [yet another temporary Government initiative] *in the 1980's followed community needs, organised community groups and community pressure in a piece meal fashion. The grants to inner-city voluntary sector groups / organisations followed the initial start-ups financed through the Urban Programme. Manningham / Toller is well resourced compared to some other inner-city areas.*

7.3 Over the past 3 to 5 years any additional monies have been absorbed through the funding of time-expiry projects. New organisations have not been able to gain a grant due to the council's budget constraints.

7.4 The opportunity for a strategic, geographical review of how resources were distributed could not have followed without affecting established groups. The funded organisations are not therefore equitably distributed throughout the Manningham/Toller area.

7.7.13.   *8.1 The majority of the community provision in the area is focused on the ethnic minority voluntary sector. The majority of these organisations are Asian with the exception of three African Caribbean Projects.*

8.2 The reporting structure and the funding arrangements within the grant-aided voluntary sector are complex. The arrangements are based on historical precedent.....

7.7.14.   *11 Council Finance*

11.1 The Council alone could not reverse the effects of urban degeneration and youth unemployment; the parameters of which include factors which rely upon/result from Central Government policies and intervention. Central Government has made and will make further reductions to the council's overall funds in the coming financial year.

11.2 Given the above constraints any recommendations or proposals for initiatives in the Manningham area will in all likelihood have to be within the Local Authority's current resources. New resources should be achieved either through rationalisation, amalgamation or redirection or through an injection of co-ordinated new external funds."

7.7.15.   We agree. There is a case, even in present circumstances, for new expenditures – but based upon a clear strategy, and closely monitored for appropriate results.

7.7.16.   The above quotations are representative of the gist of both these reports, and the fact that the first set of quotations is now three years old raises a question from their obviously continuing relevance in 1995. Why had the first report not been acted on? According to a letter from the city council's Chief Executive to the MP for Bradford West, dated 24th October 1995, what we believe to be this competent and thorough Resources survey

"has not been implemented to date. I believe that some elected members were concerned about the implications of the report and its subsequent implementation. As a consequence of these views the report was not circulated or considered by Committee.

The conclusions of this report are reflected in the recent review commissioned by the Leader of the Council into the views of young people following the riots in June and a future strategy [sic]. This study will be presented to Committee in the near future and underlines a key message in the Manningham/Girlington report which underlined the need for greater strategic coordination of resources in the area."

7.7.17.   At the time of writing this part of our Report neither the Study, nor the Review commissioned by the Leader, had been openly considered by the council or by a Committee, we were told on enquiring. Three years is a long time for such an important report as the Resources Study to have been in limbo, especially as its importance was also highlighted in the Foundation 2000 report published in late 1995. Similarly, the report urgently commissioned by the Leader of the Council in June 1995, which was available in October 1995 ought, by now, to have been considered by a Committee, as foreshadowed in the Chief Executive's letter.

7.7.18.   We can only wonder on what grounds these two reports have not been considered. We have been told that bodies such as the council are waiting for our Report, but that, at best, can be only a recent explanation applicable to the later report. Were the reports suppressed, as many of our informants alleged, because they raised too difficult issues for local politicians to want to resolve them?

Competitive Bidding

7.7.19.   Increasingly, Central Government is dictating a process whereby local authorities finance new expenditure by competitive bidding for centrally controlled allocations of funds. The particular rules governing a particular bid must obviously dictate the actual proposals of the bid put forward by the council, and their locally perceived priority can only be an influence. The development of the Congress's status and influence is necessary to strengthen Bradford's bids, and to help meet the second deficiency identified by Lord Scarman about the contribution of the private sector which we quote in para 7.9.2.

7.7.20.   As we have been writing this Report some controversy has existed over whether housing estates in the north of the city, or Manningham/Girlington, should be the location of the next bid for some Central Government funds and, if the latter, why there should be preference over other inner city areas with similar acute needs. It seems increasingly likely that the Manningham/Girlington bid will be chosen by the council. If there had been a clear, overall strategy the process could have been much easier.

7.7.21.   One particular consequence of the bidding system is that if the local authority submitting a bid has no clear, publicly supported strategy, from which the individual bid can flow obviously and naturally, the only alternative is a 'Buggin's turn' approach based on competition within Bradford between geographically limited needs and solutions. The latter is the approach which has so far been adopted in Bradford. Such an approach has many disadvantages.

7.7.22.   First, obviously it generates rivalries between different areas of the city. This leads inevitably to misapprehensions about the reasons for the priority given to one location over another, in a city where investment needs are almost everywhere. Have previous bids avoided the inner city for racial reasons? Will Manningham/Girlington be given priority because of the disorders? If so, should other areas have a riot to gain some priority? These are not our argumentative questions. Indeed, we could not take them seriously. But we have heard them again and again from people in different localities.

7.7.23.   Secondly, the process of building up demonstrable local support for a bid arouses expectations in that locality, and corresponding frustration if the bid is not pursued by the council. We were impressed by the length and depth of public involvement which had occurred on the bid involving the Thorpe Edge estate in Bradford North. At the time the rivalry of the two bids was first drawn to our attention no comparable consultation had taken place in Manningham/Girlington, despite considerable thought by some local activists. Such differences are seized upon as examples of irrational preferential treatment.

7.7.24.   Thirdly, once a locality has had its 'Buggin's Turn', it will be unlikely to have another turn for a long time, whatever the relative priorities of its continuing needs. This can be stated shortly, but its likelihood casts long shadows into the future.

7.7.25.   Fourthly, the lack of a strategic approach weakens the force of all the bids made by the city, in that each bid has to be separately justified, rather than be based on a continuing strategy whose elements have already been accepted, assuming that previous bids have proved satisfactory in their relevant practical outcomes.

7.7.26.   Fifthly, the extensive needs across the city can be exposed in an overall strategy, and thus strengthen the understanding of those Central Government civil servants who have to advise both on the allocation of grants to competing local authorities within the region and on the needs of the region to whom the central grant is first allocated nationally. Once more we urge the articulation of a clear locally adopted strategy, to focus external attention on Bradford's needs.

7.8   The Explanation

7.8.1.   The explanation we were usually given, when we pressed on this disappointing absence of a clear set of strategic priorities, was that instability in the Party political control of the city council during the 1980s had prevented the development of a consistent strategy. This excuse was supplemented by an explanation for the nineties, in which the party political control of the council seems set firm for many years, which referred to power struggles within the controlling group of councillors with consequent sectionalised power bases and no central consensus or permitted overall leadership. Obviously, this line of explanation, if correct, is a situation of Bradford's own making.

7.8.2.   A further 'explanation' was that the local political programme was perforce driven by the need for cuts in expenditure, with everyone concerned to protect their enthusiasms so far as possible, and to hang on desperately to what they had already. In these circumstances there was a lack of confidence to look into the future. This is not so much an explanation as an illustration of the criticism we make.

7.8.3.   We are not in a position to examine such matters further. We did not set out to look for evidence of this, or any other, deficiency. We have to report that this is what we have been told with sufficient frequency, and from knowledgeable people with sufficiently diverse backgrounds, that we suggest a need for examination of the processes of public decision-making within the city to clarify the basis of public policies, given the serious indicators to which we have referred.

Part 2   Reflecting Public Concerns

7.9   The Failure

7.9.1.   We now turn to the other outstanding criticism, which was made to us frequently, in various guises. It was 'The failure of the local political system to reflect public concerns which are so strongly and widely held that they ought to be obvious candidates for purposeful political consideration.'

7.9.2.   Once more, we begin with an apposite quotation from Lord Scarman's 1981 Report on the Brixton Riots:

> *"6.7. The approach to inner city problems also appears to have been deficient in two other important respects. First, local communities should be more fully involved in the decisions which affect them. A 'top down' approach to regeneration does not seem to have worked. Local communities must be fully and effectively involved in planning, in the provision of local services, and in the management and financing of specific projects. ..... Inner cities are not deserts: they possess a wealth of voluntary effort and goodwill. It would be wise to put this human capital to good use.*
>
> *6.8. A second deficiency appears to lie in the extent to which the private sector ... is involved in the process of inner city regeneration. ..."*

7.9.3.   Both these deficiencies cited by Lord Scarman have been acted upon in Bradford to a considerable extent. Nonetheless, the changes which have taken place, and will continue for the foreseeable future to take place, in the ethnic nature of Bradford's population, have enormous continuing implications for the exercise of political power in the city. It will be obvious, from what we have already reported, that we are concerned about the extent to which the local political processes have responded to these changes.

7.9.4.   We do not, of course, suggest that ethnic groups should be treated merely as influential units for purposes of Party political advantage. In any event that possibility is rapidly coming to an end. We are concerned that the real issues about life in a divided city are just not being discussed in an open, constructive, and organised way. As a consequence, there is much ignorant public muttering, in addition to the provision of inappropriate services, and the inability to make hard choices backed by public understanding, to which we have referred.

7.9.5.   It is invidious to choose examples of failure, because they will be taken to reflect badly on those people particularly associated with them. That would be unfair, and divert attention from the roots of the general problem. We are not attacking individuals, or particular organisations, but attempting to demonstrate a general state of affairs, and the inadequacy of outdated systems.

7.9.6.   We have already highlighted in this Report the concerns that so many Bradford citizens expressed to us, from very diverse backgrounds, which require purposeful political discussion. We have to conclude that the local political system is failing to pick up important public concerns. We therefore take, by way of relevant illustration, just one very general example from these already expressed concerns, and add in a second very specific example which is a source of considerable concern to many people.

7.10 The Example of Policing

7.10.1. If one takes the very widely held belief amongst young people in the Asian communities that the police are unprofessionally insensitive, and often hostile, to them, it is still not an excuse for making one's protest by violence, even though the particular community from which the violent protests emanated were holding such views so strongly. We are not dealing here with whether the belief was right or wrong, but with the fact that it was held so widely, and so strongly, and resulted in violence. The question has to be asked: why has this issue, and other concerns relating to policing, not been prominently raised through the democratic processes, and dealt with effectively, prior to the disorders?

7.10.2. Even though the city council has no significant direct involvement in the direction of the West Yorkshire Police Force, there cannot be a good answer to this question. The plain fact is that the local political system has failed to deal with a major public issue, despite the relevant concerns of so many who are actively involved in the system, and the deeply held concerns of the public. Of the topics we have raised, policing seems to be a subject almost entirely ignored by the formal local democratic political processes. The city-wide concerns of the population relating to policing have, we have been told, received only a token acknowledgement by the city council. What is an effective role for the city council in relation to the West Yorkshire Police Authority? What is the locally accountable role of the Police Authority in dealing with the policing issues we have raised on behalf of the public?

7.11 The Example of Delayed Renovation Grants

7.11.1. The other, more specific, example of the failure of the political system relates to house improvement or renovation grants. There is plainly a problem in Bradford about maintaining the long term value of sound houses heavily populated by people who have insufficient means to maintain them. Assistance with private house improvement has been a major strand of Bradford's housing policies for many years. Unfortunately, Central Government policies now severely restrict the scope of the council's financial help.

7.11.2. Yet two opposite and equally mistaken conclusions, that Asians get favoured treatment (held by Whites), and that Asians are prevented from having what Whites can get (held by Asians), are widely voiced by Bradfordians. To make matters worse there is also a view (held by both Whites and Asians) that such grants as are obtained are sometimes obtained dishonestly and/or corruptly. A frequently quoted example, of the many given to us by so many people, was that of the man who had been waiting unsuccessfully for eight years since making application, yet a neighbouring householder had twice received a grant in that period.

7.11.3. The city council has taken very determined steps to eliminate the possibility of their relevant systems being abused, but it has signally failed to get across the basic fact that there is a lack of resources to continue to fund an adequate programme, or even that there are proper, openly declared, reasons why some applicants are given priority over others who have been in the queue for much longer. Why is there such widespread misunderstanding? This misunderstanding was identified clearly in the follow up report about Service Delivery in Girlington of September 1994, yet it still persists.

7.11.4.   Is there corruption, despite the council's efforts? Or does this longstanding and widespread misunderstanding stem from the council's failure to acknowledge that the programme needs radical 'down sizing' in line with now longstanding resource constraints? Or do many of those whose responsibility it is to represent the public – the 'gatekeepers' as they are known – deliberately fail to explain the reasons to 'their' public in order to maintain the mystique of a system which they are thought by many of 'their' public to control?

7.12   Political Differentiation

7.12.1.   The historic political and numerical dominance of White people in Bradford has made it a difficult struggle for other ethnically based perspectives to be considered and taken seriously. The established political Parties are not yet comfortable associations for many Asian people, and the articulate young Asian men with whom we spoke were often very critical of them.

7.12.2.   The sheer size of some 'ethnic minority' groups can be superficially perceived as being more electorally significant than others, and this can influence the attitudes of public office holders, particularly if there is no adequate ability to distinguish beyond stereotypical generalisations. There are some issues, though not as many as is sometimes thought, which will attract overwhelming support from a particular group when its influence is organised, e.g. the struggle by Muslims to persuade the council to provide Halal meat. The temptation is to concentrate on the campaigns of such powerful, articulate, groupings, and not to hear the less powerful.

7.12.3.   Yet internal factionalism weakens the ability of the very large Asian population to elect representatives of their number. If people from the ethnic minority groups were to join in mature consideration of the issues we have outlined in this Report, dividing as necessary on the strategic responses which the council should make to problems which they share with others, instead of splintering on factors largely irrelevant to acute current concerns in Bradford, the main political Parties would have to take them, and the issues, much more seriously. Articulate young Asians are aware of this. Hence their alienation from current traditional politics. This is an important transition, requiring careful management.

7.12.4.   The same in fact applies to the people of all ethnic groups. There are Bradford-based issues affecting everyone, which are not being adequately addressed by the very people who constitute the authority of democracy. Local political choice is about more than the election of the next Government.

7.13   Local Area Panels

7.13.1.   Although we write about 'the inner city', as distinct from the city centre and the suburbs, the inner city is itself divided into many recognisably separate communities each with its own local loyalties. At this level there is the possibility of a much more real involvement of ordinary people in the political issues that affect them. This is not just opportune; it is necessary that the people who live in the inner city should be able to understand, and react constructively to, the many significant decisions which affect them and which are rarely made by people living amongst them.

7.13.2.   Indeed, such few responses as we received from the suburbs, where for many years much of the leadership of Bradford has lived, were almost entirely of a lofty distancing from the disorders, the problems, and the people, of Manningham. If that is a true reflection of how the District operates as a unit, it is small wonder if there is so little of the synergy that brings a city into being and sustains it.

7.13.3.   The council, commendably, has already established Area Panels, each based on a Parliamentary constituency, just over five years ago, to enable local people to influence the political system. Each Area Panel organises more locally based Neighbourhood Forums, based on Wards, where any local resident can raise an issue, or join in a discussion of an item raised by others, or by the council.

7.13.4.   Each Area Panel consists, we were told, of up to 12 Councillors, and reflects the balance of Party political power on the council. It has a small budget to use at discretion for local schemes which have been discussed at the Neighbourhood Forum. In Manningham, because the attendance at meetings is predominantly of middle aged Asian men, special arrangements have now been made to have meetings for women, and for young people. Unfortunately, important changes like the closure of a local Housing office do seem to bypass this part of the council's arrangements.

7.13.5.   We were told that these potentially excellent mechanisms have not been used to capture public concerns in a way which can lead to prioritisation and the development of appropriate strategies, and a common complaint was that although the Forums were used to tell the public what the council proposed, and why, there was no organised involvement of local people so that they could raise their own concerns.

7.13.6.   We have been impressed by the quality of support provided by the small staff associated directly with the two Area Panels in which we took particular interest, and we think that some of this criticism is too sweeping. But when so many people from the local communities have bothered to come to us with a small number of the same deeply held frustrations which require political action, the mechanism appears to need careful reappraisal.

7.13.7.   One mature Asian man, active in his inner city locality, said of life there:

"There is some funding, but little happens after initial studies. Local people don't see the effects or the work of the Area Panel. .... The community needs to know what the Council does

and thinks. …. Out of three Neighbourhood Forums I attended Councillor X turned up once. The other two [Councillors] *didn't turn up at all. People's perception is that if they raise matters nothing happens."*

In this Section of our Report we have already referred specifically to two Area generated reports to which inadequate attention has been paid.

7.14   Local Leadership and Its Limits

Existing Patterns of Leadership

7.14.1.   That there is potential leadership to take on the challenges to life in Bradford, we do not doubt. We have been impressed by the articulate concerns and suggestions, based on existing participation in local matters, of so many who troubled to speak to us. Of particular importance in areas like Manningham is the role of the existing and aspirant leaders of the Asian communities as the processes of political integration develop. They undoubtedly exist, often operating differently from traditional Bradfordian leadership roles, and it is therefore difficult for the White community to understand these roles and their authority. There is, however, a danger of expecting too much from them, especially as the public processes of the city become more widely understood.

7.14.2.   There are only a few issues on which the various ethnically or religiously defined 'communities' can properly be represented as being united, and as more people are born and raised here the authority systems of a distant tradition cease to be as powerful. Even where the subject matter is appropriate, discussion with a few 'community representatives' will only occasionally be a reliable short cut to consultation with a 'community', however managerially tempting such a short cut might be. Such a process would not often make sense in a White community. We suggest that its useful days are numbered in Asian communities, for most purposes.

7.14.3.   It is also important to ensure, in any discussion, that the extent of any representative's real authority is understood. We have met a number of people, young and old, who claimed to be representative figures, yet we often came to realise that their claims were exaggerated.

7.14.4.   One perceptive Asian Councillor wrote:

"Inner City Godfathers:

By design or default, the national and local political bodies seem to consult and provide services to the inner city communities through a set of local community leaders. On the face of it, it appears to be a good model: community development has been a buzz word for the last few years. But what does it actually mean on the ground…….

Using Urban Programme funding, a network of community centres / advice centres has been set up in Manningham area. But as time passes the management committee of these centres have been reduced to one or two active and vocal persons. In some cases they have become part of one or two persons' empire. Thus instead of true community development or empowerment, the local powers have become concentrated in the hands of very few community leaders. The community development model has degenerated into a "colonial model" of running inner cities. To make it explosively dangerous, the local politicians have started favouring this model because it makes their job easier. By giving out favours, and exploiting the fears, if they can control these GODFATHERS, the community will remain quiet.

The youth who rioted definitely felt that they have no significant power or influence in the city. But there were a few ... GODFATHERS who were winding them up to shake the tree in the hope that this will open up opportunities for them to gain significant influence thus creating a new set of GODFATHERS.....

My difficulty with the "Colonial Model" is that the so called leaders are not accountable in any visible way to the community. A favourable decision can be reached by flooding a meeting or by obtaining a petition, the contents of which are not clearly understood by the signatories. Thus the so called devolving of power has strengthened the voice of already vocal residents but has eroded the voice of the weakest eg homeless, abused children, women fleeing violence etc."

7.14.5.   There is a danger of giving false ideas of self-importance, or of mistakenly assimilating only a vocal few into the local political processes. In a democracy, only the process of public election can confer the authority to determine political matters on behalf of the public. That is why we look to the city council to take the lead in opening up important choices to better informed and wider public debate, as part of their clear responsibilities.

Developing a New Pattern

7.14.6.   In any area there will be a considerable number of locally based people and organisations concerned with life in that area, as distinct from the city or district as a whole, and almost all of these will be capable of giving informal responses to the choice of clearly defined priorities and their pursuit. Ideally, to choose how to meet local needs responsibly, those involved locally will have to understand a wide range of material. This will include current problems, opportunities and trends, the confusion of public finances, and the potential of inter-agency co-operation.

7.14.7.   The existing structure of Neighbourhood and Police Community Forums, and Local Area Panels, does provide a basis for such development, provided that they can connect with, and command the respect of, the informal leaders of various sections in the local communities covered by the Forum or Panel. There is urgent need for these local communities to be enabled to:

1.   discuss their concerns and aspirations, and any active plans for dealing with them;

2.   consider the redirection of the resources which already exist within these communities to match the results of 1;

3.   realise that there is little prospect of extra public resources on top of those already available, other than in very exceptional circumstances.

7.14.8.   We believe that such a process should sort out the mere talkers, and produce tough, committed, local leadership.

Part 3   Representative Democracy

7.15   Councillors

Their Power

7.15.1.   We have often emphasised the importance of the city council as the locally elected representative body for the city. Council decision-making is collegiate, and the actual influence of an individual Councillor is only commensurate with the continuous strength of her/his informal alliances with other Councillors. We wonder if this is always sufficiently realised, and whether sufficient initiative has been taken within informal groups of Councillors to share concerns, burdens, and enthusiasms. We hope that alliances could be formed about the kind of issues raised in this Report. Few of these issues can be dealt with satisfactorily by individuals, or by hi-jacking them to ethnic groupings or standard political coalitions and Parties. ·

7.15.2.   No Councillor, in law, has any individual power, but the way things are done in the Indian sub-continent is, we were told, quite different, and so leads older members of the communities who regard the Asian Councillors as their own to expect them to deliver, single-handed, favourable decisions. The different way of approaching constituents' problems which this causes excites suspicion on the part of White Councillors and Officers, who then may respond in a reserved and cautious way. It is this style of operating that encourages descriptions like 'gatekeeper' or 'godfather'.

Their Workload

7.15.3.   The workload of all Councillors is extremely demanding, but that of Asian Councillors is especially high. One Asian Councillor, speaking of his Ward, told us:

"People expect local Councillors to be fully aware of all issues, and personal circumstances. We are expected to come to their aid as soon as asked, to visit them in their homes, to attend weddings and funerals. But there are 12,000 of them! When I installed an Ansaphone, to be more available, there were many complaints – even though I always responded next day. It even became an election issue. 'He doesn't want to listen'. So I had the Ansaphone removed, and now they say 'You are never in'. People don't appreciate this, that Councillors are not full time, and that they have a family, a job, and their own personal problems to deal with too."

7.15.4.   Another told us how people of his particular ethnic background, from all over the city, would approach him for help.

Irrelevant Issues

7.15.5.   There is exasperation amongst many decent politicians, of all ethnic groups and Parties, at the irrelevant intrusion of political issues from the Indian sub-continent into the local politics of Bradford, such as clan loyalties, in the attempted manipulation of group voting patterns. In particular, the more politically aware Asian young people, from whom future leadership is likely to come, deeply resent this. One young man spoke for many:

"This is not Pakistan. We're in the middle of Yorkshire. You can't live Kashmiri village life here."

7.15.6.   But the problem, which we have repeatedly drawn to attention, is that many older people who are citizens of Bradford do live Kashmiri village life here, and if multi-ethnic freedom means anything, if sensitivity to different assumptions and practices means anything, it must surely be also meant in Political Party matters just as much as in schools or policing. Why should traditional family or political loyalties have to be abandoned just because to others they seem, or are, irrelevant to political life in Bradford? There is here, in microcosm, the challenge of the divided city, and it seems to us that the political systems, like the public services, are slow to come to manage the reality that exists.

Unfair Criticism

7.15.7.   We consider so much of the public's general criticism of individual Councillors to be unfair and exaggerated. Of course, the distinctive political agenda of young people leads to disenchantment with older 'community leaders' and Councillors. They are widely seen by Asian young people (and not just by young men) as posturing to maintain their popularity and to advance their political careers. In some cases this may be so. But this hardly represents a peculiar ethnic distinction, of the critics or of the criticised!

7.16   The City Council

7.16.1.   The problems which we have outlined throughout this Report require Bradfordian leadership of, and by, the many collective public and private forces that need to face the future with realism, and with the strength of a coalition of various forces acting with a united determination, if the problems are to be overcome. In such a controversial process the role of the democratically elected city council, as the only representative body capable of determining and implementing city-wide priorities against restricted public finances and sectional pressure groups, will be crucial, and not only in relation to its own Services and now heavily restricted powers. The city council is constitutionally designed to sort out local priorities, and it should concentrate on this role as the organised 'centre', as a counterweight to the diffusions and confusions of separate geographical, social, ethnic, financial, and operational forces of which presently it is a part.

7.16.2.   The urgent political issues which need to be confronted do not fit neatly within the orthodox organisational arrangements of the city council. Indeed, the continuous weakening of the powers of local authorities, over the last two decades in particular, means that the council will rarely command the power to develop and implement any solution itself. Maximising the needed resources of skills, equipment, manpower, and even money, will require partnerships on a hitherto unknown scale. We have heard that, despite the development of the Congress partnerships, the local authority does not like to involve, or to be involved with, people and organisations outside its direct control. Those who hold to this view are living in cloud-cuckoo-land. As the democratically elected representation of the city, the council must lead, but it cannot achieve single-handed.

7.16.3.   The kind of issues we have identified require organised consultation, and professional advice openly taken as to lines of solution. Then resources can be optimised and prioritised, and practical programmes developed, implemented, and appraised. In this way relevant leaders can emerge and be trained, and their energies constructively channelled to deal with real issues of practical achievement.

7.17   The Media

7.17.1.   Local politics is heavily dependent on the media for making available to the public the issues being considered by a supposedly open political process. The consequence of a free press and broadcasting process is, or should be, one of tension between those involved in the public representative processes and those who independently report to the public. The benefit for the public is the obstruction of an automatic peddling of the 'official line' on behalf of publicly accountable people and organisations. This idealised description fails to take account of the 'line' pursued by the different public media, which may not always be based primarily on the public interest.

7.17.2.   We have been considerably assisted in our work by some of the local media, and we express our thanks. Unlike the official bodies who were also so very helpful, the local media had no pre-commitment to our work. We trust that the commitment of the local media to serious, independent, explanation of the grave issues raised in our Report will continue. Several people who spoke to us were critical of the local media for failing to take seriously the issues which confront Bradford. We consider this subject to be beyond our ability to judge, though we did experience some disappointments in some treatment of issues which arose during our Inquiry, and which we felt were trivialised.

7.17.3.   The national media is, perhaps, no more than an irritation which Bradford has cheerfully to accept. One of the particular regrets about the disorders, which so many Bradford people share, is that they created one more item for the national media to add to a longstanding fascination with bad news about Bradford. Yet Bradford has had a good reputation amongst knowledgeable people for having, in the past, tackled many of the problems of ethnically diverse urban life in a determined and successful way. In fact, Bradford has always had such a reputation for pioneering successful ways of dealing with its succession of enormous social problems since the modern city began in the early nineteenth century.

7.17.4.   It is time to build again that reputation, to create a current political agenda for the city which is determined by the city, which is heavily influenced by the range of relevant expertise held by those who daily deal with its problems, and which builds on the enormous wellspring of common sense, honesty, and decency which is so evident in most of its people, of all ethnic backgrounds. Perhaps the media will then be more constructive.

7.18   The Challenge

7.18.1.   We have set out a political challenge which faces the people of Bradford. They, and they alone, can exert the pressure needed to improve the city's political processes if they consider that the criticisms we have made are valid.

Section 8

What Next?

8.1 The Challenge of our Report

8.1.1. In the previous Sections of this Report we have given a careful account of what we were told in the interviews with members of the public about the disorders of June 1995 and their implications, and of our conclusions, expressing the results of our consideration in summary form in Section 2. We have tried to make it clear that this Report is intended to be a series of amplifications of the issues which are of major concern to many people, concern which appeared to be justified by our enquiries, and which therefore requires thought and the creation of political strategies, and only then executive action.

8.1.2. We have sought to set out a basis for constructive discussion which could lead to focussed action. The challenge is not merely how to respond to the negative threat of future public disorder similar to that which occurred in June 1995.

8.2 What Next?

8.2.1. The formal action to be taken has to be left to those who, although they are responsible for dealing with the matters to which we have drawn attention, also carry political responsibilities for a wider range of issues. Unless they consider that they can ignore the public concerns and other material to which we have referred, they should decide openly whether they agree with our criticisms and suggestions about public services and the local political processes, and the extent to which the subject matter must have some priority over their dealing with other concerns. We are not aware of any other concern which can completely override the primacy of those to which we have referred, because the latter affect all aspects of the present and future well-being of Bradford's citizens.

8.2.2. We therefore do not think it wise to create an 'executive summary' In any event, we do not have the technical expertise, nor have we had the time, to investigate the best pragmatic steps to be taken, and we are confident that appropriate expertise and experience is already available to the authorities if they choose to use it. Executive action can only sensibly be taken after our Report has been digested by the public and by those responsible for directing the agencies involved. Our concern is that, already overbusy, those directing the relevant agencies will merely delegate the task of extracting sufficient information from the Report to produce self-justifying sound-bites to cope with the immediate, fleeting interest of the media. 'Cherry picking' a few relatively easy practical options from a list of detailed recommended executive actions is certainly not the next appropriate step; nor do we want to spare those who are responsible for policy making from reading the Report itself!

8.2.3. What happens next is up to the people of Bradford and, if they share the concerns which we have relayed, to their influence on the democratic processes of government at national and local levels.

8.3   The Communication of this Report

8.3.1.   We understand that the Congress, which is the body commissioning our Report, has already decided to publish it and we should stress that neither the Congress nor any of its partners will have seen the Report before it is publicly available. We think it would be wise for immediate comment on the Report to be restrained, at least until commentators have read it! The last thing to which we will attach any importance is instant reaction, and we urge others to take the same robust attitude. However urgent the subject matter, a reasonable time taken to think and to consult will be well spent.

8.3.2.   We have found the need for better communication within Bradford to be a recurrent feature of our Report. Despite strenuous efforts to clarify our Report, we are conscious that it is not an easy read, and that its communication raises several difficult practical issues which are themselves illustrative of the challenge facing the governance of Bradford.

8.3.3.   The interviews with members of the public were conducted, with only a few exceptions, in English, though interpretation arrangements were available from the beginning. The Report has been prepared in English, and we understand that the Congress has decided to make the Summary contained in Section 2 available, on request, in other languages used in Bradford. In subsection 6.28 we drew attention to conclusions from research which had been carried out in Girlington into the needs of people with various traditions of communication. We suggest that, once its members have had an opportunity to digest the Report, the Congress should consider, in liaison with representative organisations, what further steps can be taken to ensure the widest availability of the Report's contents within Bradford, for the purposes of useful public discussion.

8.3.4.   If there is to be the extent of involvement for which we hope in the consideration of the matters we have raised, it is necessary to base the development of publication on similar insights to those in the Girlington study. Can arrangements for discussion be made which will enable individual and group views to be compared and tested in an atmosphere which builds bridges rather than confrontation?

8.3.5.   How can such discussions be evaluated, or brought to bear on political decisions? How can they be used to amend inappropriate services so as to become efficient and effective in achieving appropriate standards of service delivery? Or to identify publicly the extent and location of racial discrimination, particularly in employment? Or to use constructively the energy and time of the unemployed insofar as jobs are unavailable and cannot be created? Or to benefit the economy of the City from its multi-ethnic strengths? Or to overcome the economic and social insecurity which promotes racism and intolerance? Or to assist voluntary associations of citizens to make their contributions? Or to enable parents, schools and other educational bodies to cope with responsibilities they are presently not discharging adequately?

8.3.6.   We must leave questions such as these, and the organisation involved, to the Congress, though the existing organisation of Area Panels, and Neighbourhood and Police Forums, may suggest some starting points.

8.4   Practical Implementation

8.4.1.   We suggest that the Congress should actively encourage the purposeful pursuit of the several subjects in this Report, at two levels: that of practical implementation of responses to accepted criticism, and that of monitoring such implementation. The Congress itself, we understand, normally relies on its most appropriate partner organisation(s) to take the lead. We see no reason for the Congress to alter this approach in dealing with this Report; the primary responsibility for dealing with the matters we have raised, with the important exception of that of the Central Government, usually lies with one or more of these partners.

8.4.2.   In addition to the organisations who constitute the Congress the individual organisations in the industrial and commercial sectors which derive their prosperity from Bradford's people, and the individual voluntary bodies who are concerned about Bradford's problems, have an essential part to play. Practical responses from all these bodies to the concerns we have emphasised ought to be realised.

8.5   Monitoring Progress

8.5.1.   We suggest that the Congress should also organise a framework for the independent monitoring of the progress made by these agencies, individually and overall, noting particularly if their internal agendas are tending to obstruct achievements which would be in the public interest.

8.5.2.   The Congress would probably be most effective if it used its range of partners, and others where appropriate, to create sub-groups for this purpose which were independent of the agencies responsible for the implementation being monitored, whose task would be to emphasise achievements relevant to public concerns, rather than to second guess the specialist methods of achievement which are the responsibility of those involved in implementation. The appropriate University specialists could offer assistance in developing a monitoring process.

8.5.3.   The Congress has no power beyond that volunteered by its participating agencies. An effective way of ensuring progress by these Bradford organisations in meeting public concerns is most likely to be established through public discussion and examination. These activities will only be meaningful insofar as the Bradford public is well-informed. Hence, our first concern about adequate communication.

8.6   The City Centenary

8.6.1.   We refer to the words with which Lord Scarman concluded his Report on the Brixton Riots:

> *"9.5. I end with the quotation from President Johnson's address to the nation, which appears at the very beginning of the US Report of the National Advisory Commission on Civil Disorders (1968):*
>
> *'... The only genuine, long-range solution for what has happened lies in an attack – mounted at every level – upon the conditions that breed despair and violence. All of us know what those conditions are: ignorance, discrimination, slums, poverty, disease, not enough jobs. We should*

attack these conditions – not because we are frightened by conflict, but because we are fired by conscience. We should attack them because there is simply no other way to achieve a decent and orderly society in America....'

These words are as true of Britain today as they have been proved by subsequent events to be true of America."

8.6.2.   These fine words require action. 10 July 1997 will be the Centenary of Bradford formally becoming a City. It would be a fitting contribution to the celebrations marking the beginning of the next hundred years if Bradford had, by then, a greater clarity and determination about **how** the challenges the next century will present are to be tackled.

Appendices

Appendix 1

The leaflet issued by The Bradford Commission inviting public views

WE ARE INTERESTED IN
YOUR VIEWS

THE MANNINGHAM
RIOTS

THE BRADFORD COMMISSION
4TH FLOOR
METROCHANGE HOUSE
BRADFORD BD1 5SG
TEL: (01274) 743000
FAX: (01274) 743050

WE ARE INTERESTED IN
YOUR VIEWS

THE MANNINGHAM
RIOTS

THE BRADFORD COMMISSION
4TH FLOOR
METROCHANGE HOUSE
BRADFORD BD1 5SG
TEL: (01274) 743000
FAX: (01274) 743050

Chair: Mr John Barratt,
Members: Professor Sheila Allen,
Mr Mohammad Taj,
Secretary: Mr Allen Sykes,
Facilitator: Ms Elaine Appelbee,
Executive Support: Yusuf Karolia,
Administrator: Ms Julie Williamson

Typeset and layout by

PRINT UNIT

PLEASE SEND TO **THE BRADFORD COMMISSION** 4TH FLOOR METROCHANGE HOUSE BRADFORD BD1 5SG
TEL: (01274) 743000 FAX: (01274) 743050 *OR* PLEASE DEPOSIT IN A SPECIAL BOX PROVIDED AT CHATA'S SUPERSAVE, OAK LANE

PLEASE CONTINUE OVERLEAF AND/OR ON A SEPARATE SHEET OF PAPER

COMMENTS

TELEPHONE NUMBER

ADDRESS

NAME

THE MANNINGHAM RIOTS

We are interested in your views.

You may telephone at the number below and arrange to give your views in person to the three Commissioners or you may write in with your views. You can use the space below to write to us if you wish. After you have done this you may post it to the Commission Office or take it to Chata's Super Save, Oak Lane and deposit this leaflet in a special box provided. You may write in any language you prefer.

[Text in Bengali, Gujarati, Hindi, Punjabi, and Urdu scripts follows in adjacent columns]

Appendix 2

Map A: **The Bradford Metropolitan Distrdict showing the area (hatched)
of the County Borough before 1974**

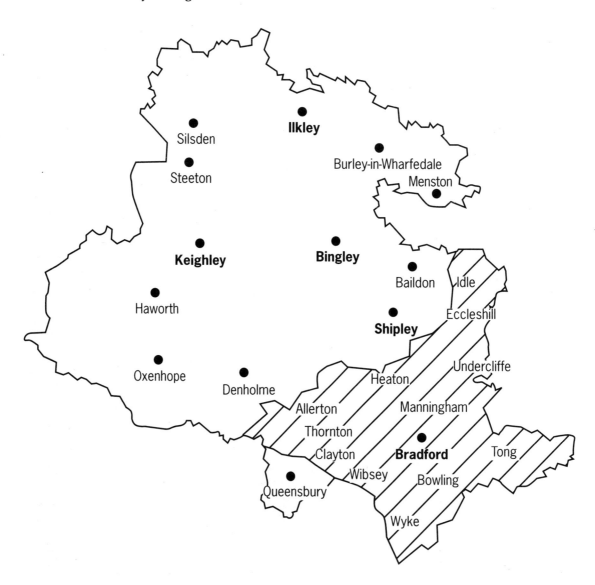

Appendix 3

Map B: **The electoral wards of the Bradford Metropolitan District with ethnic group information**

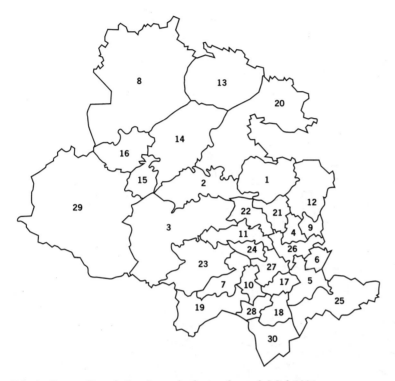

Ethnic Group: Population in each electoral ward: Mid-1991

	Ward	Total Population	Rounded percentage (%) of population in each ethnic group					
			White	*African Caribbean*	*Indian*	*Pakistani*	*Bangladeshi*	*Other*
1	Baildon	15,413	99%	0%	0%	0%	0%	0%
2	Bingley	13,080	99%	0%	0%	0%	0%	0%
3	Bingley Rural	15,536	99%	0%	0%	0%	0%	0%
4	Bolton	13,403	90%	2%	6%	2%	0%	1%
5	Bowling	18,665	74%	2%	6%	13%	3%	2%
6	Bradford Moor	18,066	47%	2%	9%	37%	2%	3%
7	Clayton	13,239	93%	1%	3%	1%	0%	1%
8	Craven	14,428	99%	0%	0%	0%	0%	0%
9	Eccleshill	15,377	97%	1%	1%	0%	0%	1%
10	Great Horton	15,556	77%	1%	9%	11%	0%	1%
11	Heaton	17,459	71%	1%	4%	22%	0%	2%
12	Idle	14,535	98%	1%	0%	0%	0%	1%
13	Ilkley	13,493	99%	0%	0%	0%	0%	1%
14	Keighley North	15,914	79%	1%	0%	16%	4%	0%
15	Keighley South	13,526	91%	0%	0%	6%	3%	0%
16	Keighley West	16,584	90%	0%	0%	8%	0%	1%
17	Little Horton	19,409	64%	5%	4%	21%	2%	4%
18	Odsal	17,475	86%	2%	3%	8%	0%	1%
19	Queensbury	16,735	98%	0%	1%	0%	0%	1%
20	Rombalds	15,180	99%	0%	0%	0%	0%	0%
21	Shipley East	14,631	98%	1%	0%	0%	0%	1%
22	Shipley West	15,578	87%	1%	2%	9%	0%	2%
23	Thornton	14,301	97%	1%	1%	1%	0%	1%
24	Toller	18,149	47%	2%	4%	45%	0%	2%
25	Tong	14,749	97%	2%	0%	0%	0%	1%
26	Undercliffe	16,704	76%	2%	3%	13%	5%	1%
27	University	22,281	27%	3%	11%	52%	2%	5%
28	Wibsey	14,041	97%	1%	1%	0%	0%	1%
29	Worth Valley	14,045	99%	0%	0%	0%	0%	0%
30	Wyke	17,605	98%	1%	1%	0%	0%	0%
	Bradford District		84%	1%	3%	10%	1%	1%
		475,155	398,021	5,847	12,610	48,962	3,883	5,832

Appendix 4

Map C: **Sketch map showing the areas affected by the disturbances
(Not to scale)**

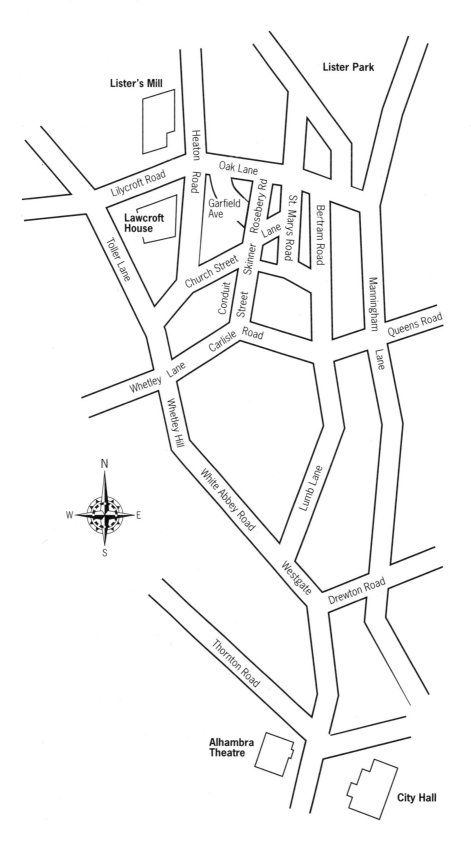

Appendix 5

Map D: **Indian sub-continent showing the areas from which emigration
to Bradford has taken place**

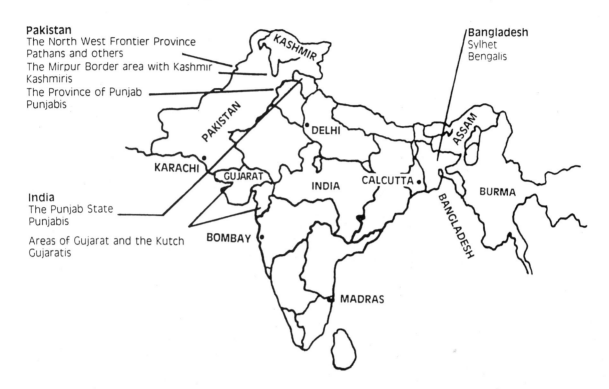

Pakistan
The North West Frontier Province
Pathans and others
The Mirpur Border area with Kashmir
Kashmiris
The Province of Punjab
Punjabis

India
The Punjab State
Punjabis

Areas of Gujarat and the Kutch
Gujaratis

Bangladesh
Sylhet
Bengalis

Source: *Why Should I Care? A multicultural approach to service delivery* – City of Bradford Metropolitan Council

Printed in the UK for The Stationery Office
Dd 303046   C20   11.96